THE ARTIST'S ESTATE

for

Ascan, Philomene & Artemis

and

Maja Stadler-Euler & Engelbert Büning

THE ARTIST'S ESTATE

A HANDBOOK FOR ARTISTS, EXECUTORS, AND HEIRS

EDITED BY
LORETTA WÜRTENBERGER

HATJE CANTZ

On Dealing with Artists' Estates

By Loretta Würtenberger and Karl von Trott

8 **Introduction**

14 **I. What Is an Artist's Estate?**

- 14 1. An Artist's Estate in the Legal Sense
- 17 2. An Artist's Estate in the Commonly Understood Sense

20 **II. How Should Estate Work Begin?**

- 20 1. Strategy Development
- 22 2. Securing the Oeuvre
- 24 3. Categorizing the Stock of Artworks

30 **III. In What Forms Can an Artist's Estate Be Administered?**

- 30 1. The Imperative of the Artist's Will
- 32 2. Administering an Estate Privately
- 34 3. Administering an Estate in an Institutional Form
- 37 4. Considerations in Selecting the Type of Estate Structure
- 41 5. Aspects of Nonprofit Status
- 46 6. Art, Taxes, and Structural Options for Estates
  - 47 a) Continental Europe
    - 48 (1) Germany
    - 51 (2) Austria
    - 52 (3) Spain
    - 52 (4) France
    - 53 (5) Switzerland

54 b) United States of America and United Kingdom
55 (1) Inheritance-Related Laws in the Anglo-American Legal Sphere
59 (2) Trusts
62 (3) Foundations and Artist-Endowed Foundations

66 **IV. Who Should Administer an Artist's Estate?**

66 1. Internal Administration
66 a) Family Members
73 b) Third Parties Unrelated to the Family
74 c) Advisory Bodies and Supervisory Boards
78 2. External Administration
78 a) Galleries
82 b) Auction Houses
83 c) Museums
83 (1) Acquisition of an Estate by a Museum
88 (2) The Dream of One's Own Museum
93 (3) The Artist's Studio as a Place of Remembrance
94 d) Other Institutionalized Administrators
96 e) Specialized Service Providers and Independent Estate Administrators

102 **V. How to Keep an Artist's Work Alive?**

102 1. Scholarly Research
103 a) The Archive
104 (1) Archival Organization
105 (2) Internal and External Custody of the Archive
109 b) The Catalogue Raisonné
110 (1) The Historical Development of Catalogues Raisonnés
112 (2) Standards, Methods, and Costs
115 (3) Catalogues Raisonnés Compiled during the Artist's Lifetime

116 c) Estates and Authentication
120 d) The Artist's Estate as a Stimulus for Academic Research
121 2. Active Collaboration with Museums
122 a) Initiating Exhibitions
123 b) Targeted Donations
125 3. Entering the Art Market: Branding and the Marketplace
126 a) Forming Active Relationships with Galleries
128 b) Market Strategy
130 c) Participation in the Secondary Art Market

132 **VI. Should an Artist's Estate Live Forever? Investments, Returns, and the Future**

133 1. Sunset and Eternity Models
137 2. Estate Expenditures
142 3. Source of Income for Artist's Estate
142 a) Selling Art
142 b) Copyright
144 (1) Reproduction and Distribution Rights
145 (2) Posthumous Editions
147 (3) Resale Rights
149 c) Real Estate
150 d) Additional Sources of Income

152 **Summary**

Interviews

158 **Michael Baumgartner**
Zentrum Paul Klee

174 **Mayen Beckmann**
Max Beckmann Estate

188 **Richard Calvocoressi**
Henry Moore Foundation

196 **Jerry Gorovoy**
Easton Foundation / Louise Bourgeois

204 **David Nash**
Gallerist of the Roy Lichtenstein and the Willem de Kooning Estate

212 **Jack Flam**
Dedalus Foundation / Robert Motherwell

224 **Christy MacLear**
Robert Rauschenberg Foundation

234 **Rainer Judd**
Judd Foundation

242 **Barry Rosen**
Eva Hesse Estate

246 **Michael Ward Stout**
Robert Mapplethorpe Foundation

254 **Gisela Capitain**
Martin Kippenberger Estate

268 **Hélène Vandenberghe**
Estate of Philippe Vandenberg

Introduction

Most people who assume responsibility for an artist's estate happen upon the role: they become custodians of a deceased artist's oeuvre because they are his or her son, daughter, or grandchild, or because they were the artist's spouse, partner, or friend. My own experience was no different. In 2009, my father-in-law passed away. Alongside his career as an art history professor, he had managed the estate of his father, Wolfgang Tümpel, a silversmith and industrial designer who had trained at the Bauhaus. This task fell to my husband, who after his father's death found himself surrounded by portfolios and boxes that he had no idea what to do with. Although Wolfgang Tümpel's work had been included in exhibitions every now and then, the estate had found no real structure in the thirty years since the artist's death. We gained first-hand experience of just how hard it is, even for members of the second generation, to distance oneself emotionally from such sensitive family matters. Yet, gaining a sense of objectivity is precisely what is needed to develop a sensible approach to the estate. My husband decided that an institutional setting would provide the best context for his grandfather's work, and set about finding a museum that would be interested. In the end, he transferred the estate to the Museum Huelsmann in Bielefeld, the city in which Wolfgang Tümpel had lived and worked for many years.

For us, this experience provided an introduction to the fascinating work with artists' estates. In 2008, we assumed joint responsibility for the sculptor Hans Arp's estate, and those of Sophie Taeuber-Arp and Keith Arnatt followed. Today we work together with several artists' estates. In addition, we founded the Institute for Artists' Estates (artists-estates.com) in order to provide estates worldwide with research findings, to facilitate networking, to make our archive on artists' estates accessible, and to provide expert advice.

From the very beginning of our work with artists' estates, I have been reaching out to other artists' estates. I wanted to learn from them just what makes an artist's estate successful. What topics are important for artists' estates to consider? What options do they have? These conversations were the starting point for the present volume. Fifty-plus conversations ensued with estates large and small, privately managed and entrusted to museums, as well as with those whose holdings eventually formed the basis of wealthy foundations. Twelve of these conversations have been incorporated into the second part of this book. These examples make it abundantly clear that estates are as diverse as artists are brilliant and unique. The common thread among them is their commitment to keeping the artist's work alive.

Despite differences among artists' estates, the living artist planning for the future or the estate itself must ask the same questions in order to develop a successful strategy. How should the estate be managed? Who should manage it? How should the estate work with museums, galleries, and academia? How will it be financed? These questions provide the structure of this book. We have attempted to provide a range of possible answers to these key questions, because we understand that each estate must draw its own conclusions. Another central assumption is that estates have life cycles that may be divided into three phases:

1. Strategic and Safeguarding Phase
2. Operational Phase
3. Expansion or Final Phase

Each phase poses challenges and questions. During the first phase of strategy and safeguarding, those surviving the artist must ask which goals the estate wishes to achieve and by which means. At the same time, the estate must be evaluated, sorted, and appraised in order to ascertain what there is to build upon. Once these questions have been answered, the operational phase begins, during which the focus is on the art as art. The estate should assemble the catalogue raisonné, open its archive to outside researchers, and focus on shaping the artist's posthumous reception. At a certain point, the estate will have had its art historical context relatively fixed, and will be positioned well enough that it no longer needs to rely upon the estate's ongoing advocacy. The estate must then ask whether the work on behalf of the artist is finished. The work of the estate is not an end in itself; its purpose cannot be keeping roofs over its employees' heads. In this phase, those managing the estate should ask what else they hope to achieve above and beyond the direct care of the artistic bequest.

This book attempts to help estates to find their own answers to these complicated questions. We hope to demonstrate that good management can go a long way for the artist and his or her legacy, even when the means are slim. The examples drawn from various estates, both large and small, are meant to promote dialogue between estates. When we touch upon the art market, we are referring to the structures and rules of the global art market, which is the appropriate frame of reference for most estates. Our discussion of legal questions pertains to the EU and the United States. Nevertheless, I would like to emphasize that this book does not provide legal advice. Rather, it concentrates on the substantive questions surrounding artists' estates. We wanted to address what comprises successful estate management, and are convinced that the answer to this question is influenced by factors above and beyond legalities. In order to consider the topic in relation to a wide range of artists' estates, it was necessary to generalize in matters of law. However, we have attempted to mitigate this choice by providing references to relevant legal sources. The explanations found here provide an initial overview of many of the pertinent legal issues, allowing readers to enter more confidently into discussions with lawyers and tax advisors. These professionals should be consulted on all legal and tax questions.

This book came about through collaboration with Karl von Trott and my husband, Daniel Tümpel. I thank both of them for our sustained dialogue on artists' estates, which continually challenged, expanded, and refined my own thinking—it was and is my pleasure. I am equally grateful to the many artists, their children, husbands, wives, and grandchildren as well as other estate stewards who spoke so openly with us. In the process, they discussed not only the managerial issues surrounding estates, but also the personal and emotional ones, which was a great gift. These conversations resulted in an enriching experience that we hope to carry on by maintaining similarly high standards through our work at the Institute for Artists' Estates.

Loretta Würtenberger
Spring 2016

On Dealing with Artists' Estates

By Loretta Würtenberger and Karl von Trott

Every Scribble on a Piece of Paper! Or, What Is an Artist's Estate?

"A scribble before breakfast can be worth $10,000 after breakfast."[1]

Helena Brack

I. What Is an Artist's Estate?

Before turning to the question of *how* the estate of an artist should be administered, it is important to understand *what* an artist's estate is. Naturally, it comprises the artworks bequeathed. But does it also include drafts, notes, or perhaps even a can of paint left in the studio? And what about copyrights or inconvenient matters such as inheritance tax? Are they also part of an artist's estate? And is a foundation established by an artist and furnished with his or her artistic legacy also part of the artist's estate in the narrower sense of the word? To answer these questions, it makes sense to take a look at the wording of the law[2] and to consider how the legal and the commonly understood sense of the term differ.

1. An Artist's Estate in the Legal Sense

The law provides the first answer to the question of what an artist's estate is. Generally, the estate of an artist is assigned the general definition of an "estate," where this is understood to include the assets and any debts left behind by the deceased. This means that the sum of all the assets and liabilities of a natural person do not die with the deceased, but will instead be transferred to his or her heirs. In relation to heirs, an estate is referred to as an inheritance.[3] From a legal perspective, this includes *everything* the artist leaves on death: the car in the garage and the pans in the kitchen, just as much as the canvas in the studio. In the context of succession, the law does not differentiate between art and other assets of an estate nor between the estate of an artist and that of another person. For the law, the only relevant question is organizing the restructuring of financial assets—including corresponding rights and obligations—that becomes necessary due to the death of an individual.

With respect to the legal definition of the term "artist's estate," it is important to differentiate between the Anglo-Saxon and continental European jurisdictions. In the Western world, these two legal systems dominate the allocation of assets on death. Correspondingly, this also explains the partially different understanding of the term estate. A distinction needs to be made between the legally separate estate as it commonly exists in the Anglo-Saxon jurisdiction (e.g., the United Kingdom und the United States) and the system of universal succession, which prevails in continental Europe (e.g., Germany and France). Depending on the laws governing the succession of the deceased, the transfer of assets takes place in different ways and at different points in time.

In Anglo-American common law, the estate as such is central to the inheritance and not the heirs or the community of heirs. Accordingly, heirs are not per se liable for debts or tax liabilities, but rather the estate itself is taxable via its executors or administrators. Lawyers in Anglo-Saxon jurisdictions normally refer to beneficiaries of an estate rather than heirs when describing individuals who benefit from an estate. In the Anglo-Saxon tradition, the estate first has to be administered by a person appointed to do so (usually an executor), who may simultaneously also be a beneficiary.[4] It is only at the end of this process that property is handed over to the beneficiaries, who may be natural persons or, in the case of artists' estates, often, additionally, a charitable organization.[5] During

---

1 Helena Brack, in Katrina Strickland, *Affairs of the Art: Love, Loss and Power in the Art World* (Melbourne, 2013), p. 12.

2 In this book, we concentrate on the legal systems of Europe and the United States of America. Insofar as that is the case, generalizing statements are only made with reference to these legal systems. When specific statements concern individual legal systems within these geographical limitations, this is indicated.

3 See *Palandt. Bürgerliches Gesetzbuch,* edited by Peter Bassenge, Gerd Brudermüller, Uwe Diederichsen, Wolfgang Edenhofer, Jürgen Ellenberger, Christian Grüneberg, Helmut Heinrichs, Hartwig Sprau, Karsten Thorn, Walter Weidenkaff, 68th edition (Munich, 2008), § 1922, Rn. 7.

4 http://www.cross-channel-lawyers.de/tag/englisches-erbrecht-erbfolge-pflichtteil/ (accessed March 19, 2016).

5 On this see, for example, the US standard work on art law: Ralph E. Lerner and Judith Bresler, *Art Law: The Guide for Collectors, Investors, Dealers & Artists* (New York, 2005) or also the extensive information material of the Aspen Institute Artists-Endowed Foundations Initiative (AEFI); http://www.aspeninstitute.org/policy-work/nonprofit-philanthropy/artist-endowed-foundations (accessed March 19, 2016).

this interim period when the estate is being administered, the period of administration, the surviving relatives are very limited in their powers of disposal, even though interim distributions and bequests are possible.

In the case of "universal succession" in continental European legal domains (like Germany, France, Italy, and Spain), by contrast, the estate as a whole is already transferred to one or more heirs upon death. In this European tradition, several heirs as a community of heirs and/or a single heir take the place of the deceased. The succession includes assets as well as liabilities. An individual item can be allocated to one heir by means of a bequest, but not inherited in a legal sense. A joint heir only obtains sole ownership of individual items in the estate by means of a separate partition agreement. If the artistic body of work was organized in the form of a business, in some countries there is also the possibility of a tax-saving continuation of operations, which we will look at later.

In practice, the legal differences between estates in the two legal spheres can mean an immediate, shared right of disposal over the works bequeathed, coupled with the person- and the portion-of-the-estate-related (tax) liabilities, as it did for the heirs of Sigmar Polke for example. After the death of Willem de Kooning, the executors who had been appointed (attorney John Eastman and daughter Lisa de Kooning) first had to clarify tax-related questions on behalf of the estate with the American Internal Revenue Service (IRS) and have the estate as such pay taxes, before Lisa de Kooning and the Willem de Kooning Foundation were able to obtain ownership of the works intended for them. In the case of Donald Judd, it took four years for inheritance-related matters to be clarified and assets permitted to be transferred to the ownership of the Judd Foundation, which had been established according to his wishes.

According to the legal classification in the two legal realms, the term "estate" is also subject to a time limitation. Under Anglo-Saxon common law the period of administration ends when the net assets have been transferred to the beneficiaries. After the estate's liabilities have been settled and administered, the beneficiaries assume the legal position of owner by virtue of the transfer, which supersedes the preferential treatment. From a legal perspective, the Rauschenberg or Judd Foundation, for example, are also not artists' estates. One speaks here instead of an artist-endowed "foundation." In the continental European system, the transfer takes place by means of universal succession upon the death of the decedent. Here, the term estate becomes legally obsolete at the latest with the expiry of the period for disclaiming an inheritance. Accordingly, in a strict sense, each individual who calls an artistic legacy his or her own is therefore no longer an administrator of an estate, but rather of his or her own legal circumstances as inherited from an estate. But what child of an artist really wants to say that he or she manages the "inherited material assets" of his or her mother or father—even though this would actually be accurate?

2. An Artist's Estate in the Commonly Understood Sense

In everyday language, the term "artist's estate" refers to the artistic legacy, hence to the physical products of the artistic process and the intangible rights to them, as well as any accompanying documentation. All other components of the estate, such as other material assets or purely private items, play no primary role for the public examination of an artist and his or her work. Rather, insofar as present, either serve as financial protection for the heirs and/or the artistic estate or are ascribed to the private sphere of the artist and his or her dependents. In everyday language, these components are therefore not included under the term artist's estate.

With respect to terminology, this understanding follows that of the field of archiving, which comprehends an estate as comprising all unofficial documents of a physical person that have arisen from their private, social, artistic-literary, or official activities and are acquired by an archive as a deposit or through donation or purchase.[6] Correspondingly, the estate of a visual artist is regarded as all of his or her works as well as working materials and tools, notes, sketches, journals, and other documents.[7] At the same time, the colloquial use of the term artist's estate strains the legal definition factually as well as linguistically. In English-speaking countries, outside of specialist circles, a difference is only rarely made between the, in itself, temporally limited estate and the artist-endowed foundation that can follow from it in the eyes of the law.[8]

In continental Europe, many different forms of organizing an artistic legacy are also referred to in this respect as an artist's estate. The spectrum of conceivable

6 As defined in the glossary of selected archive-specific terms of the der Universitätsbibliothek Frankfurt am Main; http://www.ub.uni-frankfurt.de/archive/glossar.html (accessed March 19, 2016).

7 Roger Fayet and Deborah Favre, *Umgang mit Künstlernachlässen in der Schweiz*, SIK-ISEA study of March 17, 2014, p. 6.

8 Details on legal distinctions in the United States are named, for instance, in the information material of the Aspen Institute Artists-Endowed Foundations Initiative (see note 5); for generalized usage/use of the term in the United States, see for example Magda Salvessen and Diane Cousineau, *Artists' Estates: Reputations in Trust,* (New Brunswick, New Jersey, 2005).

structures ranges from purely private-purpose, non-institutionalized administration to the purely charitable foundation set up for perpetuity, with strict legal provisions regarding the individuals who are active in it.

As a result of the conflating of artistic legacy and artist's estate in colloquial speech, an artist's estate is given its own, post-mortal identity, in which the aura of the artistic genius is still inherent. This can happen independently of whether this artistic aura receives an independent legal identity, by establishing an artist's foundation for example. In this spirit, the American artist Jill Magid poses the question of what the character of an artist's estate is. What is it really? Is it perhaps also a work of art? And do the individuals who administer an estate contribute to it creatively? In her own artistic practice, she tries to reconceptualize this question through making artists' estates the subject of her work. With her *Luis Barragán Project,* she is attempting to convince the Fehlbaums, the Swiss husband-and-wife collectors and the owners of the furniture producer Vitra, to return the estate of the Mexican architectural icon Luis Barragán to his home. This estate is currently found in the Barragán Foundation in Switzerland, which is controlled by the Fehlbaums.[9] Meant to assist in the decision is the offer of a diamond that the artist had pressed from a portion of Barragán's ashes, for which the Mexican parliament had to grant special permission. Whether she will be successful with her offer remains to be seen. Magid has already examined aspects of the estate artistically in a previous work: with *Auto Portrait Pending,*[10] she bequeathed her future mortal remains in diamond form to an art-collecting ring wearer. The term "body of work," which is always an essential part of an artist's estate, receives an entirely new, equivocal connotation. The German artist Peter Piller works from a different perspective. In the eponymous *Archiv Peter Piller,* he creates photo archives assembled from estate holdings and private collections and sorts them based on design elements as well as content-related similarities. They therefore become the work. Such approaches—as far removed as they are from precise legal definitions—can be very inspiring when one is responsible for an artist's estate. If one regards the estate as an artwork per se, one dares consider one's own role and possibilities more freely. This can be relieving, especially for the children of artists who might also see responsibility for the estate as a burden.

---

9 http://www.barragan-foundation.org/; http://www.welt.de/print-welt/article526454/Luis-Barragan-das-Phantom-von-Mexiko.html (accessed March 19, 2016).

10 http://www.raebervonstenglin.com/index/artists/Jill-Magid/images.html (accessed March 19, 2016).

No Strategy = No Goal, No Goal = No Way!
On Conditions, Aspirations, and Truths

"Strategy is an economy of forces!"[11] Carl von Clausewitz

II. How Should Estate Work Begin?

Having clarified what an artist's estate is, we can now look at the much more interesting question of *how* an artist's estate can be managed. There is no *single* answer to this question, however, and the possible answers to it are as multifaceted as the artists and estates are different.

1. Strategy Development

To find the right answers, it is necessary to ask the right questions. Successful administration of an estate therefore begins with an extensive strategy phase, which should take a look at the following questions:

1. In what condition is the estate?
    a. What is the condition of the estate with respect to organization and conservation?
    b. How is it catalogued and stored?
    c. Where does the oeuvre stand within the context of art history? How recognized is it, and what is its objective quality?
2. In which structure should the estate be administered?
    a. Was the intention of the deceased artist verbalized?
    b. Should the estate be administered in a private form?
    c. Should it be administered in an institutionalized form?
    d. Profit or nonprofit definition of objectives?

3. Who should administer the estate?
    a. Family
    b. Third party
    c. Role and composition of advisory bodies
4. What objectives do I want to achieve through working with the estate in the short, middle, and long term?
    a. Definition of objectives
    b. How do I achieve the objectives?
        I. How do I work with museums?
        II. How do I work with scholarship?
        III. How do I work with the art market?
        IV. Will a catalogue raisonné be necessary?
        V. Will an authentication committee be necessary?
5. How do I finance the achieving of these objectives?
6. Should the estate be set up for an indefinite or definite period?

Such a strategy phase requires time, and some estates take as long as three years—a period in which all external activities are reduced to a minimum. The Gordon Parks Foundation, which was created in 2006 to preserve the memory of the American photographer Gordon Parks, took an even longer time. "The very first thing the foundation decided on was to catalogue all his works and not work with any museums or galleries for the first five or so years, until we uncovered what was in the archive," the managing director Peter Kunhardt, Jr. reported.[12] Similarly, the children of the Belgian painter Philippe Vandenberg[13] closed the studio, blocked all sales as well as the mandates of galleries, and recalled all artworks to the studio after his sudden death. They then took the time they needed to analyze the situation, obtain opinions of their father's art, and develop an agenda. They also discussed their relationship to one another in connection to the estate work. Looking back, daughter Hélène Vandenberghe says that this retreat was the best decision they could have made. It enabled them to ask questions and to listen—to friends of their father, friendly collectors,

11 Carl von Clausewitz, cited according to Hans H. Hinterhuber, "1. Exkurs: Die Entwicklung des strategischen Denkens," in *Wettbewerbsstrategie* (Berlin, 1990), p. 26.

12 Quoted after: Pac Pobric, "Museums and galleries turn to the work of Gordon Parks," in: *The Art Newspaper*, Nr. 278, April 2016.

13 Philippe Vandenberg had his name changed and wrote it from then on without the letters "he" at the end. His children continue to use the original name.

artists, art dealers, curators, and museum people. It was after that the siblings developed a strategy, to which they have remained true: "In 2010 we outlined our short- and long-term goals and planned the further steps we wanted to take. To this day we still follow the very script that we wrote down six years ago. It's amazing that we intuitively felt what steps were necessary."[14]

2. Securing the Oeuvre

Parallel to developing a strategy, the estate of an artist should be secured after their death. If one of the tasks of art is bringing chaos into order, this dictum does not apply to artistis' estates. Order in an estate is the most important prerequisite for a realistic assessment of the holdings as a basis for strategic and financing options.

The artworks in the estate come first. At the time of death, they are often "scattered" in various places: in the studio, in the home, in various storage spaces, with friends, on loan to museums, or with gallerists. Although it requires effort, initially bringing all the works together is recommended so that one can get one's own impression of the condition and quality of the works. The case of an estate is like that of all art: nothing is a substitute for a direct, physical impression of the work. Doing this enables one to arrive at a realistic assessment and to truly become familiar with the oeuvre.

The work of sorting through the oeuvre should go hand in hand with cataloguing the artworks. When doing so, the following information should ideally be checked and/or compiled:[15]

1. Title, description, year of creation
2. Material and dimensions, including the size of the frame, other mounting or necessary architectural exhibition elements such as the base used, et cetera; weight in the case of sculptures
3. Inventory number and photo documentation of the work as well as signature and/or casting stamp found on the work
4. Essential requirements for conserving, storing, and exhibiting the artwork
5. Information about the process of creating the artwork and what materials were used—this can be beneficial for the long-term preservation of particular artworks
6. Current owner and location of the artwork
7. Current condition of the work

8. Invoices for the artwork
9. Correspondence about the artwork, including commissions, sales, donations, or loans
10. Exhibition catalogues or catalogue data for exhibitions of the artwork and/or exhibition history
11. Assessments and insurance documents
12. Selling prices achieved at auctions or private sales (as far as possible)
13. Information about the artwork provided by the artist, also within the context of other works or the oeuvre as a whole
14. Press articles and press photos with the artwork as their subject
15. Information about copyright, granting of use up to this point, and about license fees received

Ideally, the estate is able to refer to an inventory and organizational system that was set up during the artist's lifetime. The professionalization of the contemporary art market will simplify the estate work of the future. If an artist today achieves enough success to work with a professional gallery, the processes connected with this success alone already make it necessary for artists to have professional studio management. If this is not the case, galleries often step in with appropriate support, ensuring that a copy of the material collected in the gallery is always made available to the artist for archival purposes.

Professional studio management consists of clean accounting along with the necessary archiving of production and sales documents, including details on buyers—which will be of importance for provenance information in later indexes of works—as well as ongoing cataloguing of the artworks. If a studio has reached a certain size, then assistants and a studio manager are also necessary.

Whether during an artist's lifetime or first within the framework of estate work, there are various specialized software programs available for cataloguing works; these data sets can then be used as the basis for a catalogue raisonné. It is advisable to keep up-to-date with the current technical state of the art, since hard- and software continue to develop further, but here are a few examples of useful technology: the Vandenberghe siblings use the services of the Light-

14 See the interview with Hélène Vandenberghe in this volume.

15 This list is based on the approach recommended by the Royal Academy of Arts, London, published as: *The Artist's Legacy: Estate Planning in the Visual Arts*, Emma Warren-Thomas and Linda Schofield (eds.), London 2013.

machine Agency,[16] the estate of Hans Arp uses a software solution from Hamburg-based Trenz AG,[17] and the Zentrum Paul Klee uses the collection administration software MuseumPlus, conceived for museums by Zetcom AG,[18] which also offers alternatives for private individuals with ArtPlus. There is a wide range of other suppliers such as Artsystems, Artworkarchive, and Collectionspace.[19] When choosing a program, care should be taken that the software is able to depict catalogue raisonnés and other needs of an estate, and is not only oriented toward museum or gallery operations. Software tailored to museums or galleries often has functions that an estate does not require, while other functions that might also be quite useful at a later point are missing. The labeling of artworks should include not only the number assigned to the work, but also lasting coding such as a barcode or QR code (2D barcode) so as to make handling them more efficient. In ideal cases, the labeling can simultaneously be combined with the newest authentication technologies such as so-called bioengineered DNA technology. This involves giving artworks an artificial DNA to assist in recognizing the original artwork.[20] It is a process developed by the nonprofit Global Center of Innovation for protecting against counterfeit art and is in turn supposed to become part of an entirely new global standard for marking and identification called i2M.[21] A company providing modern solutions in this area is Tagsmart, a British company founded by artists, among others.[22] As security, digital images of the works and the master data should be stored in an online storage device or cloud service (if the inventory program is not already online-based). The same applies for the whole archive after digitization.

3. Categorizing the Stock of Artworks

"Don't throw things away. Don't even throw away cans or tubes of paint, they can become very handy down the road—as aids in documentation, in conservation, and even with regard to dealing with questions of authenticity," advises Jack Flam, President of the Dedalus Foundation, which was created by Robert Motherwell.[23] But not every brush and can of paint is worth keeping, even if the reconstruction of the London studio of Francis Bacon in Dublin with more than 7,000 individual items makes one hesitate to make such a statement. Nevertheless, at the beginning, a selection process should take place because not everything that an artist thinks, makes, and leaves behind is art and relevant to his or her work. Distinguishing between areas of an artist's life is often not clear-cut;

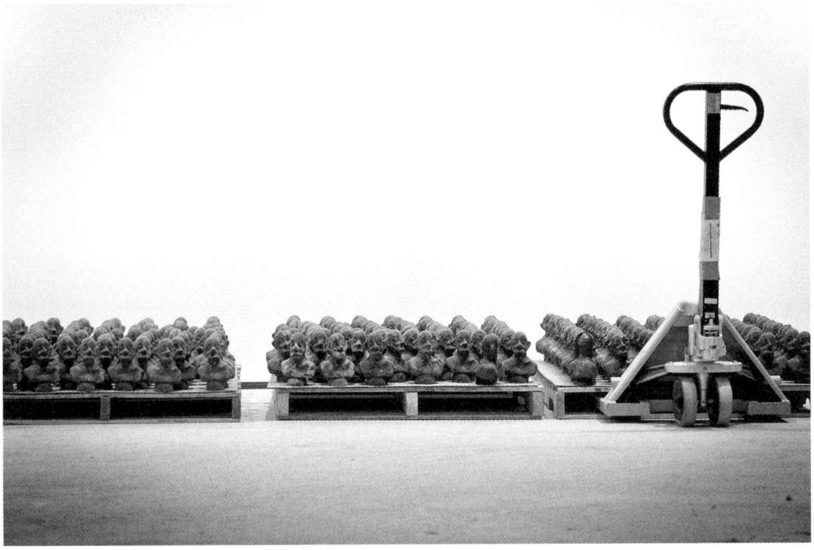

Installation of *Dieter Roth: Björn Roth* at Hauser & Wirth in New York, 2013
Chocolate casting for *Selbstturm*, 1994/2013

Every artist has a purely private, unprofessional side with corresponding remnants/legacies—be it a receipt for a restaurant visit or possibly the scribble on the notepad next to the telephone. "There's always this terrible issue of memorabilia," as the widow of the Australian artist John Brack refers to it in Katrina Strickland's book *Affairs of the Art*, further adding: "Doodles on the telephone pad are nothing to do with the artist's work whatsoever, but lots of artists think differently, so a scribble before breakfast can be worth $10,000 after breakfast."[24] But it is not only many artists who think so, many art mediators or art-collecting institutions do as well. Everything that might remotely be an expression of artistic work runs the risk of being overvalued, artistically and

16 http://www.lightmachine.agency/ (accessed March 19, 2016).
17 http://www.trenz.ag/ (accessed March 19, 2016).
18 http://www.zetcom.com/de/produkte/ (accessed March 19, 2016).
19 http://www.artsystems.com/solutions/artist-studio-software/; https://www.artworkarchive.com/ (accessed March 19, 2016).
20 http://www.aristitle.com/news/docs/Authenticating%20Art%20With%20Bioengineered%20DNA%20The%20IP%20Issues_110215.pdf.
21 https://www.i2mstandards.org/i2m-solution/ (accessed March 19, 2016).
22 www.tagsmart.com.
23 See the interview with Jack Flam in this volume.
24 Strickland, *Affairs of the Art* (2013) (see note 1).

financially. This is why no one wants to be responsible for the destruction of supposed artworks that might, in a possibly booming art market, also have great financial value.

A selection, or at least some type of sorting of artworks is inevitable for all but a few estates that have the financial resources to actually keep every object. For most estates, it is virtually essential for their survival to limit and focus themselves. And such estates that do have sufficient resources available should also undertake a sorting in order to define where their emphasis will lie. For this reason, the taking stock of the estate that always comes first should be followed by a selection process of what artworks, archival materials, and other potentially existing assets (such as real estate or artworks by other artists) will form the core of the work within the artist's estate.

At the same time as the sorting process, one is likely to arrive at the first central question of all estate activity: Does the quality of the work suffice for reasonable estate work? The answer to this question has an art historical and an economic dimension, which are connected. The more important the entire oeuvre of an artist is within the context of art history, the greater the probability that individual works will enjoy relevantly high regard long term and also generate correspondingly high sale prices that make financial planning possible. Even if there are isolated cases of posthumous discoveries, it is difficult to act if the cultural asset that has been inherited is not considered relevant or important art historically. This not only limits the possibility of financing the estate, but also puts the motivation of those involved to a tough test. Assessing the artistic work (or having it assessed) is therefore recommended—even though expectations are sometimes disappointed.

In this evaluation process, as many opinions on the art as possible should be obtained from diverse professions, as was done, for instance, by the children of Philippe Vandenberg. For them, it was crucial to know whether their artist father would be able to "keep up" on an international level, and if so how he could be situated. What ultimately concerned them was whether his work was relevant. "We wanted to know if [our father's art] would hold up in an international context, and if so, where it could be positioned," as Hélène Vandenberghe notes.[25] The response in her case was positive, and it was then that the siblings dedicated themselves to their father's artwork.

But how should one proceed with such a categorizing of the holdings of an estate? What is crucial here is the artist's own understanding of his or her work and tools, and in particular whether and in what form he or she wanted to bequeath them to posterity. Artists themselves are in the best position to decide what part of their oeuvre should be handed down to future generations or what should remain in the hands of relatives. Artists should also make up their own mind regarding artworks to which they no longer attribute any value, or at least leave instructions as to which works should only be kept within the family due to their (perhaps lack of) quality. This decision process may also involve works that are no longer the property of the artist, something that often comes to light when publishing a catalogue raisonné, as will be explained later using the example of Gerhard Richter.[26] If the artist neglected to make such a selection and left no instructions, the process has to be effected by the heirs through remembrance and assessment. The artworks being transferred to the estate can then be classified according to their importance and market value: Which are principle works, which works are rather unimportant, which are preliminary studies not intended for the market, which multiples exist in what editions, et cetera. Useful aids in this process are often notes and statements by the artist. Exceedingly few estates will, however, be able to draw on the meticulousness and self-perception that Paul Klee displayed in this regard. The catalogue by Marie Kakinuma, Wolfgang Kersten, and Osamu Okuda for the exhibition *Paul Klee—Special Class, Not for Sale* impressively reports on the artist's efforts to categorize his own oeuvre based on quality and significance and price them correspondingly. Klee used the term "special class" for the group of works that he declared not for sale. He withdrew these works from the market and thus defined the presumed core holdings of his estate and laid the foundations for a first, self-conceptualized retrospective. If one would like to follow this example and keep a core collection of five to ten percent of the artworks bequeathed, including key works, completely in the estate, one should definitely do so to benefit the estate. Conversely, this complicates the ability to finance the estate since—with great likelihood—these works will be the most coveted works from a market perspective.

As Uwe Degreif, a curator with many years of museum experience, recommends, one can group works in the categories A to D independent of whether one introduces an inalienable special class that stands above all others or not. "A-works are such works that the artist did not sell during his or her lifetime, that he or she always wanted to have around, that he or she lent for exhibitions and envisioned for catalogue illustrations, they date back to various creative

25 Hélène Vandenberghe in conversation with the author.
26 On catalogue raisonnés, see Chapter 5.

periods and generally always from the beginning of each such period,"[27] as he has noted. Works from the A-group are therefore comparable to those that Klee proactively defined as not for sale. Depending on what plans will be pursued mid and long term, targeted placement in museums or also sale to very good private collections can make sense. The works from the B-group represent the body of works that is most interesting for estate development. In Degreif's interpretation, these are good works from the main creative period. "This group is numerically larger than the A-group, but, in my experience, comprises a smaller period of time," according to the conservator.[28] The C-group, which is on the whole the most extensive, in contrast, includes all works that might be considered to be of lesser quality, such as variations, drafts, the incomplete, and the reworked: "They do not add anything of importance to the information of the A- and B-groups."[29] From a museum perspective, besides the A-group, the final D-group, to which the files with documents, photos, personal mementoes, certificates, exhibition discussions, correspondence, et cetera belong, is the most interesting, since it provides information about the artist's relationships to diverse individuals and his or her way of life.

27 http://www.artexperts.ch/fileadmin/user_upload/Publikationen/Artikel_Interview_UweDegreif.pdf (accessed March 19, 2016).

28 Ibid.

29 Ibid.

"Give me a museum and I'll fill it!"[30]

Pablo Picasso

III. In What Forms Can an Artist's Estate Be Administered?

The question of the form in which an estate should be administered is initially the most important one since the framework conditions for answering all other questions are derived from it. There are two basic models to discuss: private administration of the estate and institutionalized administration of it as a separate legal entity. It is also necessary to decide who should receive income from estate work. This will determine whether the estate will be managed for the financial benefit of the heirs or for charitable purposes. Which concrete form an artist's estate should be given therefore depends on the objectives and requirements connected with it.

1. The Imperative of the Artist's Will

The form in which an artist's estate will be administered is determined by the artist, whether he or she wants to or not, by leaving behind a last will and testament—or through not doing so. Dealing with one's own mortality can be unpleasant. Nevertheless, dealing with one's estate during one's lifetime and formulating what will later serve administrators as a guide and instructions is recommended. This occurs either by means of a will or through establishing an entity, like a foundation, to administer the estate while one is still alive. Choosing one of the two possibilities is generally based on considerations relating to tax law. In either case, how important seeking tax and legal advice is cannot be emphasized enough, since there is a wide range of possible options as well as pitfalls. I cannot, however, go into the inheritance and tax law-related details here, since they would go beyond the scope of this handbook in their complexity and differences with respect to legal systems.[31] Rather, let us concentrate on the content-related aspects of an artist's last will and testament.

Leaving behind a will has a range of benefits. Besides arranging inheritance procedures such as the correct use of tax exemption, et cetera in a tax-optimized way, the author of the will is able to specify who will take care of his or her work in the future. They can also define many details that are not directly accessible, like answering questions such as: Do I want to provide for the children differently in the case that my spouse remarries; should they be given access to their inheritance only at a particular age; or, do I want to give art to specific individuals?

With a will, artists have the ideal opportunity for self-stylization and personal mythmaking.[32] Through intentions expressed in the will, they can, for example, have all their works shown only together, as Clyfford Still stipulated: "I give and bequeath all the remaining works of art executed by me in my collection to an American city that will agree to build or assign and maintain permanent quarters exclusively for these works of art and assure their physical survival with the explicit requirement that none of these works of art will be sold, given, or exchanged, but are to be retained in the place described above exclusively assigned to them in perpetuity for exhibition and study."[33]

Another, more modest possibility, is to link one's self with an artist one chooses, as the German painter Karl von Pidoll did with that of his revered mentor, Hans von Marées. He bequeathed his paintings to the "Bavarian Crown,"

---

30 Pablo Picasso, cited according to: http://www.pablopicasso.org/quotes.jsp (accessed April 4, 2016).

31 On regulations in different countries, see for example: Herbert E. Nass, *The 101 Biggest Estate Planning Mistakes* (Hoboken, N.J., 2009); Emma Chamberlain and Chris Whitehouse, *Trust Taxation and Estate Planning* (London, 2014); Walter Zimmermann, *Rechtsfragen beim Todesfall* (Munich, 2010); Andreas Schlüter and Stefan Stolte, *Stiftungsrecht* (Munich, 2007).

32 Nicole Hegener and Thomas Pöpper, "Mit dem Tod an Bord: Künstlertestamente als Quellen der Kunstgeschichte und Künstlersoziologie," in Nicole Hegener and Kerstin Schwedes, eds., *Der Künstler und sein Tod. Testamente Europeaner Künstler vom Spätmittelalter bis zum 20. Century* (Würzburg, 2012), p. 14.

33 Geoff van Dyke, "Clyfford Still's Unyielding Will," in *5280 Magazine;* http://www.5280.com/magazine/2011/11/clyfford-still (accessed March 23, 2016).

under the condition that they would always only be shown next to those of von Marées.[34] For the purpose of their own posthumous sacralization, artists can also have a monument worthy of an emperor erected, as Antonio Canova did with his temple in Possagno.[35] There are many other examples of instructive artists' wills in the history of art: In the sixteenth century, the miniaturist Don Giulio Clovio prepared a will containing a total of three fastidious estate inventories.[36] In 1973, sixteen years prior to her death, Lucia Moholy-Nagy drafted: "My literary estate as well as my work material may be utilized after my demise … the rest of my estate goes—without public mention of my name—in equal parts to the following two entities: (a) Stiftung Kinderdorf Pestalozzi, Trogen AR … ., (b) International Rescue Committee … New York … ."[37] The stipulations of the English sculptor Barbara Hepworth were also very concrete: no posthumous castings, private administration, no levying of copyright fees, and the financing of work on her estate

Despite such examples, legally secure documentation of the artist's will nevertheless remains the exception, as is the case with most wills. Martin Kippenberger, for example, did not want to be confronted with the topic and as a result of his passivity left it to his legal heirs to decide how to regulate his estate. The inheritance provisions that legally apply in such a case leave the question of how the estate should be up to the heirs. Considered optimistically, this can mean that the artist gives those who survive him or her complete control in dealing with the oeuvre. But it can also mean that he or she is indifferent to the fate of the work, as in the sense of Eva Hesse, who said: "Art doesn't last, life doesn't last, it doesn't matter." And the less clear statements, written documents, or wills are, the more likely inheritance disputes are. Perhaps considering the estate as a "final major work" can help to motivate many artists to address the details of his or her estate while still alive. Those who tend to shy away from the topic might then understand that a will can preserve the artistic aura that is inherent in their life's work.

2. Administering an Estate Privately

Whether during one's lifetime or post mortem, a decision as to whether the estate should be maintained privately or through a separate legal entity has to be made.

Private administration of an estate means that the heirs make the parts of the estate their private property, keep them, and can dispose of them just like any other object that belongs to them. If they sell an artwork, they do so as private individuals. If there is income from copyrights or resale rights, they receive it as private individuals. If they decide to publish a catalogue raisonné, they pay for the costs from their private assets.

Most artists' estates are managed in this form. This form is the least complicated from an administrative perspective. No foundation or capital stock is needed and there are no expenses incurred through running a separate legal entity. In this private form, however, income from the estate is taxed just like all the owners' other income. This means that the heirs have to pay the inheritance tax immediately, depending on the legal system,[38] and pay income tax on ongoing sales and revenues from immaterial assets. In exchange, although the proceeds can be used privately, there are altogether fewer liquid funds available for estate work than if the income were tax-exempt. Another advantage of this form of estate administration is the freedom it gives the heirs. They can dispose of the estate with all the freedoms that private ownership entails: they can, for instance, divide up the holdings if there are multiple heirs; they can administer them jointly and make alterable civil law agreements; there are no supervisory bodies with which they have to come to be answerable to; and there are no legal provisions applicable beyond general civil law that have to be taken into consideration—as is the case with US foundation law's very strict rules on insider dealing or the specifications regarding a supervisory authority in German law. From the perspective of the artist bequeathing an estate, this freedom can, however, also have disadvantages. Particularly in the case of multiple heirs there is a danger that the estate will be broken up. Moreover, there will not be a clear entity that is visible to outsiders on an ongoing basis and able to present itself as the long-term contact concerning questions about the oeuvre.

---

34 Roman Zieglgänsberger, "Von Wahrheit, Windmühlen und Schildknappen: Das sonderbare Testament des Marées-Schülers Karl v. Pidoll," in *Der Künstler und sein Tod* 2012, p. 299.

35 Hegener / Pöpper, "Künstlertestamente als Quellen" 2012 (see note 32), p. 24.

36 Nicole Hegener, "'Diligentia in minimis maxima'—Testament und Nachlass des 'kleinen Michelangelo' Don Giulio Clovio," in *Der Künstler und sein Tod* 2012 (see note 4), pp. 105, 127 ff.

37 Sybille Hoiman," Lucia Moholy: Zur Geschichte ihres Nachlasses im Bauhaus-Archiv," in Volkmar Hansen and Ulrike Horstenkamp-Strake (eds.), *Special Delivery. Von artists' estatesn und ihren Verwaltern* (Bonn, 2011), p. 176.

38 Exceptions include the possibly privileged tax law status of income from sales of art in some legal systems, such as, for instance, in Germany, where income from the non-commercial sale of art is not subject to income tax. Very strict conditions do, however, apply in such cases, which means that many estates that finance themselves through regular sales of art are not permitted to satisfy this rule.

3. Administering an Estate in an Institutional Form

Administration by a separate legal entity means that the estate is transferred to a separate legal "person" and they become the owner of the assets found in the estate. The most well-known form for this is the foundation, but other legal forms, such as the GmbH in Germany or the limited company in the United Kingdom, are also conceivable. This is particularly so if the respective legal system also permits charitable variants of such entities to be established.

The advantage of an institutionalized structure is that artists are able to give the content-related structure of the estate work a legal basis. Added to this is the fact that nearly every legal system offers nonprofit variants substantial tax benefits, and that in the case of income more liquidity is available for estate work. A disadvantage is the fact that becoming a separate legal entity, whether for profit-oriented or charitable purposes, results in a loss of flexibility and freedom. Foundations in particular are regularly subject to considerable intervention options on the part of the state. These might comprise not only preventative measures, such as requests for information or authorization requirements, but also repressive instruments, such as the annulment of measures or the dismissal of board members. The founding of a corporation has the advantage of systematically limiting liability, but this also goes hand in hand with disclosure obligations. The German charitable GmbH (or charitable company in the United Kingdom) is also a very suitable institution for managing an artist's estate because it allows greater freedom of action than a foundation and is not subject to the monitoring of a foundation supervisory authority. Another variant is the registered association, which, in its charitable variant, is not permitted to engage in economic activities—in contrast to the charitable GmbH. Associations managing an art estate aren't usually formed until after an artist passes away, at the initiative of friends and collectors.[39]

Unlike a GmbH, an association is not required to disclose figures. While a foundation belongs "to itself," an association is supported by members as decision-makers. Associations are also allowed to use up their existing assets. In practice this means that they—if no provisions in the articles of association preclude it—can decide to dissolve the association and turn all its assets to account in advance through donations or sales. A foundation, on the other hand, always has to obtain approval from a supervisory authority in order to dissolve itself. This is so even if an objective that facilitates dissolution according to the foundation charter has been achieved—that is, if a non-perpetual endowment foundation has not been established.

Establishing an independent legal entity for administering an artist's estate gained in importance in the second half of the twentieth century. While estates were mostly managed and disposed of by gallery owners, if not bequeathed to museums in their entirety until World War II, estate administration in the form of a separate legal entity such as a foundation became the norm afterward. The motivations for such a decision and the options for structuring such an entity are manifold and revolve around the topics of money, family, self-image, and memory, as well as increasingly around the topic of benefit to the public. This approach to administering and organizing an estate naturally suggests itself for artists without descendants, although a lack of family members is the reason for institutionalization in only six of ten cases.[40] In the remaining four, what frequently plays a role is the idea of also wanting to continue to influence the work with one's own oeuvre post mortem by means of content-related provisions anchored in legal structures. This limits the heirs' scope of action, but it does not, however, mean that all possibilities to influence the estate are denied. Donald Judd and Louise Bourgeois, for example, both defined the establishment of their respective foundation in their wills, and both also made their two children, among other individuals, trustees of the foundation.

The more well-known and economically successful an artist is, the higher the likelihood that a foundation or comparable independent legal entity will be brought into being by natural persons in order to administer the artist's estate. In the United States in particular, many artists choose a foundation as the way to administer their estate and already regulate it during their lifetime. Tax issues often play a role in this, as the attorney and President of the Robert Mapplethorpe Foundation, Michael Ward Stout, confirms in the case of Mapplethorpe: "Originally, the Foundation was tax motivated, but it was also motivated by his [Mapplethorpe's] sharp business mind and his determination to shape his own legacy."[41]

---

39 Compared to a foundation, the legal form of an association, which in Germany also exists in a non-incorporated variant and which is designed for the long term just like a foundation, has the advantage of not requiring a minimum asset. The reason is that an association constitutes a community of individuals for a shared purpose and does not contain a separated asset for a specified purpose.

40 Christine Vincent, "Estate Planning Choices," in: *The Artist as Philanthropist: Strengthening the Next Generation of Artist-Endowed Foundations. A Study of the Emerging Artist-Endowed Foundation Field in the US, A Reading Guide to the Study Report for Artists and Their Family Members* (Washington, D.C., 2010), p. 4.

41 See the interview with Michael Ward Stout in this volume.

Utilizing the potential tax privileges that result from foundations, associations, and other institutions is quite frequently accompanied by a desire for posthumous recognition. Successful artists today are comparatively independent and in a position to make decisions on the fundamental disposition of assets as a result of the money that can be earned during their lifetime. Such artists are able to establish and finance institutions that possibly also bear their own name and pursue their own goals in the long term. Presented with the choice of paying taxes that finance the purposes of the state or directly supporting the community in one's own name and based on one's own ideas, the decision would appear straightforward. Lawmakers in most countries also seem to prefer this. The United States, for example, has played a pioneering role in allowing artists to set up foundations within their own lifetime. Here, the state motivates its citizens more powerfully by means of generous tax advantages, but is also more reserved in its support of social and cultural objectives. This is no doubt a result of the extensive financing of "public" cultural institutions by private individuals. Legal thinking that favors the community and the benefactor or testator finds a place in most legal systems, however.

The American Aspen Institute,[42] a nonprofit policy studies organization and a global leader in research on nonprofit artist foundations,[43] has, under the directorship of Christine J. Vincent, compiled extensive data relating to this topic in recent years. According to one study by the institute, approximately fifty percent of nonprofit artist foundations are structured by artists during their lifetime in the US, but first realized after their death; thirty percent are realized during their lifetime; and twenty percent are first set up by descendants and/or heirs after the artist's death.[44] Foundations that were established based on provisions in the artist's will include the Joan Mitchell Foundation, the Roy Lichtenstein Foundation, the Willem de Kooning Foundation, the Judd Foundation, the Calder Foundation, the Barnett Newman Foundation, and the Judith Rothschild Foundation. Foundations established during the artists' lifetime include the Keith Haring Foundation, the Cruz-Diez Foundation, the Sam Francis Foundation, and the Mark Rothko Foundation.[45] Henry Moore established the trusts that today manage his oeuvre in the United Kingdom in the nineteen-seventies; just a short time ago, the French sculptor Bernar Venet[46] and the Japanese photography artist Hiroshi Sugimoto[47] each established a foundation in their home country.

4. Considerations in Selecting the Type of Estate Structure

The most important criterion in the choice of estate form is the artist's intention and the question of which form is suitable for the artist's oeuvre. The artist ideally provides the answer to this question during his or her lifetime. If such a clear intention is not available, the heirs have to identify it. Thus, for example, Martin Kippenberger's heirs decided against an institutionalized form of estate. "Kippenberger was an extreme artistic personality, someone who presented himself publicly in such a provocative way as hardly anyone else had done. That shouldn't be disguised by the concept of a foundation," as his close friend and gallerist Gisela Capitain explained.[48] Capitain has now been accompanying Kippenberger's estate for over eighteen years along with the widow, daughter, and one sister of the artist, and her work shows that it is also possible without an institutionalized structure to do much more than simply fulfill the responsibilities of administering an estate. Capitain was a natural choice for this work since she had already been managing Kippenberger's administrative affairs, such as taxes and account management since 1978 and also had experience with the art market. Based on this relationship of trust, they were able to cooperatively develop a market and exhibition strategy, and also to advance the creation of the catalogue raisonné. Mayen Beckmann manages her grandfather's estate in a private form, and her level of efficiency in doing so extends far into the institutional sector. The Beckmann-Archiv of the Bayerische Staatsgemäldesammlungen (Bavarian State Painting Collection) is co-financed by the family using income from copyrights; by permanent loans in Beckmann's native city of Leipzig his

---

42 http://www.aspeninstitute.org/ (accessed April 3, 2016).

43 Through the Artist-Endowed Foundations Initiative (AEFI), the institute has expanded its research activities in the nonprofit sector to include the more and more relevant field of artist foundations; more information is available at http://www.aspeninstitute.org/policy-work/nonprofit-philanthropy/national-study-artist-endowed-foundations/about-aefi (accessed April 3, 2016).

44 Christine Vincent, "7. Forming, sustaining, and terminating foundations. Part B: Considerations in foundation practice," in Vincent, *The Artist as Philanthropist* 2010 (see note 40), p. 15.

45 Barbara T. Hoffman, "Reflections on the survey and other musings on the management of artists' foundations and museums," in *A Visual Artist's Guide to Estate Planning: The 2008 Supplement Update* (Colorado Springs, 2008), pp. 55 f.

46 http://www.ft.com/intl/cms/s/2/8478e89e-08dd-11e4-8d27-00144feab7de.html#slide0 (accessed April 4, 2016).

47 http://blogs.wsj.com/scene/2014/01/23/hiroshi-sugimoto-designs-his-own-museum-in-japan/ (accessed April 4, 2016).

48 See the interview with Gisela Capitain in this volume.

museum presence has been strengthened, and the estate initiates and organizes exhibitions.

It is often assumed that charitable activities take a back seat and the financial interests of heirs take priority in the administration of estates that have a private form. But, the fact that this is generally not the case is shown by the abovementioned examples.

The dictum "only the best for the oeuvre" should also apply to purely private estate administration, and all of the instruments for estate work described in what follows are available as well as usable in that model. The decision to support scholarship through grants or give works to museums remains up to the private administrator; it is only that the support then occurs using private assets. The perspective of tax authorities is different in this case, but expenses effected for the estate can nevertheless still be deductible by means of tax structuring options. Thus, for instance, research projects done in collaboration with a nonprofit institution such as a university, which can then potentially issue a donation certificate to reduce taxes, can be taken into account with respect to taxes.

The fundamental question that is decisive in choosing the form of the estate is whether the estate should benefit the children or other private individuals in a financial sense, and if so, how freely these individuals should be able to dispose of the art and rest of the estate. Should the material value of the estate benefit only charitable purposes over a longer period of time, the only choice that remains is creating an independent entity.

In connection with artists' estates, the question of the heirs' financial interests is often only discussed behind closed doors, since it is expected that in the case of artists' estates the art historical perspective should be in the foreground. In light of this goal, the financial interests of the individual quickly become secondary. Inherited art is also inherited culture, which is worthy of protection. For heirs, however, inherited art is an inheritance to which they may make exactly the same financial claims as all other inherited assets—especially since many artists bequeath "art rich and cash poor," and the art is often the sole financially relevant thing bequeathed. For this reason, surviving relatives' interests in considering the financial aspects of the artist's estate are also quite justifiable.

To achieve a balanced relationship between heirs' interests in assets and the financial necessities of estate work, mixed models are also conceivable. They can, as in the case of Henry Moore and Willem de Kooning, be structured in such a way that the children receive a particular number of artworks, while the rest can be transferred to an estate as a separate legal entity, possibly for a charitable objective. Or the testator stipulates that the art is bequeathed to the children

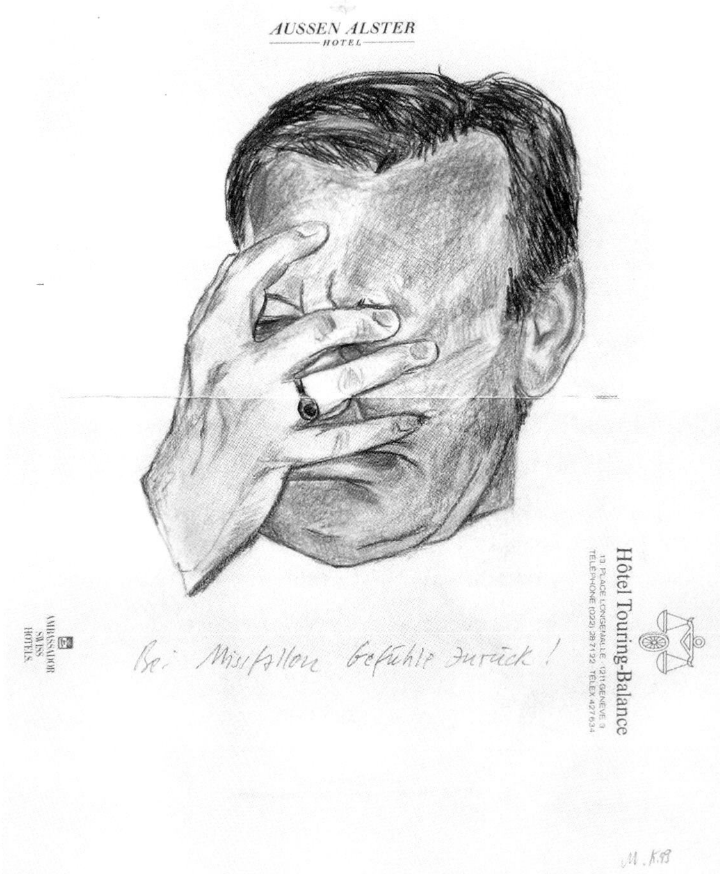

Martin Kippenberger, *Bei Missfallen Gefühle zurück (Aussen Alster Hotel/Hôtel Touring-Balance)*, 1989

under the proviso that in the case of a sale, two-thirds of the income is paid to the heirs and one-third to the estate, for example.

One should also weigh the extent to which the form of a separate legal entity—potentially subject to obligatory supervision as a result of its nonprofit status—might impede dealing with collection holdings in a flexible way. In the final chapter of this book, we will take an in-depth look at how selling collection holdings ensures financing for estate work, and how this activity in combination with acquisition activities can simultaneously be used to set in motion market impulses for the respective artist. Legal provisions regarding nonprofit status can substantially limit such activities. According to German law, for example, nonprofit organizations can only use revenue from sales to a limited extent to build up interest-earning capital stock, since they are required to pay out such income in a timely manner. In addition, market activities are quickly assessed as activities with the intention to realize profits and can therefore be harmful to the recognition of nonprofit status. The legal provisions under American law for preventing insider dealing mentioned above seem restrictive. From the standpoint of the artist bequeathing the estate, by contrast, the restrictions of freedom and flexibility that result from an institutionalized form of estate can be desired for diverse reasons. The choice of such a form also has advantages with respect to liquidity planning and the amount of the potential income available for achieving estate goals as a whole. This applies primarily in the case of nonprofit institutions. Their extensive exemption from most taxes allows the revenues that are utilized for the artist's legacy to grow. Institutionalized forms of administration that pursue no charitable purpose can also have tax advantages. For example, there may be no inheritance tax due at all in such cases, or perhaps it is possible to make better preparations for the obligation to pay—in Germany a private benefit foundation has to pay a so-called *Erbersatzsteuer* (substitute inheritance tax) every thirty years, and so the extra time allows them more potential to raise revenue.

The final question when weighing the choice between private estate administration and a separate legal entity for an estate is whether the estate is financially viable enough to finance an independent legal entity. Establishing an independent institution is only sensible when the assets of an estate are more than sufficient to be able to cover the additional setup and administration costs. At the same time, it is not possible to name a concrete amount that would make establishing a separate legal entity worthwhile. This must be determined based on the national legal provisions as well as relatives' need and desire for care.

A good indication is publically accessible information about American artist foundations as compiled in an extensive study by the Aspen Institute, mentioned above. According to this study, those foundations have annual operating costs averaging $475,000 and median operating costs—which denote the median value when all estate budgets are lined up in a row—of $100,000.[49] This makes it clear that an entity without cash assets at its disposal—either available to it from the beginning or able to be generated quickly by means of sales—is only an option for such artists who have already had economic success during their lifetime. This becomes particularly apparent through looking at the United States, where nearly all the art stars of the American half-century—who accumulated and bequeathed previously unknown fortunes—decided to take such a step. It will be interesting to see how their global successors such as Gerhard Richter, Jeff Koons, or Damien Hirst will deal with this question. These three artists alone are said to have assets of more than $1.5 billion,[50] not including works that can be monetized after their death.

All of this shows that the question of the form of estate administration is of great importance and requires very careful case-by-case examination, in which answers have to be found for the strategic questions previously mentioned and the consequences that the form will have for future actions.

5. Aspects of Nonprofit Status

If sufficient financial resources are available and the artist or his/her surviving dependents desire an independent legal entity for the estate, the next question that arises is whether this should operate as a nonprofit. Here, the work the nonprofit focuses on should be distinguished: Should it refer to the work of the artist or also include topics independent of the oeuvre? This is not only a financial, but also a strategic question that is independent of the inclinations and interests of the artist and his/her heirs.

What more or less all artists' estates have in common is the fact that at their core is the desire to preserve the artistic legacy of the respective artist, maintain his or her significance, and, in the best case, increase it. In most legal systems this is already a purpose that is sufficiently for the public benefit so as to be worthy of support according to tax law.[51] Such a public-oriented aim can be realized by means of the following measures:

1. exhibiting artworks publically
2. lending artworks to museums and other institutions
3. creating a catalogue raisonné or supporting a third party in doing so

---

49 Vincent, "Estate Planning Choices" 2010 (see note 40), p. 2.

50 http://uk.complex.com/style/2012/02/the-15-richest-living-artists/georg-baselitz (accessed April 3, 2016).

51 As a rule, all these institutions receive tax exemption/exempt status in the same manner: in the United States, based on the exempt purpose of the "advancement of education and science," https://www.irs.gov/Charities-&-Nonprofits/Charitable Organizations/Exempt-Purposes-Internal-Revenue-Code-Section-501(c)(3); in the United Kingdom based on their nonprofit purpose as a result of promoting the charitable concerns of "arts and education," https://www.gov.uk/setting-up-charity/charitable-purposes (accessed April 1, 2016); in Germany, based on promoting the charitable purposes of "art and culture" or "science and research," https://dejure.org/gesetze/AO/52.html (accessed April 1, 2016); or in Switzerland, for instance, based on the promotion of "cultural purposes."

4. providing access to archives for research
5. publishing scholarly publications
6. promoting research on the artist and/or his/her surroundings in general
7. maintaining the artist's studio and/or residence
8. operating a museum dedicated to the artist

There are, however, some restrictions on directly promoting the artistic work. For example, in the United States interaction between family members who own works themselves and a nonprofit foundation that in turn promotes the oeuvre are regulated due to the danger of insider dealing.[52] In light of possible legal consequences, specialized legal advising is therefore indispensable here.

Beyond taking care of the artistic work, many artist foundations with greater financial resources pursue broader goals, such as:

1. promoting research on particular artistic periods, genres, or styles
2. promoting education on art in general
3. awarding grants to artists, art projects, researchers, et cetera
4. awarding grants and donations to other charitable organizations for concrete projects or their general operating activities
5. promoting research on fighting illnesses
6. promoting efforts to reduce hunger or poverty, therefore benevolent purposes such as supporting individuals in need

With foundation assets of more than fifty million US dollars, the Dedalus Foundation of Robert Motherwell, for instance, fosters "public understanding of modern art and modernism through its programs in arts education, research and publications, archives and conservation, and exhibitions, as well as in the guardianship and study of Robert Motherwell's art."[53] The foundation fulfills this mission through an astounding range of educational initiatives and by sponsoring symposia and lectures, as well as grants for students and doctoral candidates. It therefore takes its place alongside a group of American artist institutions that have become a considerable influence and catalyzer in the general preservation, mediation, research, and promotion of art and artists. Its president, Jack Flam, sees the self-image and mission of the Dedalus Foundation as no less than "improving people's lives through art!"[54] Other, in particular US, foundations, also support further funding sectors in a comparable way. The Robert Mapplethorpe Foundation has made promoting photography as an art form and the fight against AIDS its mission;[55] the American artist Faith Ringgold made the focus of her foundation's work supporting African-American artists;[56] and Judy Chicago's Through the Flower Foundation seeks to increase the recognition of the role of women in history.[57]

For their charitable activities, American artist foundations are meanwhile able to access quite large fortunes: in 2010, the total assets of all 368 US artist foundations were ca. $3.48 billion—that year they gave out around $132 million for charitable purposes.[58] The biggest actors in the awarding of grants to date are the Andy Warhol Foundation for the Visual Arts with over $250 million[59] and the Pollock-Krasner Foundation with over sixty-five million US dollars.[61] The art journalist and university lecturer Andras Szanto has given this phenomenon the beautiful title: "the sleeping giants of philanthropy."[61]

In Europe, most artist foundations have dedicated themselves first and foremost to the work and memory more narrowly defined of the respective artist. They only act within a larger framework in very few cases, a fact that is mainly due to not having resources comparable to those of many US foundations—at least at the present time. Large foundation assets, like those of the Pollock-Krasner and Rauschenberg are rarely found in Europe. Additionally, ensuring the existence of art and culture is a responsibility allocated to the state in Europe, and so less emphasis in artists' estates on benefit to the public.

The Henry Moore Foundation, whose foundation capital currently totals ca. eighty-five million British pounds, represents one exception in Europe. It promotes public appreciation of the work of Henry Moore and the fine arts in

---

52 Vincent, "Estate Planning Choices" 2010 (see note 40), p. 5.

53 http://dedalusfoundation.org/foundation (accessed April 1, 2016).

54 See the interview with Jack Flam in this volume.

55 "He established an initial mandate of furthering the recognition of photography as an art form of the same importance as painting and sculpture. During the last weeks of his life, he added the second mandate of supporting medical research in the area of AIDS and HIV infection"; http://www.mapplethorpe.org/foundation/ (accessed April 1, 2016).

56 "[T]o expand the art establishment's canon to include artists of the African Diaspora and to introduce the Great Masters of African American Art and their art traditions to kids as well as adult audiences"; http://www.anyonecanflyfoundation.org/ (accessed April 1, 2016).

57 http://www.throughtheflower.org/about (accessed April 1, 2016).

58 Christine Vincent, "The Artist-Endowed Foundations," in *The Artist as Philanthropist: Strengthening the Next Generation of Artist-Endowed Foundations*. Study Report Supplement (Washington D.C., 2013), pp. xi–xii.

59 http://www.nytimes.com/2012/09/06/arts/design/warhol-foundation-to-disperse-collection.html?_r=0 (accessed April 1, 2016).

60 http://www.pkf.org/foundation.html (April 1, 2016).

61 http://www.giarts.org/article/artist-philanthropist (April 1, 2016).

general. It preserves Moore's legacy in his house in Hertfordshire and through exhibitions around the world, finances exhibitions and research on the topic of sculpture at the Henry Moore Institute in Leeds, and awards grants to arts organizations in the United Kingdom and abroad. Other examples are the German Stiftung Arp e.V.,[62] the Italian Fondazione Vedova,[63] and the English Kenneth Armitage Foundation,[64] which all award grants to scholars and/or artists. There is also a range of smaller institutions such as the Te Peerdt-Stiftung or the foundation of Horst Egon Kalinowski: The foundation of painter Ernst te Peerdt (1852–1932) supports the arts, but also supports individuals who have accidentally fallen on hard times.[65] The Karlsruhe art professor Horst Egon Kalinowski bequeathed his artistic estate to the Stiftung Kunstfonds of the State of North Rhine-Westphalia on the condition that it take care of his work and give an advancement award to young graduates of his art academy each year from the proceeds generated.[66] Another example is the Berlin-based Alexander und Renata Camaro Stiftung, which cares for the work of Alexander and Renata Camaro and makes it accessible to the public, as well as promoting the whole spectrum of contemporary art, including dance, literature, film, and music.[67]

There are also many foundations and associations in Europe that function as museums dedicated to a particular artist or institutes: The charitable Cragg Foundation of the British sculptor Tony Cragg, for instance, maintains the Waldfrieden Skulpturenpark. Besides presenting Cragg's own works, those of other sculptors are also shown and lectures on cultural topics are offered. The foundation is further dedicated to research and publications on fine arts.[68] Emil Nolde and his wife Ada established the Stiftung Seebüll Ada und Emil Nolde, which runs the artist museum in the German state of Schleswig-Holstein. He said: "All European cities and metropolises have their museums filled with thousands of artworks from ancient and modern times. This has its great beauty for many people and also the disadvantage of there being too much on offer. Every museum visitor will have experienced this. In total contrast to this, in our small place in simple, rural nature—metaphorically speaking—questing, intellectual pilgrims from all countries should find a special place where they receive some happiness and artistic-mental relaxation."[69]

Naturally, artists and their heirs are completely free in their choice of funding areas. It is nevertheless recommended that these areas not be defined too broadly or in too much detail. It is quite a beautiful burden to want to save nearly the whole world, as the cartoonist and artist Herb Block verbalized in the objectives of his foundation, endowed with ca. fifty million US dollars: "[The foundation's

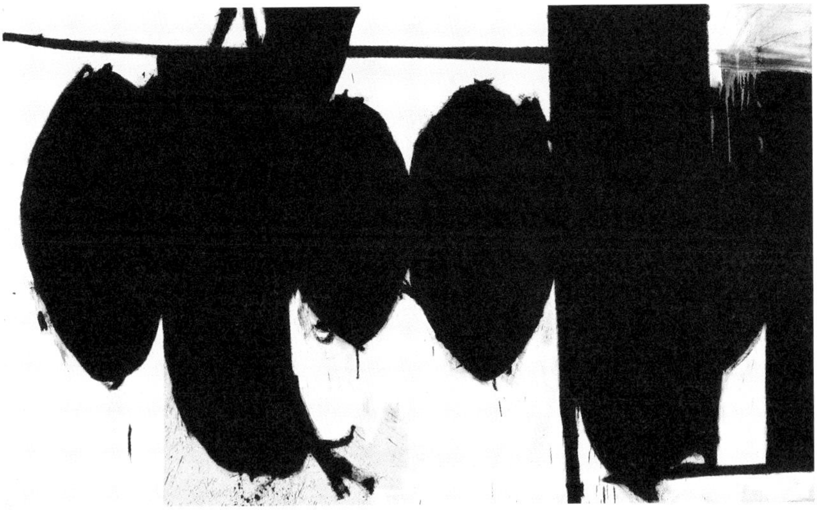

Robert Motherwell, *Elegy to the Spanish Republic No. 70*, 1961, The Metropolitan Museum of Art, New York

mission is] to preserve Herb Block's works and to conduct and sponsor charitable and educational programs to aid the poor, distressed and underprivileged, promote civil rights, fight prejudice and discrimination, advance freedom of expression and improve democratic government. To receive Herb Block's cartoons, sketches, paintings and manuscripts, as well as his residence, most of his investments ($49 M) and any future income generated by the investments."[70]

As is so often the case, the solution lies in the middle. The desire to promote everything and everyone can overtax representatives and paralyze them due to a lack of concept, while specifications that are overly concrete can impede the flexibility necessary to adapt over the years. Christy MacLear, managing director of the Rauschenberg Foundation, puts it in this way: "It's very valuable to have

62 http://stiftungarp.de/forschungundprojekte/stipendien/?setlang=en (accessed April 1, 2016).
63 http://www.fondazionevedova.org/en/foundation/aims-and-goals (accessed April 1, 2016).
64 http://www.kennetharmitagefoundation.org.uk/about_fellowship.jsp (accessed April 1, 2016).
65 http://www.te-peerdt-stiftung.de/web/satzung.html (accessed April 1, 2016).
66 http://www.kunstfonds.de/kalinowskistiftung.html (accessed April 1, 2016).
67 http://www.camaro-stiftung.de/content/stiftung_stifterin.htm (accessed April 1, 2016).
68 http://skulpturenpark-waldfrieden.de/skulpturenpark/cragg-foundation.html (accessed April 1, 2016).
69 http://www.nolde-stiftung.de/de/97/selbstverstaendnis.html (accessed April 1, 2016).
70 http://www.sharpeartfdn.org/supplement/D-3_A-Listing-of-Some-Deceased-Visual-Artists.pdf (accessed April 1, 2016).

latitude, but equally, if not more valuable, to have a sense of direction. It's exceptionally helpful if the artist can define the topics / issues / subjects that were critical to them and allow for the fluctuation of that over time. Rauschenberg was very open in terms of his interests, when faced with materials to define the direction of the foundation he checked every single box on the tax form: education, environment, AIDS medical research, etc. etc. It was almost too much, as if he wanted to be everything. So in this case we had to prioritize our focus based on our resources. Additionally, you have to assume that things will transform. So being too definitive is not good and won't allow for changes over long periods of time to adjust."[71]

In the end, broad objectives can only be realized if the financial means allow. Everyone should only act within the realm of possibility. And so the president of the Andy Warhol Foundation, Joel Wachs, warns against too much ambition: "... one size doesn't fit all when it comes to this work, because everyone isn't in the same situation. There are many different ways that artists can use their assets to help other artists and arts organizations. Each foundation has to find the path that's right for it, and its namesake."[72]

6. Art, Taxes, and Structural Options for Estates

With the death of an artist, as with every other individual, taxes are incurred. These might be inheritance taxes or they might be income taxes, depending on how the artist organized his or her production in legal form. For artists' estates, this issue is of particular importance since they are generally "art rich and cash poor" and need every cent for the future responsibilities of estate administration. For artists' estates, it is therefore a legitimate objective to pay as little in taxes as possible and to take advantage of legitimate legal instruments for tax optimization. It is not possible to provide a detailed description of the corresponding instruments for all relevant legal and tax regulations within the framework of this book. However, I would still like to give an overview in order to facilitate understanding of this topic for individuals responsible for an estate and to help simplify the necessary conversations with tax advisors and attorneys.

As a rule, legal systems that levy an inheritance tax have no special provisions for artists as a professional group or for art found in an estate as an asset, even the artist's own works. This becomes clear in connection with cases of inheritance where an artist built up a large collection, as with Willem de Kooning for example. Both his works and his collection of art by friends and contemporaries were subject, without exception, to American inheritance tax and the valuation process that applied at that point in time.

Inheritance tax law in many countries does, however, provide various kinds of preferential treatment and creative possibilities with respect to the asset value of art on a subordinate level. Heirs in Germany can obtain an exemption from tax liability of up to 100 percent for particular works of art pursuant to § 13 *Erbschaftsteuergesetz* (ErbstG: inheritance tax law), or pay this tax in accordance with § 224 a *Abgabenordnung durch Kunstgegenstände* (tax code for art objects), as an example. The latter is also possible in the United Kingdom (acceptance in lieu) or Mexico, but not, for example, in the United States.[73] There, however—with regard to the artist's own artworks in his / her estate—it is possible to reduce the taxable base using the so-called blockage discount, a markdown that takes into account a depreciation in value when a large number of works is sold at the same time.[74] In addition, most jurisdictions provide various models for organizing the administration of artists' estates that allow for tax benefits.[75]

a) Continental Europe

In all countries, the taxes to be paid after the death of an artist depend on the existing structures or forms in which his / her production processes and assets were organized. If the artist already created his / her own asset subject while alive, by establishing a private benefit foundation for instance, in most legal systems this entity is not required to pay taxes after the artist's death. The large majority of artists, however, pursue the profession as so-called freelancers, in which case

---

71 See the interview with Christy MacLear in this volume.

72 http://philanthropynewsdigest.org/5-questions-for/joel-wachs-andy-warhol-foundation (accessed April 1, 2016).

73 http://www.forbes.com/sites/robertwood/2014/09/10/paying-tax-with-art-is-legal-in-uk-mexico-why-not-in-us/ (accessed April 1, 2016).

74 On this, see in general Alan Breus, "Valuing Art for Tax Purposes," in *Journal of Accountancy*, July 1, 2010; http://www.journalofaccountancy.com/issues/2010/jul/20092096.html (accessed April 1, 2016).

75 At the same time, if the legal construction is primarily designed to secure an optimal fiscal structure, it should be noted that the tax laws and regulations may be subject to change in the different states. As a result, the estate tax exempt amounts, the methods for calculating the basis for fiscal assessment, the effects of endowments by the artist during his or her lifetime or upon death, as well as the rules and mechanisms for assessing art can change. Therefore, the choice of the legal form can only ever me made in light of the current legal options. Against this background, the following is meant to provide a mere orientation on which institutionalized models of administration of an estate with which fiscal effects could currently come into consideration.

restrictions are set on tax planning strategies. Exceptions are gifts given during the artist's lifetime to spouses or descendants in order to benefit from tax-free allowances, which are often granted again after a certain period of time.

(1) Germany

Germany provides an interesting tax structure for estates if the production of art was organized in a commercial operation. European legal systems are also familiar with the so-called blockage discount in US tax law, with respect to income tax that is possibly also due. This can happen in Germany when the artist organized his / her production in a business form, whether as a sole trader or in another form of business recognized by commercial law, and the business is not intended to exist after his / her death. As a result of the consequent termination of business, the hidden reserves—mainly existing artworks in the possession of the business—are revealed and have to be taxed at a rate of forty-five percent, but the total taxable sum can ultimately be reduced through deductions that can be negotiated.[76]

Termination of business in Germany is a "right to influence" that is available to heirs, which means that it may be exercised, but need not. Once exercised, however, it can no longer be revoked. For this reason, one should have a comparative calculation drawn up with the support of tax advisors, since the possible continuation of the business may also have tax advantages that are greater than the deduction to be granted. The decision which variant is less expensive can then be reached on this basis, while whether or not to terminate the business should also be clarified, since the business continues automatically otherwise. When the business continues, its hidden reserves are not revealed. Income tax is only due in such cases when art from the business assets are actually sold. At the same time, the business can benefit from a privileged inheritance tax status if continued.[77]

Establishing a legally independent foundation, which would be the usual case for an artist foundation in Continental Europe, has completely different tax implications. What is concerned in this case is an institution that is supposed to advance a purpose defined by the founder with specific assets and organization in the long term.[78] The phrase "in the long term" should, however, not be equated with "in perpetuity," and a foundation's end can be clearly defined in the bylaws. Such a foundation is independent because it, as a legally responsible legal entity, has rights and obligations and achieves legal independence at the point in time when the founder establishes it. Although the founder has great latitude in designing the foundation with respect to its funding aims, organization, and capital basis, after acquiring its legal capacity, he/she has hardly any more influence; especially since the foundation does not "belong" to the founder and also not to anyone else, because as a corporate body, it has neither members nor partners or other owners.[79] In contrast to other legal persons in German law, such as companies (GmbH, AG) or registered associations, which have to be listed in the trade or association register, independent foundations however have to be officially recognized. The process of recognition—which requires the foundation to accept strict formal provisions and government auditing rights—quite plainly shows the founder the fundamental irreversibility of the endeavor, but also protects him or her from acting rashly.[80]

To effectively constitute a foundation in Germany, it is necessary to fulfill various formal criteria. But it is also required to have a sufficiently sound capital basis. The so-called "endowment capital" is supposed to represent the material basis for the foundation; from which it generates revenue and which may not

---

76 Inheritance tax has to be paid in addition, even though a deduction in accordance with § 35b ErbstG does occur to a certain extent. The taxable base, therefore the total value of all taxable operating assets, can, as far as artworks are concerned, be reduced through negotiating with tax authorities, whereby an average of thirty to forty percent deduction is granted. According to tax advisors who deal with this topic, it is, however, to recognize increasing resistance on the part of the state to overly high reductions.

77 Even if the artist is no longer alive and the production of art has been discontinued, for the continuation of the business, the continuation of the trade aspect suffices. In this case, for example, inheritance taxes can be avoided completely if artworks are first sold after seven years, since after this period of continuing a business it is completely exempt from the perspective of inheritance tax. If art is, however, sold from the business after six years, for instance, besides the income tax, only one-seventh of the value is estimated for the retroactive payment of inheritance tax. These advantages are, however, linked to the preservation of jobs. If these are eliminated, the tax advantages can also occasionally be reduced completely. Currently, this coupling between tax reprieves and preservation of workplaces is only regulated for businesses with more than twenty employees, the relevant company size is, however, supposed to be reduced to the number of three employees during the course of 2016 as part of inheritance tax reform, so that artist businesses will in future also be affected by this much more quickly. Correspondingly, sample calculations should also include personnel planning and wages. Such tax reprieves for businesses also exist in other European countries. The motivation on the part of lawgivers is the fact that the continuation of businesses not only preserves jobs, but fundamentally also contributes to general economic productivity and the ongoing payment of other taxes.

78 Schlüter and Stolte, *Stiftungsrecht* 2007 (see note 31), p. 31.

79 Ibid., p. 54.

80 Depending on how the foundation's bylaws are drafted, under certain conditions, rescission and/or dissolution is still conceivable during the founder's lifetime. Such dissolution is much more difficult, if not impossible, if the foundation is first formed after death based on the will, and then namely only under very restricted statutory conditions.

be touched, but can be increased through endowment contributions.[81] This results from the principle of asset preservation depending on the structure and planned lifespan of the institution, and the extent to which deviations are permitted by the structure of the bylaws or charter.

The type of endowment capital is not fixed and may comprise investments, cash deposits, or securities. It must, however, be able to yield income without touching the capital. For an artist foundation, this means that although it is possible for copyrights to be part of the endowment capital, artworks alone do not suffice, at least not to begin with. They may increase in value, but only bring revenue when sold. For the foundation's basic endowment, if it cannot be obtained from other sources, the sale of works is generally necessary prior to its establishment. The possibility of utilizing later proceeds from works transferred to the foundation for increasing the foundation capital naturally remains unaffected. An exact amount of endowment capital has not been defined in Germany, and is instead determined in a case-by-case assessment by the state authorities, though 50,000 euros has been established as a minimum.[82]

As a legal person under private law, the private law foundation in Germany is subject to unlimited corporate tax, currently at a rate of fifteen percent. If it maintains a business enterprise, it is also subject to business tax. Germany, like most other countries, only grants tax incentives if the state is relieved of burdens. This is the case when a foundation, or another corporate body such as an association or a corporation, operates charitably and advances aims that serve the common good.[83]

In contrast to independent foundations, fiduciary foundations, also called dependent foundations, have no legal identity and correspondingly no narrow legal provisions. This is because this legal model does not participate independently in legal transactions and has no external effect. A core element here is either a trustee agreement between the founder and the trustee, who can in turn be a natural or legal person, or a stipulation with which the founder connects the funds.[84]

In principle, the legal structures in other Continental European countries are nearly or for the most part identical. Insofar as an artist was active and "felt at home" in several countries, and there is therefore a cross-border context, doing some "forum shopping" to find the right legal model and checking whether the differences between countries might have a positive effect on the realization of the respective objectives of the estate can be advisable.

(2) Austria

Austria differentiates between nonprofit foundations and nonprofit funds, as well as private foundations, which have existed in their current form since 1993.[85] As everywhere else, the Austrian private foundation may pursue any objective as long as it does not violate the law or common decency. To make the confusion complete, it can, however, also be established in a charitable form, as the Hundertwasser charitable private foundation in Vienna is.[86] It was established based on the so-called *Privatstiftungsgesetz* (private foundation law), whereas other (exclusively) charitable foundations are established according to the foundation law of the respective Austrian federal province. Private foundations as well as nonprofit funds[87] are permitted to use their endowment capital. The

81 Schlüter and Stolte, *Stiftungsrecht* 2007 (see note 31), p. 59.

82 Ibid.

83 As a rule, in the case of an artist's estate, tax privileges are obtained as a result of the nonprofit goal of advancing art and culture. It is, however, possible to pursue multiple objectives in parallel. Thus, for instance, the foundation of Ernst te Peerdt, a painter of the Düsseldorf and Munich schools, benefits from tax privileges, on the one hand, because it promotes art, and on the other, however, because it supports people in need and is thus benevolent. The exemption from taxes that can be realized in this way includes gift and inheritance tax, corporation and business tax, property tax, and value added tax, as long as an ideal purpose is pursued with the commercial activity. Investments in securities, real estate, and shareholdings, which are still classified legally as asset management, and revenue from them also belong to the corporate tax-exempted area of a foundation. Economic activity that goes beyond this is also permitted, but may not predominate with respect to the ideal mission established in the charter. For such activities, the tax privileges are then dropped. Schlüter and Stolte, *Stiftungsrecht* 2007 (see note 31), pp. 61–64.

84 For them, law of obligations and inheritance law provisions apply and not foundation law. One example of such a fiduciary foundation is the organization of the estate of the already mentioned, German Informel artist Horst Egon Kalinowski. The fiduciary, in this case the Stiftung Kunstfonds of the State of North Rhine-Westphalia, in this model may not be identical with the founder; it can be organized in a charitable manner, but does not have to be. When establishing a foundation, the charitable status, if desired, it is necessary to commit and adhere to the fact that the means can only be used for the tax-privileged objectives defined by the founder. As in the case of Kalinowski, here, the objective of the foundation has to be coordinated very precisely with the area of responsibility of the fiduciary that is envisioned. This suggests already establishing a fiduciary foundation during one's lifetime. Dependent foundations are not subject to any state supervision; in the case of tax exemption, however the tax authority monitors compliance with relevant tax regulations; http://www.iww.de/erbbstg/archiv/stiftung-die-treuhaenderische-stiftung-f47916 (accessed April 4, 2016).

85 On this and on the differences in detail, see http://www.verwaltung.steiermark.at/cms/beitrag/11683750/75853088 (accessed April 4, 2016).

86 http://www.hundertwasserfoundation.org/impressum/ (accessed April 4, 2016).

87 A fund from the perspective of Austrian foundation and fund law denotes assets with a legal identity that a founder of a fund does *not* dedicate long term. The assets can be used up until the fund dissolves, and they have to be intended for the fulfilling of charitable or benevolent purposes.

private foundation model also has advantages with respect to taxes in its noncharitable variant, even though Austrian law relativized tax privileges by abolishing inheritance and gift tax in 2008.[88]

(3) Spain

In Spain, foundations organized under private law are only permitted when they pursue goals that benefit the public. That means that advancing general interests can be the aim of a foundation, but the law explicitly rules out private economic self-interests as well as the promotion of relatives.[89] Such a nonprofit foundation can, as in other countries, also be established during a person's lifetime or as a result of death. They can set up long-term or be dissolved once an objective is achieved. The law stipulates that the endowment capital necessary is at least 30,000 euros, and at least seventy percent of income has to be used to achieve the aims of the foundation. Corresponding to their nonprofit status, they are fundamentally exempted from corporate tax, where there is a differentiation between income from a special-purpose enterprise and income from other types of operations.[90]

(4) France

In France preferential tax treatment is less extensive, an aspect that combined with a strong government is presumably the reason for the much lower number of foundations than other, similarly developed nations. Here, in addition to the foundation benefitting the public (Fondation reconnue d'Utilité publique), there are the company foundation (Fondation d'Entreprise) and the so-called sheltered foundation (Fondation abritée), which—comparable with the German fiduciary foundation—has no legal identity and whose assets are administered by an umbrella foundation, often the Institut de France.[91] The definition of the status of benefitting the public is quite broad in France. But, as in Spain, even only partially preferential treatment of the founder or relatives is forbidden, as well as the pursuit of political and religious objectives. A foundation is also not permitted to seek to make a profit.[92] Foundations are subject to permanent government monitoring, which goes so far as the state dispatching two compulsory members to foundation advisory boards. Apart from the difficult search for suitable real estate, the extensive control options and lack of flexibility in foundation laws were possibly also one reason why the French businessman and art collector François Pinault established his museum first in Venice and not in Paris as originally planned.[93] Meanwhile, however, Pinault and the city of Paris have agreed on a location for the Paris branch of his collection.[94]

(5) Switzerland

Swiss foundation law is considerably more liberal. As in the case of the private foundation in Austria, in the Swiss private foundation model the aim of the foundation can be amended later or the foundation revoked under particular conditions. It can therefore be used as an instrument for private asset planning and serve not only altruistic purposes, but also the founder's for-profit wishes.[95] Here, a foundation can be established as an *Unternehmensstiftung* (company foundation)[96]—in the form of a holding foundation or foundation with a corporate sponsor—or as a foundation pursuant to Art. 80–86 *Zivilgesetzbuch* (ZGB: Swiss Civil Code). Family foundations are also possible to a limited extent in accordance with Art. 87 and 355 ZGB, where due to the ban on maintenance foundations they are only allowed insofar as they pay the costs for the education, outfitting, and support of family members in need. All foundations are subject to regulatory supervision. Swiss nonprofit foundations in accordance with

88 Nonetheless, non-charitable private foundations only have to pay a corporate tax in the amount of twenty-five percent for income from agriculture and forestry, commercial enterprise, and rents and leases—for shareholding none at all. Under what type of income tax authorities subsume revenue realized through the sale of artworks owned by a foundation is not known. It is, however, clear that the model chosen by the Austrian artist Franz West was interesting both in terms of cementing his desires and also for tax reasons—the more so since revenue from capital assets such as bank deposits and funds here only pays an interim tax rate of 12.5 percent as long as it is reinvested. After payout to beneficiaries, such income is subject to a twenty-five percent capital gains tax, while the foundation receives a credit in the amount of the interim taxation.

89 http://www.ra-becker.de/535997972d0a59b03/53599798cf0a0c301/535997972d0f29144/index.php (accessed April 4, 2016).

90 Income from non-special-purpose enterprises is subject to a tax rate of ten percent. The Dalí Foundation, for instance, therefore had to pay taxes on income from assets that were not generated by the so beautifully worded aim of the foundation—"to promote, foster, explain, give prestige, protect and defend, both inside and outside the Spanish territory, the artistic, cultural and intellectual oeuvre of the painter"; http://www.salvador-dali.org/fundacio-dali/en_index/ (accessed April 4, 2016).

91 http://archiv.ub.uni-heidelberg.de/volltextserver/18051/1/Charnitzky_Milena.pdf (accessed April 4, 2016).

92 Capital gains are tax-free for a French foundation, and all other income is taxed at a rate between ten and twenty-four percent rather than the usual/standard 33.33 percent.

93 The French company foundation is subject to less governmental supervision, but can only be brought into being by a company and also has to pursue charitable objectives. The Fondation Louis Vuitton in Paris has this type of legal nature. As a rule, company foundations are, however, precluded as a legal form for administering artistic estates.

94 http://www.nytimes.com/2016/04/28/arts/franois-pinault-private-museum-paris.html?_r=0.

95 http://www.rwi.uzh.ch/lehreforschung/alphabetisch/jakob/lehre/unterlagenfs2011/europaeischesprivatrechtII/EuPRII_Ueberblick_foundation law_Schweiz_Jakob_FS11.pdf.

96 Swiss law is not familiar with the concept of the company foundation as such.

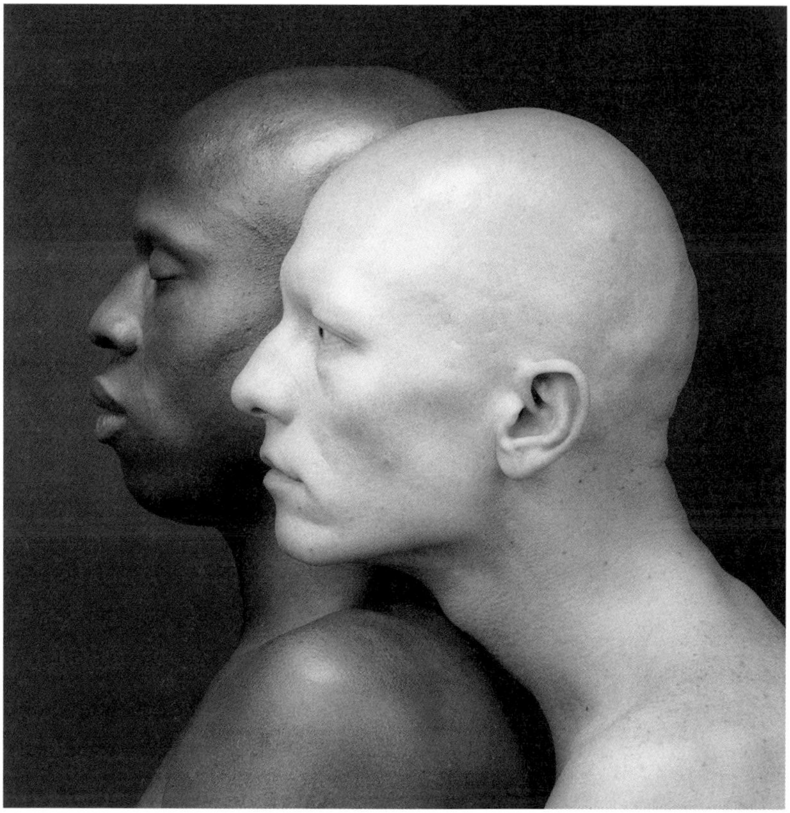

Robert Mapplethorpe, *Ken Moody and Robert Sherman*, 1984

Art. 80 ff. ZGB include the Fondazione Marguerite Arp and the Max Bill Georges Vantongerloo Foundation,[97] which the second wives of the artists established.[98] Non-nonprofit foundations in Switzerland are subject to a national corporate tax of 4.25 percent and low cantonal taxes; income from shareholdings is tax free as well as income from capital yields;[99] nonprofit foundations are completely exempt from tax on profit and capital.[100]

b) United States of America and United Kingdom

In Anglo-American jurisdictions, trusts and foundations especially are common legal tools to give effect to the intentions of an artist as well as to potentially achieve tax optimization. These also exist in tax-privileged nonprofit form as charitable trusts or tax-exempt foundations. If a beneficiary of an artistic estate is not defined in a will or a trust or foundation is not established for this purpose during the artist's lifetime, statutory intestacy rules will apply. These determine the heir to the estate but not necessarily in accordance with the wishes of the deceased.

Therefore, if Robert Mapplethorpe had not structured his estate during his lifetime, under succession rules in the state of New York, it would have gone to his parents, which he specifically did not want.[101] In the last days of his life, he decided to leave each member of his family an artwork, and to leave $100,000 to his brother.[102] The statutory order of succession in the United States is, as in most legal systems, determined by family relationship, so that unmarried partners or stepchildren are also not recognized.

(1) Inheritance-Related Laws in the Anglo-American Legal Sphere

Depending on the decedent's place of residence, different current inheritance tax provisions take effect on the date of death. Besides the tax-exempt amounts, the United Kingdom and the United States offer further possibilities for reducing the basis for assessing inheritance tax independent of trust or foundation models. Tax-reducing gifts might be particularly interesting for established artists.

---

97 http://www.steueramt.zh.ch/internet/finanzdirektion/ksta/de/steuerfragen/steuerbefreite_institutionen/_jcr_content/contentPar/downloadlist/downloaditems/verzeichnis_der_steu.spooler.download.1434349121601.pdf/2015-06-12_Verzeichnis+der+steuerbefreiten+-Institutionen+JP.pdf (accessed April 4, 2016).

98 The proposals for foundations that Bill's son from his first marriage presented during his father's lifetime were apparently unpersuasive. After Max Bill's death, his son then established his own Bill foundation, the Max, Binia und Jakob Bill-Stiftung, as well as the Bill-Stiftung. It was not possible to discover whether these two foundations are considered charitable according to Swiss law, but they do—just as the Max Bill Georges Vantongerloo Foundation—have the promotion of scholarly research on Max Bill as well as the development of a collection and making it accessible to the public as core tasks; https://en.wikipedia.org/wiki/Max_Bill (accessed April 4, 2016); http://www.bill-stiftung.ch/stiftungen.htm (accessed April 4, 2016).

99 There is no anticipatory tax such as in Austria, and the tax burden first becomes noticeable in the payout of revenue to beneficiaries. Of Western European countries, therefore, only Switzerland and Liechtenstein offer similar tax-saving conditions for purely private foundations as does Austria; foundations are in part only permitted in a nonprofit form. If some EU member states, such as Cyprus or Ireland, there is low corporate tax rates, meaning that it is possible there to achieve similar effects of low current taxation as in the case of private foundations in Austria; it is, however, still essential for the functioning and work of a foundation the extent to which gifts of private assets are subject to taxation (e.g., by means of inheritance and gift tax) and the extent to which distributions by foundations to private individuals are subject to taxation; see Otto Farny, Ani Degirmencioglu, Michael Franz, Gertraud Lunzer, and Martin Saringer, *Stiftungsbesteuerung in Europa*, Studie der Kammer für Arbeiter und Angestellte für Wien, March 2009.

100 http://www.stiftungsrecht.ch/steuerliche-aspekte (accessed April 4, 2016).

101 http://codes.lp.findlaw.com/nycode/EPT/4/1/4-1.1 (accessed April 4, 2016).

102 See the interview with Michael Ward Stout in this volume.

In the United States, this tax-exempt amount, called unified credit, is subject to change on a yearly basis.[103] Here, however, all previous gifts to the person inheriting have to be taken into consideration and not only, as in the United Kingdom, gifts during a review period of seven years prior to death (ten years in Germany). In the United States since 1970, gifts to charitable organizations during a person's lifetime ("*inter vivos* transfers") are only tax deductible with respect to the amount of the material costs and no longer in the amount of the market value of an artwork. In addition, the copyright also has to be transferred along with the work in order to obtain the tax deduction.[104] With respect to tax law, during the artist's lifetime artworks are assessed as income property and not as capital assets that result in capital gains in the long term.[105] With the death of an artist, this status changes and gifts to charitable organizations due to death can be deducted in full from the assessment basis for inheritance tax. This tax advantage in the case of a "testamentary transfer" applies for bequests to public charities or tax-exempt organizations / private foundations. Copyrights should then be transferred separately from the artwork as an independent ownership right and listed in the will as such, so as not to run the risk of forfeiting tax advantages, something that depends on the interpretation of wills according to the judgment of the respective US state in individual cases.[106] Bequests to spouses are completely exempt from inheritance tax in the United States. Such a marital bequest can, however, collide with bequests on death to charitable institutions—called outright bequests—if more than fifty percent of the estate is supposed to be transferred to a charitable body. This is because certain minimum requirements can be made with respect to the amount a spouse inherits according to the law.

The obligation to pay inheritance tax in the United States arises after nine months, although, as mentioned above, tax-exempt amounts for heirs are much higher in comparison to Europe—although all gifts to heirs as from 1976 are counted to assess the total value of the bequest. If one does not only want to bequeath one's estate to charitable organizations, it is recommended, as in other legal systems, to give significantly early on, so that the increase in value that potentially occurs at the end of an artist's career is not also taxed. This is, however, rarely a realistic option.

If tax-exempt amounts are exceeded in the United States, the abovementioned blockage discount therefore becomes relevant. This tax privilege, originally developed for securities, reduces the taxable base. If the estate comprises largely the same general type(s) of property, the necessary simultaneous liquidation recovery of assets will affect the value of all assets if need be.[107] There are no fixed values, and cases are assessed individually, since such a market mechanism depends on the individual artworks—what size, what medium, their price structure so far, the reputation of the artist, among other things. The most well-known examples of the use of the principle are the estates of David Smith, Louisa Calder, Georgia O'Keeffe, and Andy Warhol—with very different results, as Ralph Lerner and Judith Bresler describe in their standard work on art law.[108] David Nash also referred to them in assessing the estate of Willem de Kooning, which he undertook on behalf of the executor of the estate, John Eastman: "We divided the works into three groups: The first group would be the handful of best works and we recommended no discount for them. We felt that they all probably could be sold within a short space of time at full market value. The second group would be the less good paintings, which was obviously a much larger group. We recommended a twenty-five or thirty percent discount for them. The balance of the works, which were mostly drawings, would constitute the third group and we recommended a sixty percent discount."[109]

Since Warhol bequeathed his estate to the general public, the question about such a blockage discount only arose because one of the attorneys involved was supposed to be compensated based on the value of the estate and, unsurprisingly, a dispute about the total sum erupted. The court gave a twenty-percent discount for paintings and photos and thirty-five percent for drawings and prints, so that the total value that ultimately emerged here lay within the usual range of markdowns; up to seventy percent as a result of blockage discounts is possible.

---

103 In 2015, it amounted to $5.43 million, and in 2016 to $5.46 million; https://www.irs.gov/Businesses/Small-Businesses-&-Self-Employed/Whats-New-Estate-and-Gift-Tax (accessed April 3, 2016).

104 Lerner and Bresler, *Art Law* 2005 (see note 5), pp. 1767 f.

105 Ibid., p. 1767.

106 Ibid., p. 1778.

107 "The concept of blockage is essentially one of timing. A discount may be allowed where a large quantity of any type of art is offered on the market at one time and would substantially depress its value"; ibid., p. 1748.

108 In the case of David Smith, the tax court assessed the estate, for instance, at $2.5 million, while the IRS initially estimated twice that and calculated a value of $710,000 for the estate; Calder's widow, Louisa, inherited over 1,000 gouaches, which the IRS initially assessed as being three times higher, but the widow was ultimately granted a much higher discount of sixty percent. The estate of O'Keeffe provides a clear example of the three-group model that the IRS's Art Advisory Panel uses for assessing blockage discounts, among other things. According to it, in the case of O'Keeffe, a total estate value of nearly seventy-three million US dollars was calculated, whereby for works with a value of more than $500,000 no discount was granted, for works with a value between $500,000 and $200,000 a discount of twenty percent, and for works below this value fifty percent; ibid., pp. 1749–65.

109 See the interview with David Nash in this volume.

Whatever the case, the experts chosen on the part of the estate should present the IRS with a realistic assessment, since otherwise penalties amounting to twenty percent of the shortfall may be due.[110]

In the United Kingdom, inheritance tax (IHT) currently amounts to forty percent of the assets inherited and has to be paid within six months after the succession, where a tax-exempt amount of 325,000 British pounds is permitted. Taxation therefore only takes effect if the total assets exceed this amount, the so-called inheritance tax threshold.[111] There is a range of further tax reliefs;[112] for example, gifts or legacies to spouses[113] are fully exempted from the inheritance tax.[114] Moreover, for artists or artists' estates, other instruments for substantially reducing taxes can also come into consideration.[115]

The most relevant of them is surely the so-called business property relief (BPR), according to which the British, like many other legal systems, grant tax exemptions for business assets. Corresponding to the continuation or termination of business as described above based on German law, how the artistic work is organized at the time of death can have an advantageous or disadvantageous effect with respect to taxes in the United Kingdom.[116] Artworks can also be transferred to the state in the United Kingdom in lieu of paying tax liabilities, in which case a "presentation of offers" has to be submitted to the Arts Council,[117] which does not, however, have to adhere to any specific guidelines in reaching its decision. Works of art that have previously been classified as sufficiently relevant can be found in the annual *Cultural Gifts Scheme and Acceptance in Lieu Report.*[118] This option for tax reduction already exists during an artist's lifetime in connection with income tax and capital gains tax.

For the tax assessment of gifts, the time of the gift and recipient are decisive. The value of gifts to natural persons, for instance descendants, is added to the taxable estate if less than seven years lie between the gift and the death. This means that gifts should be given early on, when it is still necessary to keep any available nil rate band amounts/the threshold in mind. The same process also applies to settlements on trust.[119] In the United Kingdom as well as the European Union, gifts to charitable institutions, just as gifts to a charitable institution that one has created oneself are completely tax-free.[120] The abovementioned reduction of inheritance tax rate from forty to thirty-six percent as a result of bequeathing ten percent of an estate to charitable institutions therefore applies in the case of artists' own charitable organizations created by the artist him or her self. Awareness of such incentives makes it possible to reduce the tax burden and simultaneously to position artists by means of targeted gifts to reputable institutions, is something that should be part of all estate planning in any case.

The tax options connected with this should therefore also be utilized. Insofar as this is supposed to occur through the transfer of artwork and not, for instance, through direct financial support, for example, of (art) schools or grant-awarding organizations, what should more precisely be considered is who, or where is given what: this step is irreversible and can be beneficial or detrimental to the reception of the artist.

Like in Europe, the determining factors for tax and therefore for tax optimization here are: Which natural or juridical person gets which asset, at what point in time, and for which purpose? What is the tax-exempt amount at the time of death? For charitable institutions and non-charitable? In the Anglo-Saxon jurisdictions two major legal instruments are used in the context of legacy planning and tax optimization.

(2) Trusts

The purpose of a trust, and similar to a foundation, is the transfer of specific assets, which consequently constitute an independent body of special purpose

---

110 Lerner and Bresler, *Art Law* (2005) (see note 5), p. 1765.

111 https://www.gov.uk/inheritance-tax/overview (accessed April 3, 2016).

112 For particular asset classes such as agricultural property, the inheritance tax rate is further reduced here to thirty-six percent if ten percent of the total assets benefit nonprofit and/or charitable purposes; Anghard Palin, "Where there is a will, there is a way," in: *The Artist's Legacy. Estate Planning in the Visual Arts*, eds. Emma Warren-Thomas and Linda Schofield (London, 2013), p. 20.

113 For an overview of structures of charities in the United Kingdom, see https://www.gov.uk/guidance/charity-types-how-to-choose-a-structure#types-of-charity-structure (accessed April 3, 2016).

114 *The Artist's Legacy* (2013) (see note 112).

115 Upon request, artworks can be classified as "assets of national artistic interest," just as buildings can also be ranked as "assets of national historical interest," and excluded from the total assets to be taxed for this reason. The prerequisites for this are, however, very demanding, and such a classification is connected with maintenance obligations and making the asset(s) accessible to the public; ibid.

116 If the artist works through a company or as a sole trader, in addition to standard business equipment and/or resources, artworks and copyrights are also assessed as such and exempted from inheritance tax up to 100 percent, whereby the concrete business structure is decisive and discussions with the tax authority often become necessary. While a separate studio is assessed as a business resource without further ado, this is already more difficult in the case of real estate for residential and working purposes due to its twofold function.

117 http://www.artscouncil.org.uk/what-we-do/supporting-museums/cultural-property/tax-incentives/acceptance-lieu/ (accessed April 3, 2016).

118 http://www.artscouncil.org.uk/sites/default/files/download-file/Acceptance_in_Lieu_guidance.pdf (accessed April 3, 2016).

119 Jacqueline Hruby, "Gifting Works of Art," in *The Artist's Legacy* (2013) (see note 112), p. 27.

120 Ibid.

assets.[121] In the case of a trust, the owner of segregated assets that he or she holds on behalf of beneficiaries is called a trustee. The trustee is also responsible for liabilities connected with the segregated assets that he or she will have to administer, which the trustee will have to administer separately from his or her private assets. The trust assets are therefore also beyond the reach of the trustee's personal creditors. The so-called settlor or grantor, who establishes the trust through transferring property to the trustee, can, in contrast to the case of a foundation, retain the right to dissolve the trust at a later point and withdraw the remaining assets. However, in many jurisdictions, a right to resolve the trust at a later stage will result in tax consequences.

British and US law are very similar in this respect, which is also not surprising in light of their shared legal history—the trust as a legal institution has its origin in England. Differences exist, for instance, in difference in vocabulary, in the trustee's right to remuneration, which only exists in the United Kingdom if the trustee is explicitly specified by the settlor, and in the number of trustees who can be appointed for particular asset classes—for real estate in the United Kingdom no more than twenty-five. Further differences exist in the legal consequences in case one of the trustees dies—in the United Kingdom, a deceased trustee's executors inherit the position until they appoint a new trustee, while in the United States his/her tasks then fall to the court—as well as in trustees' rights to delegate and the opportunities for exculpation.[122]

Trusts can be used for all kinds of purposes and the options for structuring them are correspondingly multifaceted, and the specific advice necessary can therefore be extensive. Depending on how a trust is organized, over a specific period of time, it can give gifts or payouts to the beneficiaries, support art programs, or award grants. Trusts can be limited in time, be set up for very long periods of time, and benefit one single person or a range of individuals.[123] Naturally, a trust is only as able to pursue its objectives as it is—as a rule, financially—equipped to do so. Artists can, however, also transfer artworks and copyrights to a trust as assets. If an artist, for instance, does not wish to rely on his or her relatives to manage the estate, he or she can create a trust for this purpose in which the trustee assumes the management based on the artist's specifications, and relatives only participate financially.[124] Trusts can be structured as purely charitable legal institutions, but can also be designed as instruments solely for private use, as well as a mixed model. The so-called charitable remainder trust *inter vivos* according to US law makes it possible, for example, to combine charitable and private benefit (split-interest). For the duration of a maximum of twenty years, one or several individuals can benefit financially each year, where at least one person is non-charitable. Upon termination of the private benefit portion, the remainder has to be paid out to a tax-privileged organization. Charitable trusts are exempt from income and capital gains tax and the settlor/grantor receives a tax credit in the amount of the remainder. The various possible structures are manifold, but are always oriented toward the two basic concepts of payout amount that is a fixed yearly sum (annuity trust) or based on value (unitrust). In this way, it is possible for an established artist to support his/her partner and descendants with tax advantages by means of cash payouts: the artist would then transfer a number of works to such a trust, where these works—ideally sold from time to time to museums—generate the liquidity for the payouts.[125] A charitable trust in the United States is dealt with as a tax-advantaged private foundation for as long as it adheres to the rules for a public charity and thus comes under the tax rules that apply for such institutions.[126]

Examples of US trusts include the Renate, Hans and Maria Hofmann Trust,[127] which has dedicated itself to advancing the work of the abstract expressionist

---

121 Continental Europe is only familiar with this Anglo-American legal institution in the financial centers of Switzerland, Liechtenstein, and Luxemburg.

122 http://www.mayatrust.co.uk/article.419.pdf (accessed April 4, 2016).

123 http://callresources.org/estate-planning-workbook/ (accessed April 4, 2016), p. 13.

124 It should, however, be kept in mind that a trustee usually receives some kind of remuneration for his/her services and certain administrative costs can also reduce the assets in this case.

125 Since it will generally not be possible to sell all of the art brought into a trust within one year, the so-called NIMCRUT (net income method charitable remainder trust) suggests itself for artists. This subtype of charitable trust can be equipped with a so-called makeup provision, according to which the trust is able to first settle previous obligations in the following year if the revenues allow. A mandatory requirement for such a type of trust is, in any case, always the readiness of the artist to transfer ownership of works, which requires an ability to let go and trust the trustee chosen. Such a trust can also be set up based on a will. So that the privileges are able to develop their effect, as already described, copyright also has to be transferred to the trust. The trust is seen as having come into being upon the death of the artist, even if the trust assets are first constituted later. A reasonable period of time for asset formation is granted by the trustee and his/her obligation to disburse payouts is deferred correspondingly; if it is, however, not possible to turn artworks to account at all, for instance, the outstanding payments might ultimately be settled through their transfer; Lerner and Bresler, *Art Law* (2005) (see note 5), pp. 1775–81.

126 In addition, the point in time at which the trust is set up is also decisive for the use of privileging provisions. If it is set up during the artist's lifetime—it has to go through an "organizational test" just as all preferred institutions—it becomes a charitable trust at the point in time when the first assets that are considered tax-deductible from the standpoint of the Internal Revenue Code are transferred; this differs from the case of establishment on account of death, where the trust is created upon the death of the artist, but the "period of settlement/administration" first has to be concluded for a positive tax classification; https://www.irs.gov/Charities-&-Nonprofits/Private-Foundations/Charitable-Trusts.

127 http://www.hanshofmann.org/thetrust/ (accessed April 4, 2016).

Hans Hofmann as well as supporting individuals in need; the Jay DeFeo Trust,[128] whose mission is advancing the art of Jay DeFeo and the arts in general within the context of art history; as well as the Robert Rauschenberg Revocable Trust. The latter, established by the artist in 1994 and became irrevocable upon his death in 2008, inherited Rauschenberg's artistic estate and other assets and transferred them after a period of transition to the nonprofit Robert Rauschenberg Foundation in 2012. Apart from the Henry Moore Sculpture Trust, another British trust connected with an individual artist is the Gabo Trust, which was brought into being by the family of the sculptor Naum Gabo after his death in 1988 and supports the advancement of conservation techniques for sculpture as well as the training of conservators for this artistic medium.[129] The British Barns-Graham Charitable Trust was set up by the Scottish artist and main representative of the St. Ives School, Wilhelmina Barns-Graham, in 1987 for the ongoing advancement of her work and the fine arts in general, including through stipends.[130]

(3) Foundations and Artist-Endowed Foundations

In the United States, all exclusively nonprofit forms of organization are subsumed in terms of (tax) law under the generic term nonprofit organization. This includes all US organizations that correspond to the requirements of the Internal Revenue Code, section 501(c)(3). They are consequently exempt from income tax, and donations to them are deductible. They may be organized as well as run exclusively for nonprofit purposes ("exempt purposes"), and no payouts may be distributed to private shareholders or individuals.[131] Such a charitable organization is either a public charity or a private foundation.[132] So-called artist-endowed foundations are private foundations in this sense. There are no foundations in the United States that are not nonprofit.[133]

The reasons of benefit to the public that justify exemption from taxes are also defined quite broadly here.[134] Andy Warhol's testamentary wish to support the further development of the fine arts with a foundation to still be established was surely subsumed under the advancement of education as grounds for exemption. At the same time, the concrete plan and its structuring by professional advisors has to be coordinated with the IRS in individual cases. After all, not every activity of a foundation must fall under these regulations regarding nonprofit status, but might instead also be qualified as "unrelated trade and business,"[135] even if the main purpose of the foundation is to benefit the public, and tax exemption is therefore in principle a given. Most institutions that are established by artists for artists and/or the arts and therefore charitable come into being as private foundations.[136] They are defined as a nonprofit entity that is financed and/or provided with financial resources by one source (individual or family).[137] So-called public charities, in contrast, receive at least one third of their funding from public resources such as the Noguchi Foundation of the Japanese-American artist Isamu Noguchi.[138] But this does not mean that private foundations are excluded from receiving any support from public means, only that the state has no long-term financing obligations on a greater scale in such cases.[139]

Private foundations can be differentiated with respect to their internal organization and operations: Private non-operating foundations are foundations that carry out their activities through awarding grants to other qualified foundations and organizations. The factor that differentiates a private operating foundation from a private non-operating foundation is only the direct or indirect way in which funds are utilized with respect to the aspect of benefit to the public.[140] The non-operating foundation has the advantage that the expenditure of costs

---

128 http://www.jaydefeo.org/.

129 http://www.gabotrust.org/about-us/history (accessed April 4, 2016).

130 http://www.barns-grahamtrust.org.uk/The-Trust/About-Us.html (accessed April 4, 2016).

131 https://www.irs.gov/Charities-&-Nonprofits/Charitable-Organizations/Exemption-Requirements-Section-501(c)(3)-Organizations.

132 A US charitable trust is also subsumed under private foundation in terms of (tax) law; https://www.irs.gov/Charities-&-Nonprofits/Charitable-Organizations/Life-Cycle-of-a-Public-Charity-Private-Foundation.

133 Comparable results are achieved in the US by means of a non-charitable trust. A foundation that pursues exclusively self-serving goals such as the family foundation according to German law does not exist there.

134 https://www.irs.gov/Charities-&-Nonprofits/Charitable-Organizations/Exempt-Purposes-Internal-Revenue-Code-Section-501(c)(3).

135 https://www.irs.gov/publications/p598/ch03.html (accessed April 4, 2016).

136 Hoffman, "Reflections" (2008) (see note 45), p. 54.

137 Many of these foundations are registered in the state of Delaware due to its less strict and tax-optimized state law, even though their operative headquarters are, for instance, in New York; thus, for instance, the Lichtenstein Foundation, the Willem de Kooning Foundation, or also the Richard Avedon Foundation; ibid., pp. 53 f.

138 The Isamu Noguchi Foundation and the Garden Museum receive one part of their support from public funds of the New York City Department of Cultural Affairs in partnership with the City Council, the New York State Council on the Arts, supported by Governor Andrew Cuomo and the New York State Legislature, as well as the Institute of Museum and Library Services; http://www.noguchi.org/museum/mission (accessed April 2, 2016).

139 Another difference from public charities is the fact that these/such institutions have an extensive fundraising program and receive financial funding from many sources, including the broader public, public authorities, businesses, foundations, or other public charitable organizations, and/or are active as fundamental supporters/benefactors for one or more public charitable organizations; https://www.irs.gov/Charities-&-Nonprofits/Charitable-Organizations/Life-Cycle-of-a-Public-Charity-Private-Foundation.

and time remains more manageable. It only has to choose what institutions to support and oversee the correct use of the funds donated.

Examples of non-operating foundation are the Larry Rivers Foundation, the Milton and Sally Avery Arts Foundation, the Dan Flavin Art Foundation, the Samuel L. Francis Art Foundation, and the Robert Mapplethorpe Foundation.[141] The Andy Warhol Foundation, also non-operative,[142] for example, under the presidency of Archibald Gilles between 1989 and 2001, awarded over forty-one million dollars in grants for charitable initiatives. It supported not only obvious projects such as the Andy Warhol Museum in Pittsburgh or the conservation of Warhol's video and film works by the Museum of Modern Art in New York, but also the establishment of the Creative Capital Foundation, which directly supports artists, or the Warhol Initiative, terminated in 2012, which supported smaller charitable art organizations financially and through consultancy.[143]

Depending on one's point of view, one "disadvantage" of a private non-operating foundation is the fact that it is able to react less flexibly in its charitable activities—or it is an advantage that diverse purposes can be supported on an alternating basis. Private operating foundations are characterized by more active programmatic agendas than merely providing funding to private non-operating foundations and are also able, for instance, to award direct support in the form of grants. This means that they do not only pursue their aim of benefiting the public through intermediaries. In addition to grants to other charitable organizations, such foundations can also develop direct charitable activities through their own program, be it as a training institution or a study center, with a museum or exhibition space, or by means of a residency program for other artists or researchers. The vast majority of American artist foundations are private operating foundations.[144] The Josef and Anni Albers Foundation,[145] for example, maintains a study center in Connecticut and funds exhibitions and research, as well as art classes for children and in prisons; training and research programs are offered by Motherwell's Dedalus Foundation,[146] the Calder Foundation,[147] as well as the Willem de Kooning Foundation.[148]

Traditionally, the term "foundation" has no specific legal meaning in the United Kingdom, but charitable organizations especially tend to include it in their company name. The legal framework in such cases is generally the (charitable) trust as discussed above. The private-benefit Henry Moore Trust and the nonprofit Henry Moore Foundation and the Henry Moore Sculpture Trust are thus all trusts from a legal standpoint.[149] In the United Kingdom there are, however, further legal structures for pursuing charitable goals in addition to charitable trusts. The charitable company, which is comparable to the German charitable GmbH, the charitable incorporated organization (CIO), or the unincorporated charitable association have up to now appeared rarely if at all in connection with artists' estates. Whether they represent more suitable alternatives to the (charitable) trust in individual cases has to be determined based on the specific needs and aims of the estate.

---

140 "These organizations are called private operating foundations because they are private foundations that actively conduct their own charitable, educational, or other exempt programs and activities. Examples of operating foundations include museums, zoos, research facilities, libraries, etc. In contrast, a private foundation that principally provides grants to other entities or to individuals for charitable or other exempt purposes would not qualify as an operating foundation, and instead would be called a 'non-operating foundation'"; https://www.irs.gov/pub/irs-tege/eotopicn84.pdf (accessed April 4, 2016).
141 http://www.sharpeartfdn.org/supplement/D-3_A-Listing-of-Some-Deceased-Visual-Artists.pdf (accessed April 4, 2016).
142 Ibid.
143 Hoffman, "Reflections" (2008) (see note 45), p. 54.
144 Ibid., p. 55.
145 http://www.albersfoundation.org/about-us/mission/#slide3 (accessed April 4, 2016).
146 http://dedalusfoundation.org/foundation/programs (accessed April 4, 2016).
147 http://www.calder.org/ (accessed April 4, 2016).
148 http://www.dekooning.org/the-foundation/programs (accessed April 4, 2016).
149 https://www.henry-moore.org/hmi/about-us/history-of-the-institute (accessed April 4, 2016).

More Feudalist than the King? On those Who Create an Artist's Estate

> *"Heirs have to subordinate their interests to the will of the decedent."*[150]
>
> MUNICH CIVIL CODE COMMENTARY

IV. Who Should Administer an Artist's Estate?

Once an artist or his/her heirs have selected a form for the estate, an important question arises: Who should administer the estate? While administering an artist's estate was historically the responsibility of the family and/or heirs of an artist, the twenty-first century has seen the advent of a range of possible administrators. This includes art dealers and galleries, museums, public archives, or service providers specializing in artists' estates. This has substantially broadened the options of who can be entrusted with an artist's estate.

1. Internal Administration

a) Family Members

In most cases, family members are still usually the first supporters for an artist's oeuvre. They generally take on this role out of a deep feeling of responsibility. "It was like things were aligned this way—in a way that we had been emotionally and educationally primed for. There is something about being Donald Judd's kids. There was nothing else we could do, except doing the right thing, for him and his world,"[151] as Donald Judd's daughter, Rainer, describes the apparent need to dedicate herself to the estate. The fact that this feeling can also have an effect on the second generation, is illustrated by Max Beckmann's granddaughter Mayen Beckmann: "When you grow up with his paintings, you've been 'brainwashed' by the time you're twenty in any case, so that you're basically only able to see by means of the pictures."[152]

The task of administering an estate is very demanding both professionally and emotionally for family members. Although, as an estate administrator from within the family is often the first contact person and decision-maker when the work of one's relatives is concerned, one nonetheless ultimately still stands in the background. In the foreground is always the "genius," whose work is irreplaceable and irreproducible. One has to be able to endure this. The widow of the Australian artist Howard Arkley decided against it: "Left in this position you do have a certain responsibility. It is almost as if their career continues, and that in itself is difficult, to be looking after someone else's legacy. I did it myself for a short while, but I found it overwhelming and consuming, and not what I wanted to do with my life. I think for me it would have been suffocating. I want to have a memory of Howard that is different to just being focused on keeping the legacy straight."[153] The perceived obligation to preserve a life's work and manage and promote it in line with its creator's intentions can collide with what one wishes for one's own life. One puts one's father or mother at the center of one's professional life at a stage in life when one is typically more independent from them. When artists' children manage the estate they have to evince closeness and distance to their parents at the same time. It is no surprise that many children of artists very rarely speak of the estate depositor as "mom" or "dad," but instead frequently use their names, using "Don [Judd]" or "Keith [Arnatt]" as an expression of an attempt at achieving emotional distance for example.

To attain a balance between family burden and the search for something of one's own in estate work, it can help to think "outside the box" and—inspired by the artistic works of Jill Magid or Peter Piller mentioned above[154]—to see the estate itself as an artistic work, perhaps purely as a mental game. One can ask: What is the oeuvre and what is work *with the* oeuvre? Can I playfully elevate the estate work to become my own work, and hence—at least in my mind—become an artist myself? How might my approach to working with the estate change as a result? Such mental games can help one consider one's own role and individual options more freely. Rainer Judd thus perhaps gives the most important tip

---

150 Franz Jürgen Säcker, Roland Rixecker, Hartmut Oetker, and Bettina Limperg, *Münchner Kommentar zum Bürgerlichen Gesetzbuch: Grosskommentar zum BGB*, 7th edition (Munich, 2015), § 2301, Rn. 7; (Munich Civil Code Commentary).

151 See the interview with Rainer Judd in this volume.

152 See the interview with Mayen Beckmann in this volume.

153 Strickland, *Affairs of the Art* 2013 (see note 1), p. 181.

154 See Chapter 1 above.

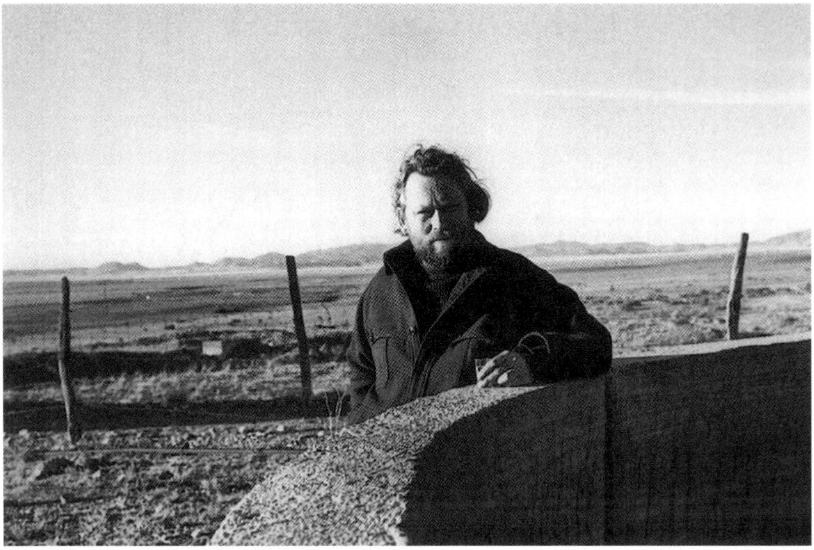

Donald Judd in Marfa, Texas

for dealing with an artist's estate from the perspective of a child: "Don't do things out of guilt. Do it out of inspiration."[155]

When family members take over estate work, they are no longer only surviving dependents, but simultaneously become individuals responsible for an economic entity, which requires professionalism. It is therefore particularly important that family members honestly ask themselves whether they are suitable for this task—both emotionally and professionally:

1. Do I as widow, as child, as grandchild really want to take responsibility for managing the estate?
2. Can I financially afford to take on this task? Do I have another job for earning a living or does the estate also have to generate sufficient revenue to support me?
3. If yes, how do I then have to modify my life in order to do so?
4. If not, who else could do so?
5. What skills do I have for working with the estate and what skills do I lack?
6. Can I handle the estate administration alone or do I need assistance?
7. Who could help me?

Family members often underestimate what specialist knowledge is required. Some think they can qualify merely as a result of the family bond. Nonetheless, only very few surviving partners or children are truly prepared for the task. They often have no specific training focused on working with an estate and little exchange with people in the same situation. This can sometimes lead to actions that outside parties are not able to understand at first glance. And there is thus an astonishingly large number of negative sayings, especially about the role of an artist's widow: "One can't be careful enough when choosing one's future widow."[156] The London art dealer Julian Agnew sheds a more empathetic light on the role of widows: "The widows are in a funny position. They're not the creators of the work, but they are often more feudalist than the king. Suddenly they're landed with moral and financial responsibility—they're guarding the house, the treasures, the memory, the reputation, and at the same time they have to deal with the brutal realities of the commercial art market, and their own grief and personal lives. It requires a very steady head and hand to navigate your way through these difficult waters."[157]

For the success of an estate, it is important that the surviving dependents remain unified, particularly if several family members are entrusted with and/or benefit from the administration of the estate. Family disputes lead to insecurity, which then brings incalculable risks for gallery owners, collectors, and curators. The oeuvre could cease to be worked with, either for exhibitions or with a view to sale, and the probability of scholarly examination is reduced as well. In the worst case, a case like Oskar Schlemmer's threatens, in which disputes among his heirs prevented the oeuvre from being appropriately presented or appreciated over decades. A similar fate was experienced by the deceased photographer Vivian Maier, who the online art magazine *Hyperallergic.com* placed on its 2014 list of the "most powerless people in the art world"[158] due to the disputes about her work and copyright.

To avoid disputes, clear agreements between the parties involved are important. A good example of this is the retreat of the children of Philippe Vandenberg. In the time following the death of their father, they withdrew form the art world in order to find a strategy for the entrusted oeuvre. This process found its conclusion in a fourteen-page contract with which the three children specified their

155 See the interview with Rainer Judd in this volume.

156 http://www.zeit.de/1960/15/kuenstler-witwen (accessed April 7, 2016).

157 Quoted after: Strickland, *Affairs of the Art* (2013) (see note 1), p. 15.

158 http://hyperallergic.com/170748/the-20-most-powerless-people-in-the-art-world-2014-edition/ (accessed April 7, 2016).

respective rights and obligations to the legacy. The core aspect of this agreement is that all decisions have to be made unanimously. There are no other decision-makers and no advisory body, even though friends and advisors are consulted in the case of individual questions. Revenue from sales is divided into four: one-fourth for each of the three siblings and one-fourth for the estate, to help finance it. This clever agreement makes it possible for the heirs to reconcile personal interests and the financial necessities of working with the estate.

There are many other examples of how families have successfully taken responsibility for an artistic legacy. I would like to single out two that are not only notable because the family members did so much correctly, but also because success was not guaranteed, since the deceased artists were not "superstars." The first example is Lyn Williams, the widow of the Australian artist Fred Williams. In her book *Affairs of the Art,* about the wives of artists Down Under, Katrina Strickland dedicated an entire chapter to her, which bears the apt title "The Gold Standard," and describes Lyn Williams's exemplary handling of her husband's estate. "She's never been greedy for income. Our business is supply and demand. Lyn Williams knows that and has controlled the supply. As a result Fred has probably had the most consistent price growth of any artist, without an actual boom," stated Paul Sumner, director of the Mossgreen auction house in Australia.[159] Williams invested more than thirty years of her life in this process, and has meanwhile come to the opinion that she has said everything possible about her husband's art. She received support from her husband in a tragic, but beautiful way. Faced with his approaching death from cancer, he acted with foresight: he put his estate in order, signed works that had not yet been signed, and earmarked works that were supposed to be sold first—an ideal scenario for all surviving dependents. The couple also discussed the estate's personnel structure and decided, since Lyn Williams was just forty-five years old at the time, against appointing an artistic executor. The goal was to give her as much freedom as possible and not to limit it by appointing other individuals.

What Lyn Williams sees as the most important aspect for successful estate work is strictly observing two fundamental principles: "follow as closely as possible what [the artist] might have done with his own artworks, and try not to make decisions on the basis of money."[160] Lyn Williams knew that she could have sold many works, that there were buyers interested in them, and also who they were, but first wanted to analyze what the estate comprised. Since Williams's gallerist died a short time after him, new gallery representation had to be organized. Lyn Williams entered into successful cooperation with two galleries that

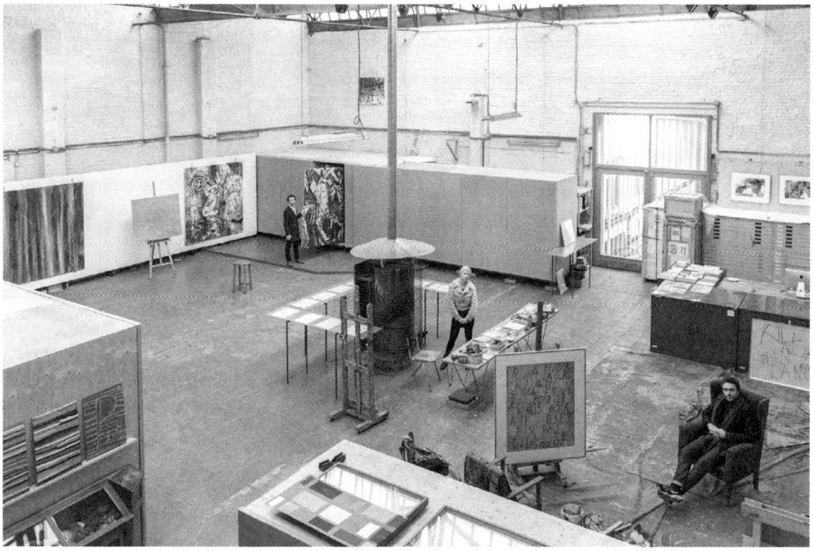

Hélène, Guillaume, and Mo Vandenberghe in the studio of their father, Philippe Vandenberg

could be regarded as blue chip galleries in the Australian market at the time, and remained loyal to them. Together they curated one exhibition every two or three years. This neither flooded the market nor starved it, which led to a steady increase in prices for Fred Williams's works. At the same time, Lyn Williams took an essential step in estate administration, and one that also justified the increase in the price of the oeuvre: she created an electronic database and possibly the best systematic organization of an artist's estate anywhere in Australia. She hired employees for this task and opened a central depot where works could be re-framed. She opened all the artist's archives to curators and researchers, including the journals that he wrote in the final twenty years of his life. Furthermore, she donated important works to museums—and did so on an international level—so that his oeuvre would be recognized beyond the borders of the continent where they had been created. Some luck was also involved. With James Mollison and Patrick McCaughey, Lyn Williams received the support of two central figures in the Australian art world; they wrote about her husband as "really no other Australian artist has been written about."[161] Last but not least, the assets that the artist had built up during his lifetime provided the family with a basis for support.

159 Cited according to Strickland *Affairs of the Art* (2013) (see note 1), p. 120.
160 Ibid., p. 127.
161 Ibid., p. 127.

Another estate activist who looks after the interests of a family estate in an equally exemplary way is Muna Tseng.[162] She is the sister of Tseng Kwong Chi, the American photographer and performance artist of Chinese origin who died in 1990 at the age of thirty-nine. As a result of her twenty-five years of work, his oeuvre occupies a place he would have wanted for it. "Over the past twenty-five years, I worked to build the legacy so his work is seen both as contemporary and through a historical lens—it has become a part of the artistic canon of the New York nineteen-eighties alongside his contemporaries, as both an artist and documentarian,"[163] as his sister describes her work with her brother's oeuvre. He perceived himself as a citizen of the world, for whom art was global and had no home. As a result of his cosmopolitan background, the artist saw his primary task as bringing the East to the West, and vice versa. Starting in 1979, the "unofficial ambassador of China" created his possibly most well-known work, a conceptual and serial photograph project with the title *East Meets West.* Tseng Kwong Chi fell ill with HIV in the mid-nineteen-eighties. His impending death allowed Muna Tseng to ask her brother how he wanted to have his legacy preserved. From this she developed her understanding of her role as a "trustee" of the estate with the task of preserving it, becoming informed about the work, and facilitating access to it for others. There have been thirty exhibitions between Tseng Kwong Chi's death and 2015, with two further shows planned for 2016.[164] Muna Tseng also reorganized gallery representation. Today, her brother's work is represented by Ben Brown Fine Arts, with locations in London and Hong Kong, as well as by Paul Kasmin and Eric Firestone in New York and East Hampton; Muna Tseng's focus in the meantime, in addition to research on Tseng's oeuvre, is on the East-West theme and the downtown New York art world of the nineteen-eighties in general. Through his work Tseng Kwong Chi inspired many Chinese artists who are prominent today, including Ai Weiwei, Zhuang Huan, and Cai Guo-Quiang. This broadens the research possibilities for Kwong Chi's estate. Moreover, the estate owns one of the largest photo archives on the artist scene of the New York City of the nineteen-eighties.

To conclude, I'll mention one more example of the family bond in art: the "Vier Corinther" (Four Corinths), as the widow of the German Impressionist Lovis Corinth, Charlotte Berend Corinth, called her family. She understood her task as an "inner vow to dedicate my love to you [Lovis Corinth] for as long and as far as it is necessary in all directions so as to preserve everything here that constituted your life's work."[165] Their son, Thomas, was no less committed. He collected thousands of newspaper clippings about his father, organized exhibitions, provided information, and published postcards of artworks.[166] When he died in 1988, his sister, Wilhelmine, stated: "I now bear full responsibility for taking care of everything. And to preserve the memory along with Lovis's art and the written estate, only that alone is still my task!"[167]

b) Third Parties Unrelated to the Family

Not every child can, let alone wants to, dedicate his or her life to the memory of their parent's work with such intensity. There is a number of reasons why estates are not exclusively managed by family members, but why non-family members are entrusted with this task. Such reasons include:

1. The family members decided against this responsibility.
2. In addition to the involvement of the family, additional personnel are also needed.
3. The family takes on the task of the supervisory board and hands the day-to-day management over to an external director.
4. The bequeathing artist stipulated that no family members be involved.
5. There are legal aspects, such as insider dealing aspects according to US foundation law, which make this step necessary.
6. The range of tasks connected with the estate has grown so much that professional management by individuals with many years of experience in other fields becomes necessary.

As with every business, the choice of the individuals involved is of great importance in the case of artists' estates, especially since they represent a particularly complex field of activities due to the combination of knowledge about art and management. The same professional requirements exist for internal managers, the executive board of an estate for instance, as for advisory and supervisory bodies. For an internal manager, there is also the additional challenge of coping as a single individual with many of the requirements that can be distributed

162 http://www.munatseng.org/muna-tseng/ (accessed April 7, 2016).

163 Muna Tseng in a talk at Paris Photo, the manuscript of which she kindly made available to the author.

164 http://www.paulkasmingallery.com/__data/c28f097c1848672943ea6975c9678714.pdf (accessed April 7, 2016).

165 Anke Maletowski, "Vom Umgang mit dem Erbe: Die estate administration der Corinther und das Archiv der Akademie der Künste," in *Special Delivery* 2011 (see Chapter III), p. 54.

166 Ibid., p. 57.

167 Ibid., p. 59.

onto many shoulders in the case of an advisory or supervisory body. The core abilities that every estate management team needs are:

1. Knowledge of the oeuvre and the artist
2. Knowledge about archiving and cataloguing
3. Understanding of the structure of the academic world
4. Understanding of the structures of the museum world
5. Understanding of the art market
6. Contacts to actors in these areas who are important for the estate
7. Basic understanding of the law and tax law
8. Finance and management know-how

The final two areas in the abovementioned list are often neglected. I would stress, however, that an estate—regardless of whether it is oriented for public or private benefit—is nothing other than a medium-sized business, which should be managed professionally. The economic basis for estate work is only available when the financial side adds up: only then can personnel be paid, only then can the possible charitable objective be realized, only then can a catalogue raisonné be published. Accordingly, in addition to art (historical) knowledge, management know-how is also part of estate work. For example, Christy MacLear, who currently manages the Robert Rauschenberg Foundation, brings with her many years of experience in managing cultural institutions, such as the Glass House[168] or the museum campus in Chicago, as well as a large network.[169]

c) Advisory Bodies and Supervisory Boards

Missing areas in the knowledge that is described above as essential for estate work can also be acquired through an advisory body or a supervisory board. Moreover, such a circle creates the opportunity to keep up-to-date with the respective fields through regular exchange with third parties. Many estates therefore decide, irrespective of their legal structure, to have an advisory or supervisory body in addition to their management.

Depending on the country and the legal structure, the functions of advisory and supervisory bodies can overlap or coincide; thus, the (governing) board of directors in a US foundation has executive functions, unlike a foundation's advisory board under German law. At the same time, however, that board is also supposed to have comprehensive advisory functions. The trustee or trustees, in the case of a trust, or board members of US foundations are ideally selected by the bequeathing artist and/or in such a way that understanding of the oeuvre and relevant expert knowledge are covered—otherwise the executor has to make this choice. After existing for a certain period of time and when the organization reaches a particular size, the number of members in such bodies usually increases. In the US, they have an average of five trustees or directors,[170] and even more in the case of larger institutions. The Rauschenberg Foundation, for example, has nine directors, the Joan Mitchell Foundation eight.

When selecting the members of such bodies, there is much to be said for choosing individuals in such a way as to cover the areas of expertise that are important for the estate.[171] To this end, clearly defining the fields in which one requires support as well as what qualifications and networks individuals should bring with them is recommended. Such board members of artists' estates are typically recruited from the following areas:

1. Curators
2. Museum directors
3. Friends and companions of the artist
4. Art dealers / Gallery owners
5. Collectors
6. Specialized estate administrators
7. Managers of other artists' estates
8. Attorneys

Good examples for the composition of an advisory council are the Calder Foundation and the Robert Rauschenberg Foundation. The advisory board of the Calder Foundation includes representatives of the art market with Arne Glimcher of Pace Gallery and his Parisian colleague Daniel Lelong; the perspective of American and European museums is represented by Alfred Pacquement, former director of the Centre Pompidou, and Ann Y. Smith, as well as David Collens;

168 A museum site in Connecticut that includes Philip Johnson's Glass House.

169 MacLear was therefore elected et al. to the Board of Trustees of Stanford University in 2015; http://news.stanford.edu/news/2015/july/new-alumni-trustees-071415.html (accessed April 7, 2016).

170 Hoffman, "Reflections" 2008 (see Chapter III, note 45), p. 60.

171 The US tax authority, the IRS, also recommends that the "supervisory board be composed of individuals who are knowledgeable about the activities and finances of a nonprofit institution and are active in its management in this regard"; ibid., p. 61. Alternatively, the governing board of a foundation or the circle of trustees can also be kept smaller and a non-governing board / advisory board, which has an advising but no supervisory function, can be established in addition.

the academic side is covered by the Sorbonne professor Arnauld Pierre and Elizabeth Hutton Turner, University Professor of Modern Art at the University of Virginia; the curatorial side is taken care of with Marla Prather, consultant and curator at MoMA, the Spanish curator Carmen Giménez, and her colleague Mark Rosenthal from the Detroit Institute of Arts.[172] The Robert Rauschenberg Foundation has a similarly impressive board of directors, if with different emphases. The current nine members include Roy Lichtenstein's widow, Dorothy, the investor Allan Fulkerson, Elizabeth Glassman, CEO of the Terra Foundation (one of the most important American art foundations), the foundation specialist Drummond Pike, as well as Michael Straus, who is simultaneously the chairman of the Andy Warhol Foundation, and Rauschenberg's son, Christopher.[173]

Different individuals can be important for the diverse phases of an estate. In the initial period, these are often an artist's associates. Even if an artist formulated parameters for how the estate should later work, questions will arise post mortem that the artist did not address. Such issues have to be answered as closely as possible to the artist's presumed intentions. For this, besides the family, close associates will naturally be called upon. With respect to the involvement of friends, artists should, however, bear in mind that, as in the case of family members, emotional situations that impede important decisions and entail unforeseen consequences can arise; the now settled dispute about remuneration between the trustees appointed by Robert Rauschenberg and the Robert Rauschenberg Foundation being only one of many examples.[174] At the same time, the emotionality and closeness to the artist and his/her work in the case of friends and associates is desired. This tricky situation can be solved by means of clearly defined structures and explicit provisions, which should also apply to remuneration and compensation for expenses. Furthermore, the number of friends who are involved in the administration of the artistic legacy after the death of the decedent should be limited in order to achieve a balance between detachment and emotionality. If an estate is given a structure while the artist is alive, the descendent is able to assess the effectiveness of the contributions of friends and adjust the composition if need be. Mike Kelley initially appointed exclusively friends to the board of the Mike Kelley Foundation for the Arts, which he established during his lifetime. After the artist's death in 2012, the board grew from these two to five members[175] and professionalized its activities at the same time.[176] Kelley's foundation is exemplary for the establishing and beginning phases of an artist-endowed foundation. Kelley not only established the foundation during his lifetime, but also was active in collaborating with the foundation and brought in friends with expert knowledge—an art historian and a museum director. In this way, the spirit of the artist is also represented after his or her death and facilitates lively interpretation and realization of the goals pursued by the artist in a positive way.

A second group of individuals, often discussed quite controversially within the context of possible board membership, is that of attorneys. There are those who regard them as absolutely necessary for an advisory body. Michael Ward Stout of the Robert Mapplethorpe Foundation—himself a lawyer—considers the involvement of an attorney absolutely indispensable. Others, such as Jerry Gorovoy or Rainer Judd also recognize the compelling need for legal advising for an estate, but nonetheless reject actively involving lawyers in a board. "Get a second opinion," recommends Rainer Judd. "For example, if an art dealer is saying, I give you this for that, just go and get a second opinion. Because even if you have known the person all your life and they fed you baby food, they're still a business person, and you as well should become a business person and get a second opinion. I would definitely recommend consulting with outside experts while not listening to others too carefully. I think lawyers should always be listened to with suspicion, logic, and reason. Lawyers as well as many institutional consultants are applying prescribed systems onto an artist foundation and they don't realize that artists have their own prescribed systems. There is often a gap of comprehension."[177] If, as in the case of Michael Ward Stout, the attorney is both a close friend of the artist and an expert on the oeuvre, the risk of a gap in comprehension is surely not as high.

Irrespective of how exactly the membership of an advisory body ultimately looks, it is important to clearly communicate to the individuals selected what legal rights and obligations the body and the individuals have, whether and which voting rights they have, and what is expected of them in terms of content. Whether board members are paid compensation or only an expense allowance or whether their activities are effected free of charge is matter of negotiation. As far as is permitted under the respective legal system, compensation or expense allowances could take place in a way that protects liquidity through the ceding of artworks, for example.

---

172 http://www.calder.org/about/trustees-and-advisors (accessed April 6, 2016).

173 http://www.rauschenbergfoundation.org/foundation/board-directors (accessed April 6, 2016).

174 https://news.artnet.com/art-world/rauschenberg-trustees-respond-to-foundation-lawsuit-78912 (accessed April 7, 2016).

175 http://www.mikekelleyfoundation.org/#!/about/mission (accessed April 6, 2016).

176 http://www.insidephilanthropy.com/los-angeles/2015/6/16/what-the-mike-kelley-foundation-is-suddenly-doing-for-small.html (accessed April 7, 2016).

177 See the interview with Rainer Judd in this volume.

2. External Administration

It the artist or his/her family decides to relinquish the estate administration as a whole, the following alternatives are available:

1. Estate administration by galleries
2. Estate administration by auction houses
3. Estate administration by museums
4. Estate administration by specialized service providers

a) Galleries

Classically, after the death of an artist, his or her gallerist is the first contact person for family members. Family members or representatives often continue the business relationship that existed during the artist's lifetime, due to satisfaction, attachment, habit, or all of these reasons together. To be successful, every estate is ultimately reliant on good cooperation with an experienced gallerist.

The types of relationship that can exist between galleries and estates are quite broad, and so it is worth looking at some possibilities in detail. To the outside, what is usually said is: Gallery X represents estate Y. But what does this actually mean? A wide range of agreements can be concealed behind this statement. They range from commercial representation in the art market, in which the gallery concentrates on selling works from the estate, to taking complete responsibility for managing the estate. The respective cooperation largely depends on the needs of the estate and negotiations with galleries. More precisely, the possible spectrum of work that galleries perform for estates comprises the following services:

1. Selling works from the estate
2. Cultivating relationships with curators, museums, and private collectors
3. Coordinating loans
4. Complete estate management

From the perspective of galleries, estates are very interesting, since "the price developments, supply problems, and reassessments of rather neglected artists have created new incentives," as the journalist Christiane Fricke characterized the market trend in the *Handelsblatt*.[178] Added to this is the so-called "memory boom," which the Schweizerisches Institut für Kunstwissenschaften SIK-ISEA (Swiss Institute for Art Research) describes as follows:

"According to the historian Jay Winter, the Western world currently finds itself in a phase of a 'memory boom,' which has long since no longer been limited only to academic circles .... The reasons for the 'memory boom' are manifold. The philosopher Hermann Lübbe correlates it to the dynamic of progress in modern civilizations and to the ongoing processes of obsolescence it causes: 'It is first as a result of progress that obsolescence occurs and becomes more obtrusive complementary to the dynamic of progress,' and it is first as a result of progress that the problem of preserving the relics of earlier evolutionary stages arises .... The benefit that results from relics of practices that have become obsolete not being disposed of, but rather preserved for the present and future consists, according to Lübbe, of the fact that this makes it possible to counteract, in a compensatory way, the loss of cultural familiarity that the frequency of change due to progress brings along with it as a 'side effect.' In an environment that is changing ever more rapidly, by depositing familiar elements—and above all by exposing them in a meaningful way—museums [as key players in the memory boom] provide offerings, at least in excerpts, for experiencing continuity.

Jay Winter locates the reasons for the heightened interest in the past and in retaining it in the et al. social and political stability connected with prosperity and the 'rising general level of education' that has been made possible by the higher expenditures on education since World War II. In the 'dying out' of newspapers, one of the 'most serious crimes and catastrophes in the annals of human history,' the cultural scientist Jan Assmann also sees another ground for the virulence of the topic of memory and remembrance. While Jan and Aleida Assmann argue from a cultural studies perspective, a publication by the theologian Thomas Laubach focusing on the ethics of remembering provides a compact summary of the current state of research. Laubach takes up insights from both the humanities and social sciences. Under the question 'Why should we remember?' he subsumes approaches from psychology, neurobiology, cultural studies, philosophy, sociology, and theology, whose 'findings specific to the respective field' are examined 'with respect to their ethical content.' The increasing significance for society of storing the past and the related hope of being able to safeguard essential parts of the past for the future is the cultural backdrop before which a greater interest in preserving artists' estates has developed ... ."[179]

---

178 http://www.handelsblatt.com/panorama/kultur-kunstmarkt/kuenstlernachlaesse-kampf-um-ressourcen/8665614.html (accessed April 7, 2016).

179 Roger Fayet and Deborah Favre, *Umgang mit Kunstlernachlässen in der Schweiz*, SIK-ISEA study of March 17, 2014, pp. 10–12.

The development of the art market reflects this trend. In the past fifteen years, artworks from the nineteen-sixties have doubled their percentage, from nine to seventeen percent, in the 1000 most valuable works on the market.[180] The relevant players are currently positioning themselves to clarify what is supposed to become particularly worth remembering after Gutai,[181] Zero,[182] and Tansaekhwa.[183] Large galleries in particular have adjusted to this and, in the last ten years, have developed from a market shaped by contemporary art into a combination of contemporary positions and "estate artists." How they present themselves to the outside and communicate the representation of deceased artists has also changed. Today, an estate is incorporated into the program of a gallery like a living artist, and accompanied by corresponding PR.

From the standpoint of galleries, the attractiveness of important estates is easy to explain: the work of the artist is self-contained and can be classified and assessed retrospectively. In addition, the prices are either already high or gallerists rate the works bequeathed so highly that the prices will be able to develop through concentrated gallery work. The current hierarchy in the extremely competition-oriented art trade, with a few globally active galleries with high turnover measuring in the hundreds of millions and many smaller and medium size galleries, is also becoming apparent in work with estates. "Without question, financially strong dealers such as [David] Zwirner or Hauser & Wirth have elevated dealing with estates to a commercially high-end level that is very capital-intensive and therefore not easy to surpass," finds the Munich art dealer Fred Jahn, who also manages estates.[184] The allusion to capital intensity has several facets. On the one hand, it is good for estate work if the gallerist is able to look at it in the mid to long term and, as a result of financial strength, is not forced to sell quickly. On the other hand, large estates have meanwhile come to expect galleries to be able to make advance payments through, for example, purchasing works from the estate up front, and not only taking them on commission, or financing the posthumous production of sculptures or other works. Moreover, a financially strong gallery is able to support the oeuvre of the artist on the secondary market and hence contribute to a value-adding synchronization of primary and secondary markets.

Some galleries also get involved in the creation of catalogue raisonnés. One prominent example of this is the Wildenstein Institute. The Wildenstein gallery-owning family began creating catalogues of works for its artists in 1922. With Renoir, Rodin, Manet, Monet, and Modigliani, their list of publications reads like an evening sales catalogue from one of the big international auction houses.[185] Other examples are the gallery owner Achim Moeller with the Lyonel

Feininger Project and the Mark Tobey Project,[186] or Gagosian Gallery with the catalogue raisonné of the paintings of Ed Ruscha.[187] Pace Gallery has even established a publication unit, called Artifex Press, which supports the digital creation of catalogue raisonnés. Artifex has published the catalogue raisonnés of the paintings of Chuck Close and the sculptures of Jim Dine, among others.[188] Such engagement is, however, not as selfless as it might appear: for a gallery there is no better instrument for gaining transparency of the secondary market for an artist than being involved in the creation of a catalogue raisonné. Afterward, the gallery knows exactly where each work can be found and perhaps purchased.

From the standpoint of an estate, the details of the relationship to a gallery largely depend on how interesting the estate is for galleries on the level of the art trade. The more important the artist's market position is, the better the estate's negotiating position. The estate can use this in deciding to hand over as much or as little responsibility for the estate to the gallery as possible. There are solid grounds for both options. If one entrusts one of the big galleries with responsibility for an estate, in the best case, all its market power benefits the oeuvre. In addition, there is then clarity regarding who represents the artist on the market and the challenge of having to coordinate the actions of various actors on the market does not arise. Such a step, however, also denotes great dependency. Galleries rarely work on the non-commercial side of an estate. And they seldom work as extensively on one artist as an estate management team, which is also able to dedicate itself to research and relationships with museums. In recent years, there has therefore been a trend in "big" estates toward developing internal know-how and distributing sales to others. Such estates are able to negotiate

180 http://www.artmarketmonitor.com/2015/01/15/works-from-the-sixties-climb-to-market-dominance/ (accessed April 7, 2016).

181 http://www.economist.com/news/books-and-arts/21650068-rise-and-rise-important-20th-century-modernist-movement-japan-other (accessed April 7, 2016).

182 http://www.handelsblatt.com/panorama/kultur-kunstmarkt/marktbericht-rekordpreise-fuer-zero-kunst/10147464.html (accessed April 7, 2016).

183 http://www.newyorker.com/culture/culture-desk/the-koreans-at-the-top-of-the-art-world (accessed April 7, 2016).

184 http:/www.tagesspiegel.de/kultur/archive-und-kuenstlernachlaesse-gruss-vom-grossvater/12280126.html (accessed April 7, 2016).

185 http://www.wildenstein-institute.fr/spip.php?page=wildenstein-publications-artistes&lang=en (accessed April 6, 2016).

186 http://www.moellerfineart.com/moeller-projects/lyonel-feininger-project and http://www.moellerfineart.com/moeller-projects/mark-tobey-project (both accessed April 6, 2016).

187 https://www.gagosian.com/shop/catalogues-raisonns (accessed April 7, 2016).

188 https://artifexpress.com/ (accessed April 7, 2016).

certain freedoms with art dealers with respect to the sales side and to regulate their representation by galleries geographically. The Robert Rauschenberg Foundation has done this for example. After Rauschenberg's death in 2008, Gagosian Gallery was the sole representative of the estate, but in 2015 it lost this mandate to Pace Gallery, with its four locations in New York, London, Beijing, and Hong Kong, as well as Galeria Luisa Strina in São Paulo, Brazil, and Galerie Thaddaeus Ropac in Salzburg and Paris.[189]

Whether one works with one or several galleries, the estate should in any case be seen as representing its own interests on the market. For this, it is necessary to acquire the relevant knowledge and to closely follow the market for the artist—as well as the art market in general—through visits to fairs, price monitoring, and observing auction events. The estate should also help to provide opportunities for gallery exhibitions and develop its own strategy for choosing works to be sold. This does not only apply to big estates. Knowing about the intricacies of the art market is also particularly important for smaller and medium size estates. Even they can achieve a high level of success in repositioning an artist through good gallery work. Thus, for example, the positioning of the estate of Keith Arnatt with Sprüth Magers or that of Philippe Vandenberg with Hauser & Wirth was decisive in re-contextualizing the oeuvre, making it visible on an international stage, and getting new collectors excited about the oeuvre.

b) Auction Houses

It is not only galleries that have discovered artists' estates as a business; auction houses have as well. The auction house Christie's, for example, represents the estate of the Japanese-American artist Ruth Asawa and showed her work in New York in 2013 and in Tokyo in 2015.[190] Since the end of 2013, the Van Ham auction house in Cologne runs a department called Van Ham Art Estate, which describes itself as a "competent partner" in the "managing and marketing of artists' estates."[191] The range of services offered includes: viewing, evaluating, storing, processing, promoting, and marketing.

Up to now, auction houses in Germany have only looked after artists' estates under particular conditions. The Munich-based Karl & Faber auction house, for instance, took over one part of the estate of the animal painter Alexander Koester (1864–1932) from the Free State of Bavaria. The owner of Karl & Faber, Rupert Keim, is more skeptical regarding the topic of estate administration than his colleague Markus Eisenbeis of Van Ham in Cologne, and refers to the long-term timescale and additional costs in comparison to pure sales. His point is that taking care of an estate responsibly and comprehensively typically exceeds the possibilities of an auction house. "The question is who binds the work to their leg? We are not a gallery," he says.[192] A huge amount of documentation and exhibition work is necessary, particularly in the case of lesser-known artists who did not succeed in gaining recognition during their lifetime. In an interview in connection with estates in 2013, Markus Krause of the Villa Grisebach auction house in Berlin also referred to the added work that mediating exhibitions to museums, the lending of work connected with it, and cooperating with dealers requires.[193]

c) Museums

Alternatively, an artist or his/her heirs can hand the estate over to a museum. This can occur by the estate being absorbed into the holdings of a museum. A further possibility is to establish a dedicated exhibition space in the respective permanent collection of a museum, or by including the artist in the title of the museum. A difference is therefore made between a so-called museum estate, a more or less complete estate comprising all phases of work and including a range of key works, and a so-called partial estate, in which case substantial and significant but only partial holdings are entrusted to a museum-like institution. Finally, there is also the residual estate—the holdings of an estate that are still in the possession of the family or institution managing the estate after many years of actively working with the estate—that need to find a home. These forms should in turn be differentiated from a targeted gift or partial gift of individual or groups of works to a museum.

(1) Acquisition of an Estate by a Museum

Today, acquisition by a museum is not as easy as it was in the past. Museums have become considerably more selective. "The twentieth century left behind such a mass of artworks; the warehouses are full and the present pushes past eras into the background, sometimes even up against the wall," as Uwe Degreif, curator at the Museum Biberach explains.[194] Museums are pleased about the donation of an estate in the case of artists of international standing or particular local

189 http://observer.com/2015/04/rauschenberg-foundation-now-repped-by-triplet-of-blue-chip-global-galleries/ (accessed April 7, 2016).

190 http://www.christies.com/exhibitions/2015/ruth-asawa-exhibitions.

191 http://www.van-ham.com/en/van-ham-art-estate.html (accessed April 6, 2016).

192 http://www.handelsblatt.com/panorama/kultur-kunstmarkt/kuenstlernachlaesse-kampf-um-ressourcen/8665614.html (accessed April 7, 2016).

193 Ibid.

194 http://www.artexperts.ch/fileadmin/user_upload/Publikationen/Artikel_Interview_UweDegreif.pdf (accessed April 11, 2016).

significance; in most other cases, estate management is perceived as a burden. "Our museum looks after several estates in its collection, including those of the formerly important animal painters Anton Braith and Christian Mali. In the past one hundred years, a maximum of twenty percent of the roughly one thousand works have been used for exhibitions and publications; the rest ... are almost without value—either for research or for exhibiting. If these holdings had not found their way into our museum, nobody would miss them," says Degreif.[195] Even very large institutions can consider an estate a burden, as the estate of Scott Burton illustrates. The American sculptor bequeathed his estate to the Museum of Modern Art in New York in 1989 with the comment that he "wanted his work in a public place as opposed to private gardens."[196] For its part, MoMA did not see itself as being able to provide the estate work and museum-quality exhibiting necessary to meet Burton's request. In Burton's case, a confused market was the result of his estate not finding a home at the MoMA, and prices for his works steadily decreased. London gallerist Inigo Philbrick notes the reason for this: "There needs [to be] someone in a position to say: 'I represent the estate and stand behind this work.'"[197] Museums, however, have to try to maintain a distance from the art market. From the perspective of estates, the market is nonetheless just as important as the academic and museum world. Since museums are not able to resolve this inherent conflict, the question that arises is whether a museum is the right place at all for the management of estates. The estate specialist Barry Rosen gives a negative answer to this question: "Museums are not really set up to represent artists."[198]

If an artist would nevertheless like to bequeath their work to a museum, it is only possible through individual solutions and by so-called hybrid models. One such form is dividing the estate up into museum and saleable works, where the estate work to be done by the museum is financed by the sale of works from the second category. The estate of American landscape painter William Thon provides an example of this model: He bequeathed a few key works to the Portland Museum of Art and stipulated that the rest of the remaining works be sold. From the proceeds, a curator position at the museum was created in his name.[199]

Another type of hybrid model can be joint estate work by a museum in cooperation with an independent estate that continues to exist. In such case, the museum takes over the task of permanently presenting (one part) of the oeuvre, while the estate is responsible for the other areas of work necessary: the art market and research. One successful example of such a cooperation is the estate of the British sculptor Barbara Hepworth. On the museum side there is The

Hepworth Wakefield, and on the other the private Hepworth Estate, managed by Hepworth's granddaughter Sophie Bowness. The Wakefield Art Gallery, established in the city where the artist was born in 1923, was renamed The Hepworth Wakefield in 2011 after the family of Barbara Hepworth donated forty-four sculptures from all periods of her work in the form of plaster and aluminum working models. The family also transferred drawings, prints, and lithographs, as well as artworks by artist friends from Hepworth's collection to the institution.[200] The gifted work was integrated into the permanent exhibition, with its own wing designed by David Chipperfield, and made The Hepworth Wakefield both an artist's museum and a city museum.[201] Besides The Hepworth Wakefield, another museum-like location was created in the studio of Barbara Hepworth in St Ives, which was taken over by the Tate Gallery in 1980 and is today run by the Tate St Ives as the Barbara Hepworth Museum and Sculpture Garden.[202] In this way, the family put the museum representation of the oeuvre in the best possible hands, while it continues to be active in the fields of the art market and research. Sophie Bowness manages relationships with galleries, follows publications, and is available as a contact person for the planning of exhibitions in other museums, and she is also responsible for the catalogue raisonné.[203] Resale rights and rare sales of works finance the estate work. All market activities are controlled by the British New Art Centre,[204] which makes sales decisions and develops the exhibition program in consultation with the family. The estate of Barbara Hepworth is an impressive example of how two sides can win: the artist, who has a museum that is dedicated to their work and preserves it, and the city, which gains a considerable cultural benefit. At the same time, the ongoing,

---

195 Ibid.

196 Brenda Richardson, former curator of the Baltimore Museum of Art in http://theartnewspaper.com/market/art-market-news/moma-struggles-to-fulfil-sculptor-s-last-wishes/ (accessed April 11, 2016).

197 Ibid.

198 Ibid.

199 http://old.theartnewspaper.com/articles/The-dos-and-donts-of-artists-bequests/26759 (accessed April 11, 2016).

200 http://www.hepworthwakefield.org/collection/the-hepworth-family-gift/ (accessed April 11, 2016).

201 http://www.hepworthwakefield.org/collection/ (accessed April 11, 2016).

202 http://barbarahepworth.org.uk/st-ives/ (accessed April 11, 2016).

203 http://barbarahepworth.org.uk/catalogue/ (accessed April 11, 2016).

204 The New Art Centre, already established as a gallery in London in 1958 and meanwhile located in Wiltshire, is a center for sales exhibitions of/by British sculptors in particular, and in this respect manages the estates of Barbara Hepworth, Kenneth Armitage, and Ian Stephenson, among others.

independent estate work by the family makes it possible for the reception of the artist to remain lively and flexible.

The director of the Berlinische Galerie, Thomas Köhler, agrees that such mixed forms are preferred by museums.[205] The Berlinische Galerie has devoted itself to artists' estates from the very beginning. When the institution was established in 1975, it had no collection of its own, and today holds as many artists' estates, including the estates of Hannah Höch, Benno Berneis, Naum Gabo, and Raoul Hausmann, as well as the archives of Heinz Uhlmann and Lotte Laserstein. Each year, the Berlinische Galerie receives enquiries from between twenty to thirty estates but is only able to absorb a fraction of them into its collection. There continues to be no acquisition budget for this,[206] and partial estates—as described above—are preferred.

Another example of successful museum estate work is the Gerhard-Marcks-Haus in Bremen, which possesses the partial estate of Gerhard Marcks, an important German sculptor of the twentieth century. It was created after Marcks bequeathed 224 of his sculptures and 5,000 of his drawings to a foundation supported by the city of Bremen and the Bremen Kunstverein (art association) during his lifetime. The museum opened in 1971 and at first exclusively presented works by the artist, with the aim of "trying to immerse oneself in the artist's oeuvre, to experience it in scope and content." Ten years later, after the artist's death, another 7,000 drawings and other objects in the estate were transferred to the museum. Since then, the holdings have been supplemented by purchases of main works, when they—something that rarely occurs—are placed on the market. At the same time, the family and the museum agreed on a sensible division of tasks, according to which the museum took responsibility for the topics of research, conservation, and exhibitions, and the family remained responsible for the sale of works, including the posthumous castings planned by Marcks. It is worth noting that the community of heirs donates a percentage of the revenue realized on the market to the circle of friends of the museum and therefore underscores the financial connection between the family and museum. The art market in turn has accepted the museum as the authority on all questions relating to Gerhard Marcks.

Today, the museum does work that extends far beyond Marcks's oeuvre. The institution began expanding its model soon after the artist's death. The goal was officially broadened to include the "historical and art-historical surroundings of the work of Gerhard Marcks until the present,"[207] and the museum's mandate was supplemented to involve research on (figurative) sculpture in the twentieth century. It then began to make an active effort to acquire other estates that fit this particular profile. Today, in addition to the works of Gerhard Marcks, the museum's collection also includes the (partial) estates of the sculptors Waldemar Grzimek, Edzard Hobbing, Hanna Koschinsky, and Gerhart Schreiter. The long unappreciated artists Koschinsky and Schreiter have been repositioned in art history as a result of exhibitions and publications by the museum.

The strategy of the Gerhard-Marcks-Haus—as also, for instance, that of the Museum Beelden aan Zee in the Netherlands or the Pallant House Gallery in the United Kingdom—points to an important aspect: at a time when acquisition budgets are becoming ever smaller, artists' estates can also be a good opportunity to expand a museum's particular collection. The collection of the Gerhard-Marcks-Haus consists almost exclusively of estates that were transferred to the museum at no cost. Through the careful selection of these estates, the collection has a clear, individual profile. And for the estates, acquisition by a museum is a great opportunity to become anchored to an institution long term, which, in this category of "secondary masters," amounts to a guarantee of survival.

These examples and insights show that if the right model is found then museums can be good partners for estates. For this reason, it is advisable to contact possible institutions as early as possible, to realistically assess the capacities of the institution as well as one's own artistic format. This contact will also aid in developing a structure that brings both sides together in a mutually beneficial arrangement. To this end, one should think about the following questions:

1. For what museum could the estate be a good fit?
2. How does the collection profile of the desired museum look?
3. Does the institution have the appropriate spatial capacity?
4. Does the institution have a budget for acquisitions / for looking after the estate? Or can I possibly acquire / bring in third-party funds?
5. How well is the estate set up: sorted through, organized, archived?

---

205 Talk by Dr. Thomas Köhler, "Deep-Storage—Welche Aufgaben kann ein Museum bei Künstlernachlässen übernehmen?" within the framework of the symposium *Management von Künstlernachlässen / Wie kann man das Œuvre eines Künstlers lebendig halten?* Van Ham Fine Art Auctions, Cologne, January 20, 2016.

206 In 2015, however, it became possible with the help of third-party funds for the Sprengel Museum Hannover and Bauhaus Dessau Foundation to jointly acquire the estate of the Bauhaus photographer Otto Umbehr (Umbo) for around 3.3 million euros; https://e-government.hannover-stadt.de/lhhsimwebre.nsf/DS/1978-2015 (accessed April 11, 2016).

207 Arie Hartog, museum concept for the Gerhard-Marcks Haus, 2014, p. 2.

The better an estate is set up, the higher the likelihood a museum will readily accept it, since preparation denotes work and financial burdens for the museum. What is usually at issue is the financial burden of acquiring and maintaining an estate.

Institutions such as the English Art Fund or The Institute for Artists' Estates have a good overview of the collection profiles and possibilities of individual museums, and can help find an appropriate museum for the respective estate.

(2) The Dream of One's Own Museum

With great probability, a museum of one's own is the wish of many artists. The desire to guarantee one's legacy, to be the sole focus of a museum's attention, to reach an "Olympus of importance," or all of these together is a difficult desire to realize due to the immense financial means required.

If one approaches this venture intellectually, the first question that arises is whether the idea of a museum dedicated to one's work corresponds with the art-historical significance of the oeuvre and whether the goal of having the oeuvre protected by a museum is commensurate with the oeuvre's worthiness of protection.[208] The answer to this question can be subjective. Such a step should only be considered when the fulfillment of the other main tasks of estate work, such as archiving, are ensured and there are clear ideas of which tasks such an institution should fulfill—in the future. One then comes to the crux of any museum planning: financing. The financial question can be structured into two areas: museum development and operations. It is difficult to name concrete figures for this, since every project is unique and requires individual planning. However, as a rule, the financing requirements for construction alone amount to millions, and for ongoing operations at least to the hundreds of thousands—which have to be secured year after year. There is almost no estate that is able to master this long term without help from third parties. And an estate can solely finance almost no museum. As Arie Hartog of the Gerhard-Marcks-Haus has said: "No artist museum can be financed solely by an estate—since it is then sooner or later dead."[209] This was the fate of the former museum of the Basque sculptor Eduardo Chillida; it closed for financial reasons on December 31, 2010.[210]

Realizing an artist museum almost always requires the support of third parties, whether public authorities or private sponsors. Such parties can take over building costs, provide a property, or support ongoing operations: The Lehmbruck Museum in Duisburg would not have been completed without the support of commercial enterprises based in the region, such as Haniel and Thyssen-Krupp;[211] there would be no Museo Morandi in Bologna if a son of the city,

Carlo Zucchini, had not provided the real estate;[212] and the Zentrum Paul Klee would likely not stand in Bern if not for the medicine entrepreneur Maurice E. Müller, who facilitated the construction of the museum with a total of 110 million Swiss francs.[213] The Andy Warhol Foundation in association with the Carnegie Institute and the DIA Art Foundation created the Andy Warhol Museum in Pittsburgh;[214] the construction of the Musée Magritte in Brussels was financed with support from the Belgian-French corporation GDF Suez, and its ongoing operations are possible because it has become part of the Musées Royaux des Beaux-Arts de Belgique.[215] The Swiss hyperrealist painter Franz Gertsch has already been allowed, while still alive, to enter a museum named after him that was sponsored by a collector.[216] The Hepworth Wakefield mentioned above is a municipal museum, and the two Picasso museums in Barcelona and Antibes, which were built during his lifetime, also came into being and were financed by third parties.

How can such supporters be found? If one looks at the examples, a regional connection seems to be decisive: The Andy Warhol Museum is located in Pittsburgh, Warhol's city of birth; the Georgia O'Keeffe Museum is in Santa Fe, a place important for the artist's work and the place of her death. The city of Berlin accepted the legacy of Georg Kolbe, who bequeathed his studio and estate to the city. These examples show how geographical closeness can motivate municipalities and local businesses to provide an artist museum dedicated to the son or daughter of a city. Today, many smaller cities or rural regions are prepared to erect a museum dedicated to their outstanding artists. Established artists and their descendants are equally willing to entrust their treasures to small cities or regions that shaped their life, but are perhaps a bit out of the way.

To illustrate the very individual structures that are possible for such artist museums, I would like to single out three examples: the Lehmbruck Museum in

---

208 On this, see also Fayet and Favre, *Umgang mit Künstlernachlässen* 2014 (see note 7).
209 Arie Hartog and Kai Fischer, *Hans Arp Skulpturen. Eine Bestandaufnahme* (Stuttgart 2012).
210 http://elpais.com/m/diario/2010/12/02/cultura/1291244401_850210.html (accessed April 11, 2016).
211 http://www.rp-online.de/nrw/staedte/duisburg/lehmbruck-gefeiert-aid-1.1019621 (accessed April 11, 2016).
212 http://www.mambo-bologna.org/en/museomorandi/history/ (accessed April 11, 2016).
213 http://www.swissinfo.ch/ger/zentrum-paul-klee-eroeffnet/4571410 (accessed April 11, 2016).
214 http://www.warhol.org/museum/about/ (accessed April 11, 2016).
215 http://www.musee-magritte-museum.be/Typo3/ (accessed April 11, 2016).
216 http://www.museum-franzgertsch.ch/de/das-museum/museum-franz-gertsch/ (accessed April 11, 2016).

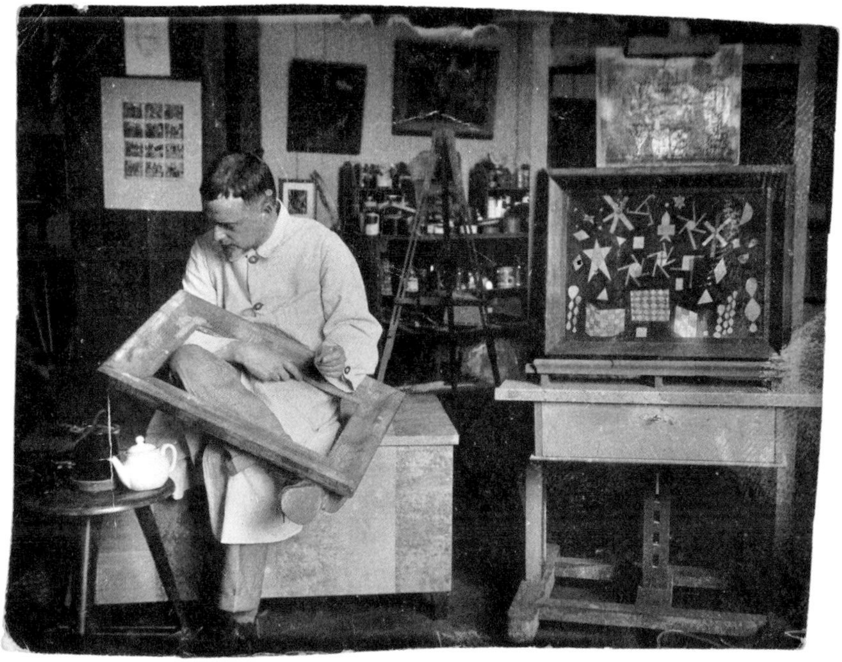

Paul Klee in his studio at the Bauhaus in Weimar, 1924, photo: probably Felix Klee, Zentrum Paul Klee, Bern, gift of the Klee Family

Duisburg, the Christian Schad Museum in Aschaffenburg, and the Zentrum Paul Klee in Bern.

Prior to achieving its current, stable form, the Lehmbruck Museum had a particularly eventful history: the director of the Duisburg museum association succeeded in obtaining a large number of works from the estate of Wilhelm Lehmbruck as a loan to the city in 1925, but the National Socialists labeled the sculptor's work as "degenerate" and the works were returned to the family. The family managed to keep them safe until the end of the National Socialist era through considerable and at times dangerous actions,[217] and reconciled with the city in 1964. Through the construction of the Lehmbruck Museum, the city once again received an extensive range of works on loan, which the city could finally purchase from the family in 2009. "The fact that I am still alive to experience this—that, where Lehmbruck stands on the outside, Lehmbruck is also inside and belongs there," commented Hans-Heinrich Grosse-Brockhoff, the then-State Cultural Secretary of the State of North Rhine-Westphalia, on the final reconciliation between city and artist and the joy regarding the artist's museum.[218]

The example of Christian Schad, for whom the city of Aschaffenburg is currently erecting a museum, shows that artist museums are also being realized in times of smaller budgets for culture. The widow of this important representative of Neue Sachlichkeit established the dependent, city-administered Christian-Schad-Stiftung Aschaffenburg in cooperation with the city of Aschaffenburg in 2000, and transferred the entire estate comprising 3,000 works to it[219] shortly before her death. Half of the construction costs, amounting to 4.6 million euros, were divided between the city and federal government.[220]

The Zentrum Paul Klee in Bern is exemplary for a museum-managed artist's estate in various respects. In the case of Paul Klee it, however, took more than fifty years for the final form to be found. World War II also initially led to a tragic situation here. "To understand the different backgrounds for the dividing up of the estate, one has to go back to 1946, when Lily Klee died in Bern ... as a German national. In May 1946, Felix Klee, Paul and Lily Klee's only son, who had been called up for military service in Germany in 1944, returned to Germany from captivity in Russia as a prisoner of war. And Paul Klee, who died in 1940 as a German national as well, had lived in Germany as an artist until 1933. Two days prior to Lily Klee's death, the Bern collectors Hans Meyer-Benteli and Hermann Rupf purchased the artist's entire estate from her in order to save it from the liquidation that threatened under the terms of the treaty with Washington," explains Michael Baumgartner, director of the department of collections, exhibitions, and research at the Zentrum Paul Klee.[221] Based on bilateral agreements between the victorious Allied powers and Switzerland, there was the possibility to expropriate (private) German assets. The buyers first founded the Klee-Gesellschaft along with the Bern collectors Rolf Bürgi and Werner Allenbach, and transferred the estate to its possession. Then, on September 30, 1947, they established the Paul-Klee-Stiftung, which they furnished with around half of the works present in the estate as the inalienable property of the foundation. When Paul Klee's son, Felix, returned to Switzerland after the war in 1948 a legal dispute erupted and ended in the dividing up of the estate. From the Klee-Gesellschaft, Felix Klee received works that had been in

---

217 http://www.lehmbruckmuseum.de/?page_id=213 (accessed April 11, 2016).

218 http://www.rp-online.de/nrw/staedte/duisburg/lehmbruck-gefeiert-aid-1.1019621 (accessed April 11, 2016).

219 http://www.christian-schad-museum.de/?page_id=233 (accessed April 11, 2016).

220 http://www.art-magazin.de/kunst/kunstgeschichte/13924-rtkl-christian-schad-museum-aschaffenburg-der-sachliche-rebell (accessed April 11, 2016).

221 See the interview with Michael Baumgartner in this volume.

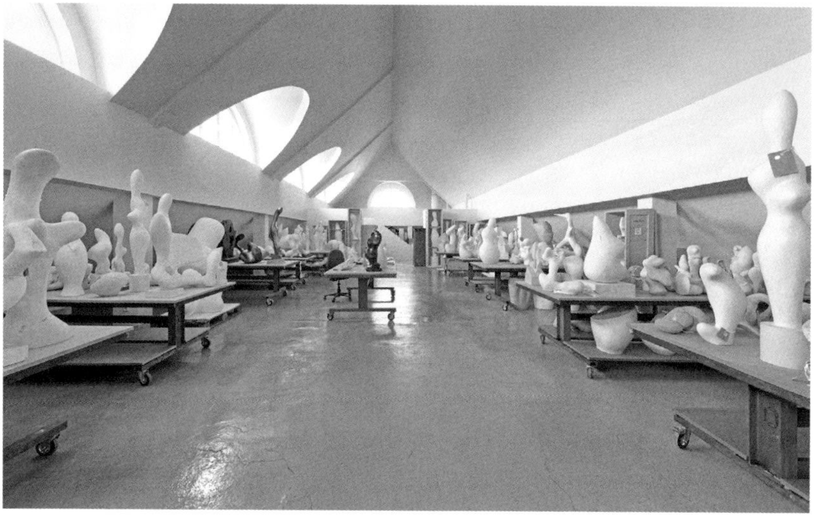

The open warehouse of the Stiftung Arp in Berlin, 2014

its possession and one portion of the holdings of the Paul-Klee-Stiftung, as well as half of the written estate. The estate of Paul Klee was thus split up. This situation began to change at the beginning of the nineteen-nineties, when Felix Klee's son from his first marriage, Alexander Klee, and Livia Klee-Meyer, Felix's second wife and Alexander's stepmother, offered the city of Bern 650 paintings under the condition that a Klee museum be erected. This was the basis for the creation of the Zentrum Paul Klee, which opened in 2005. The portion from Alexander Klee was given to the museum on permanent loan, and Livia's portion as a gift. The archives, which initially developed in parallel, were brought together as a result of a family gift in 2008. This step was a quantum leap for work for the estate: "The Zentrum Paul Klee created a completely new dimension, and for a long time there was criticism that the foundation was completely separate from the Kunstmuseum. There's a different tendency today and we have already been working actively with the Kunstmuseum for a longer period of time. The solution that we have now found is that, as of 2016, we have a joint foundation board, but remain in two separate institutions. By doing so, we have established the prerequisite for being even more present on an international level," as Baumgartner explains the positive development.[222] The institution continues to come up with new focuses and contexts to help keep Klee's oeuvre relevant and internationally interesting. Content-related research emphases currently include the theater of the Bauhaus or music that was inspired by Klee's works.

Seen as a whole, the history of the Zentrum Paul Klee seems to be a miracle—the fact that, after such a long time and so many obstacles, the estate did not suffer any damage and that the institution today is something of a role model for how an estate can be managed by a museum beyond the exhibition of works.

(3) The Artist's Studio as a Place of Remembrance

There are alternatives to the artist museum, including the posthumous preservation of an artist's studio in the form of a *Schaulager* (show-storage space). This approach to presenting an estate is being taken by more and more estates, and not only for financial reasons. In such personal surroundings, visitors feel close to the artist and can experience the work with a museum-like quality at the same time.

One example of the successful realization of a *Schaulager* is the estate of Hans Arp. In 2012, the Arp Stiftung opened a space in Berlin with over 800 square meters, in which the world's largest collection of works by Arp is not only stored, but are also easily accessible and visible. Curators looking for inspiration for exhibitions and loan requests, and scholars examining Arp's oeuvre can "stroll through the works" in a very real sense and therefore work with them that much more intensively. The library and the archive that are a part of the show-storage space are a starting point and supplement to the scholarly on-site work with the oeuvre. Tours are given for interested public. At the same time, the space costs no more than other storage spaces; the only additional costs that arose were the conversion costs and exhibition quality lighting. The holdings of the foundation are therefore made accessible, but without incurring anywhere near the costs necessary for a museum. And a lively meeting place for curators, scholars, and visitors has been created at the same time.

The Henry Moore Foundation decided to preserve Henry Moore's direct working and living environment. In Perry Green, the foundation maintains the studio of Moore with adjacent sculpture garden. There, visitors are able to contemplate Moore's works for a large part of the year (the property is closed in the winter). The building also houses the archive and the library. The Henry Moore Foundation could surely have found long-term government support and found a home elsewhere, but it nevertheless actively chose this presentation solution.

The choice of the Louise Bourgeois estate for a studio variant was also deliberate: "[Louise's] art and life were totally merged, and I think visitors feel this immediately. Having two adjacent properties has allowed us to set up the

---

222 Ibid.

archives, a residency program, and a research center, while still keeping the house intact," notes Jerry Gorovoy.[223]

The Judd Foundation has taken a similar approach in the case of Donald Judd's former home in New York as well as the many properties that Judd owned in Marfa, Texas. Besides awarding grants, the core mission of the Judd Foundation is preserving his living and working environment. In his home in the SoHo neighborhood of New York City, his "permanent installations" are shown in the form in which they were found at his death. His archive is housed in a former bank vault in Marfa, where it is accessible for researchers. In the case of Judd, however, the costs connected with this form of management can definitely keep pace with the costs of an entire museum: the renovation of the building in SoHo alone cost twenty-three million US dollars,[224] which were in part covered by the sale of thirty-five of his works.[225] A wide range of public and private sponsors further supported the preservation of the building in SoHo.[226]

The estate of the painter Magda Bittner-Simmet from Munich shows that the studio model can be a good solution for medium-size estates as well. The painter was one of the most sought-after portrait painters of the time after World War II. The nonprofit foundation that was established after her death maintains a studio museum in the Schwabing district of Munich in the multi-family dwelling that she also bequeathed,[227] with rental income from the apartments located above the studios within the residence financing the museum space.

d) Other Institutionalized Administrators

Since, as mentioned, only few museums still undertake the task of estate management and only a very few artists will receive a dedicated museum, other public and private initiatives are trying to fill this gap. There are, for instance, the Forum für Nachlässe von Künstlerinnen und Künstlern in Hamburg,[228] the Gesellschaft zur Nachlassverwaltung Schweizerischer Bildender Künstlerinnen in Switzerland,[229] or the American Artists' Legacy Foundation,[230] which have made it their goal to preserve written estates or oeuvres (or both).[231] In Germany, the Berlin Academy of Arts as well as the German Art Archive of the Germanic National Museum in Nuremberg are longstanding places to turn to, especially for written estates of artists. Moreover, probably as a result of its federal structure, over the last years Germany has enjoyed a markedly growing number of other organizations that are dedicated to the issue of artist estates, with different thematic and especially regional focus. This includes, for example, the Rhenish Archive for Artist Estates, the Initiative Private Artist Estates in the *Land* of Brandenburg, or the Research Center for Artist Estates in Saarlouis in Saarland.[232]

They all have a somewhat similar structure to that of the German government-funded Archiv für Künstlernachlässe der Stiftung Kunstfonds at the Abtei Brauweiler,[233] which we will take a closer look at.

Established in 2010, the Archiv für Künstlernachlässe assists in the professional cataloguing, securing, and preserving of entire bodies of work. A committee decides which estates will be included. Thirty-two estates are currently being looked after, but a decision was made in January 2016 to expand capacities by means of extensions.[234] The focus of the archive is on "preserving the bodies of work entrusted to the archive as a whole or in substantial portions and making them available for research and exhibition projects."[235] The works are also supposed to be made accessible to the public through loans to museums, collections, and the art trade. Sales are made in individual cases, as in the case of the dependent Kalinowski-Stiftung, whose trustee is the Stiftung Kunstfonds, and awards sponsorship prizes to visual artists.

All these institutions pursue a worthy goal, but also one that is difficult to realize, as a study by the Schweizerische Institut für Kunstwissenschaft (SIK-ISEA: Swiss Institute for Art Research) on the handling of artists' estates describes in detail.[236] The less than surprising realization contained in that study is that "the task of preserving cultural records is not independent of the resources that are available for doing so."[237] This applies to newly established institutions too, which all have to ask themselves the fundamental question of "how one deals with the material without preserving it as a whole,"[238] as Thomas Köhler of the Berlinische Galerie puts it.

---

223 "Good Housekeeping: Lasting Legacy," in *Sotheby's Magazine* (Fall 2015), p. 22.

224 http://www.nytimes.com/2013/05/31/arts/design/donald-judds-restored-home-museum-in-soho.html?_r=0; http://www.npr.org/2013/07/21/198412320/for-judd-family-home-is-where-the-rectilinear-art-is (both accessed April 12, 2016).

225 http://www.nytimes.com/2006/04/24/arts/design/24judd.html?_r=0 (accessed April 12, 2016).

226 http://www.juddfoundation.org/restoration.htm (accessed April 12, 2016).

227 http://www.magda-bittner simmet-stiftung.de/stiftung.html (accessed April 12, 2016).

228 http://www.kuenstlernachlaesse.de/ (accessed April 12, 2016).

229 https://www.archivarte.ch/ (accessed April 12, 2016).

230 http://www.artistslegacyfoundation.org/ (accessed April 12, 2016).

231 On this, see in general http://www.artexperts.ch/fileadmin/user_upload/Fachartikel/Nachlass/Gazzetta_2_2013_.pdf.

232 http://www.rak-bonn.de/; http://www.kuenstlernachlaesse.de/.

233 http://www.kunstfonds.de/kuenstlernachlaesse.html (accessed April 12, 2016).

234 http://www.kunstfonds.de/newsdetails+M514adc4a30f.html (accessed April 12, 2016).

235 Ibid.

236 Fayet and Favre, *Umgang mit Künstlernachlässen* 2014 (see note 7).

237 Ibid., p. 16.

e) Specialized Service Providers and Independent Estate Administrators

As becomes clear, there is a great need for experienced specialists who are able to take on the management of estates on behalf of families and who focus exclusively on their interests. What are concerned are specialists who bring together knowledge about profit and nonprofit aspects of an estate and are independent enough to represent the interests of the estate and the oeuvre in the complex interaction between museums, scholarship, and the art market. At the same time, they have to be able to have a long-term vision for estates and be able to make this happen. For estates, such an external solution often has advantages in comparison with an internal estate administrator: the estate can benefit from specialists' experience in dealing with other estates, and the remuneration structures are more flexible—in comparison to internal managers, who expect high, ongoing salary payments.

One very prominent example of this group of specialists is Barry Rosen. He looks after the estates of Eva Hesse, Allan Kaprow, Lee Lozano, and Dieter Roth, and explains the necessity of his position as follows: "People who have inherited responsibility for artists' estates are very often simply overwhelmed. Some of them are concerned about every detail, which can on the whole make success more difficult; others follow the advice of family lawyers or other advisors who perhaps do not really understand the importance of the legacy. For instance, a lawyer once asked: How long does it normally take to liquidate an artist's estate?"[239] Rosen got his start in estate work with the estate of Eva Hesse, and his handling of her oeuvre is a textbook example of how good estate work by a professional advisor can look. Since Rosen has been looking after Hesse's estate, there have been more than fifty-seven museum and gallery exhibitions of her works. He has suggested or acted as a consultant for them, introduced new focuses, and called for scholars and critics to examine her oeuvre. Rosen sees realistically assessing the importance of an estate and its core legacy as part of the formula for success and as the greatest challenge for an estate. "Clarifying the legacy. Encouraging focused exhibitions, building a context for advanced and continuing scholarly inquiry,"[240] in his opinion, is the trick that has to be accomplished. The more one knows about "oneself" in the sense of the estate, the better one is able to concentrate on what is important and to reach and excite individuals in order to keep the legacy alive. Rosen also dedicates himself to the oeuvres of his wards with the same tenacity. After four years of work lobbying MoMA in New York and no less than thirty-two conversations with various members of the board of trustees, he succeeded in getting Eva Hesse's work *Vinculum II* hung differently. Hesse considered various possibilities for installation when conceiving her works, but the photos that the MoMA curators used for orientation in hanging them came mainly from the first extensive retrospective on the artist at the Guggenheim Museum. There, the work hung on the wall like a canvas. The three-by-three-meter-large filigree sculpture of wire and fields of latex is now hung so that it stretches into the space—to greater effect.[241] This episode is only one of numerous initiatives that Rosen has undertaken since the premature death of Eva Hesse in 1970 at the age of only thirty-four. The fundamental work on the estate was much more comprehensive, and Rosen's focus till today is particularly on the scholarly analysis of the oeuvre.

Fine Art Partners has also dedicated itself to the external management of artists' estates and is responsible for the estates of Hans Arp, Sophie Taeuber-Arp, Keith Arnatt, and Wolfgang Tümpel. We advise a range of other estates on questions of strategy, on the correct choice of galleries, on financial planning and issues, on catalogue raisonnés, and other aspects of estate management. With the Institute for Artists' Estates, we have also created a platform through which estates can exchange information and scholarly research on this topic with each other.

As one example of the work we've done, I would like to single out the estate of Hans (Jean) Arp, which represents a special case of estate management as a result of its history. When we started dealing with this estate, it found itself in a difficult phase. Hans Arp, who died in 1966, was recognized during his lifetime—with solo exhibitions at MoMA and the Guggenheim, and was a winner of the Grand Prize at the Venice Biennale—as one of the most important sculptors of the twentieth century. His very hardworking second wife, Marguerite Hagenbach-Arp, who as a collector was knowledgeable about the art world and acted with the best interests of her husband's oeuvre in mind, managed the estate until 1977. She then transferred it to a newly established nonprofit association, the Stiftung Hans Arp und Sophie Taeuber-Arp e.V. Although she lived until 1994, she withdrew from active management due to an age-related progressive illness and ceded this work to the art dealer Johannes Wasmuth, who was also chairman of the association. Wasmuth had an in-depth understanding of Arp's oeuvre, but he did not always pay strict enough attention to the line between his commercial

238 Köhler lecture (see note 206).

239 Barry Rosen in a personal interview with Loretta Würtenberger.

240 See the interview with Barry Rosen in this volume.

241 Interview with Barry Rosen in *Monopol* (March 26, 2009);
http://www.monopol-magazin.de/der-mann-im-hintergrund (accessed April 12, 2016).

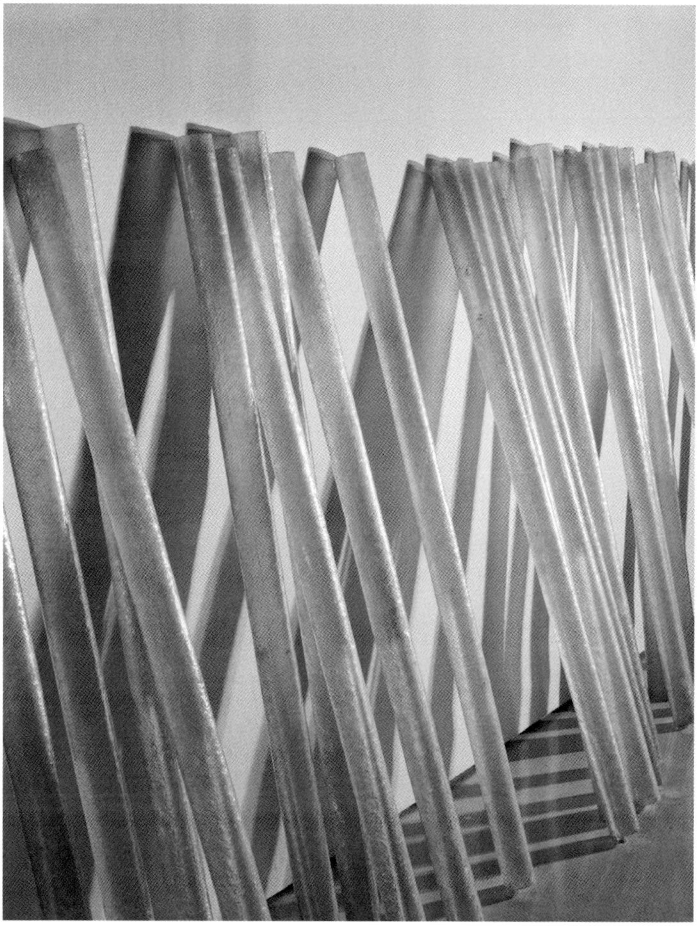

Eva Hesse, *Accretion*, 1968 (detail), Kröller-Müller Museum, Otterlo, the Netherlands

interests as an art dealer and the interests of the estate. Furthermore, he also chose to interpret the casting rights for the sculptures, although also covered by the copyright, to include more than the number foreseen by the artist and his widow. This resulted in the creation of a series of posthumously cast sculptures that had not been foreseen in the original list of casting rights, even though Arp had agreed in principle to posthumous castings. This damaged the reputation of the oeuvre and the foundation, which we were then faced with reestablishing confidence in. In a one-year strategy phase, during which we had in-depth discussions with the board of the foundation about options and opportunities, we developed a mission statement for reorienting the association with the goal of becoming *the* center for research on Hans Arp. The first and most important step in doing so was completely opening up the archive for independent research and the creation of a catalogue raisonné.[242] The catalogue provides an overview of Arp's entire sculptural oeuvre and deals in a totally open way with the previously less than transparent topic of posthumous casting. The new focus was expressed spatially in the opening of the *Schaulager* already mentioned. The association supports the scholarly work through awarding research grants and organizing symposia. The art market has also regained confidence in the oeuvre of Hans Arp, which is today jointly represented by Hauser & Wirth, Mitchell-Innes & Nash, and Galerie Thomas.

In Europe, the British DACS (Design and Artists Copyright Society) is also active in advising artists' estates. With its Art360[243] initiative the organization supports living artists in structuring their estates, with respect to questions of archiving and appropriate legal structures in particular. Technical advice for the archiving, conservation, and logistics of estates is also offered by the FM Centro d'Arte Contemporanea based in Milan.[244] The for-profit enterprise houses, among others, the archives of the Italian artists Dadamaino, Gianni Colombo, and Ugo Mulas.

In the US, the topic of artists' estates, their organization and management, as well as their role as increasingly important supports in the nonprofit sector has already been receiving a lot of attention and important backers for some years. The economic success of many American artists in the second half of the twentieth century made the need for professional contact people visible earlier on and more clearly than in Europe. The Aspen Institute has dedicated itself to the topic of nonprofit, artist-endowed foundations with the Aspen Institute Artist-Endowed Foundations Initiative (AEFI),[245] which is accomplishing pioneering work in this area on both theoretical and practical levels. The knowledge acquired through intensive research is published and shared in seminars with professional consultants and forums in order to promote best-practice methods and assist other artists in their nonprofit projects.[246]

---

242 Arie Hartog and Kai Fischer, *Hans Arp Skulpturen. Eine Bestandaufnahme* (Stuttgart, 2012).

243 https://www.dacs.org.uk/latest-news/apply-to-art360-for-bespoke-legacy-support?category=For+Artists&title=N (accessed April 12, 2016).

244 http://www.fmcca.it/ (accessed April 12, 2016).

245 http://www.aspeninstitute.org/policy-work/nonprofit-philanthropy/national-study-artist-endowed-foundations/about-aefi (accessed April 12, 2016).

246 On the research and the programs of the AEFI, see http://www.aspeninstitute.org/policy-work/nonprofit-philanthropy/artist-endowed-foundations (accessed April 12, 2016).

At the same time, US artist foundations have also set themselves the task of supporting other artists and their relatives in estate planning, whether for-profit or nonprofit. A leader in this regard is the Joan Mitchell Foundation with its CALL (Creating a Living Legacy) program.[247] With this initiative, more than twenty-five artists, including Mildred Howard, Mimi Smith, and Marcos Dimas, have been supported in documenting and archiving their life's work since 2007. Collected materials are publically available at www.callresources.org. A comparable guide for estate planning for American artists was co-financed by the Judith Rothschild Foundation.[248]

247 http://joanmitchellfoundation.org/artist-programs/call (accessed April 12, 2016).
248 http://www.sharpeartfdn.org/estateplnbook/visual_artists_estate_plan.pdf.

"Art is a force for life, not death!" Clyfford Still

V. How to Keep an Artist's Work Alive?

The real work begins after a strategy has been developed and it has been decided how the estate should be administered. An artist's estate is successful when it is able to keep the work alive. When successive generations of artists draw inspiration from the work and when curators, scholars, and collectors continually find new approaches to it, then an artist's estate can consider its job a success. This happens when the estate itself facilitates discourse, contextualizes the work, initiates exhibitions, and encourages contemporary artists to engage with it.

Three institutions line the path to this goal: the university, the museum, and the art market. These three pillars of successful estate work are inherently intertwined and must be attended to equally. Scholarly research inspires curators, while exhibitions arouse the curiosity of scholars and collectors. Furthermore, art that is successful on the market likewise influences the museum landscape.

1. Scholarly Research

The first of the three pillars is the scholarly assessment of the estate's holdings. It is especially significant because it lays the groundwork for the academic and curatorial reception of the artist's oeuvre. In addition to its role as an instigator of discourse, which includes sparking new projects by external researchers and curators, the estate is the essential point of departure for the catalogue raisonné, and very often for authentication as well.

a) The Archive

The archive is the point of departure for all materials in the above-defined Group D, such as files of notes and documents, photographs, personal mementos, certificates, documents pertaining to exhibitions and other correspondence, as discussed above.[249] It is defined as an organizational structure for the systematic compilation, preservation, and care of such documents.[250]

The archive is the key to the estate's collection. "Archives are essential for art history because they reinforce the cultural indicators that are often only hinted at in the work."[251] An archive does not just document a life; it makes it seem more immediate. The archive forms a counterpart to the artist's life in texts and objects, which help to humanize him or her and make them more understandable. Dan Chiasson's lively description of his visit to the Robert Rauschenberg Archive demonstrates how archival documents can put the artist's life and work into perspective: "And then there are his papers. In a file cabinet, personal letters from the choreographer Trisha Brown and Al Gore shared folders with a clipped-out *New York Times* review of a sushi place and a cartoon of a guy taking his pet radish for a walk. The impression is of a life in which making art was, to a remarkable degree, an extension of friendship. Each of these correspondences hints at the wider social and political worlds in which Rauschenberg held a stake; indeed, one of the most unusual things about an archive like Rauschenberg's is how many items within it could be in someone else's archive. A 'Christmas List' from 1978 includes such names as Woody Allen, Jimmy Carter, William S. Burroughs, and Andy Warhol. There is a warm thank-you note from Onassis for an unspecified Christmas gift, alongside the typed application (marked 'PLEASE DESTROY') Burroughs made for a Guggenheim Fellowship, with Rauschenberg's concise recommendation clipped to its back."[252]

At the same time, the term archive also encompasses the building that houses and preserves its holdings. The French philosopher Jacques Derrida addressed the archive's dual significance in his exploration of Foucault and Freud's understandings thereof: "Every archive is at once institutive and conservative. Revolutionary and traditional ... it keeps, it puts in reserve, it saves, but in an unnatural

249 See Chapter II.3.

250 http://www.duden.de/rechtschreibung/Archiv.

251 Gertrude Cepl-Kaufmann, Director of the Institut Moderne im Rheinland at the Heinrich-Heine University Düsseldorf; quoted from: Christiane Fricke, "Rekonstruktion von Erinnerung," in: *Handelsblatt*, October 12, 2009.

252 http://www.nytimes.com/2015/06/03/t-magazine/robert-rauschenberg-endless-combinations.html?_r=0.

fashion, that is to say in making the law ... which is the law of the house *(oikos)*, of the house as a place, a domicile, family, lineage or an institution. ... There is no archive without ... a certain exteriority. No archive without an outside."[253]

(1) Archival Organization

Just as an architect is needed to build a house, a professional archivist is necessary in order to create a veritable archive from boxes of letters, photographs, mementos, and lists. The archivist assumes the responsibility of unpacking, evaluating, and securing these contents for long-term preservation.[254] The Archives School in Marburg, Germany, has defined the role of archivist as one that is dedicated to advising on the proper stewardship and assessment of documents. In addition to material conservation and preservation, these include giving titles to archival objects and creating searchable catalogues.[255] The Dresden State Art Collections outline how these duties take shape in its description of the Gerhard Richter Archive, which was founded in 2006: "The Gerhard Richter Archive conceives of itself as a center for research and communication about the work of the artist. It therefore collects and documents all of the books, catalogues, magazines and magazine articles, photographs, videos, and CDs that are published on Richter as well as other information that is relevant to the context of his work. Unpublished writings, documents, correspondence, and photographs comprise a significant portion of the archive's holdings. Furthermore, the Gerhard Richter Archive organizes exhibitions and symposia both independently and in collaboration with other institutions, and it publishes its own series of papers as well. An important research project is the development and publication of the six-volume catalogue raisonné of Richter's paintings and sculpture with lavish reproductions and full documentation of their provenance, exhibition history, and literature."[256]

Professional archival work takes time and money: just how much depends upon the state of the materials of each estate. In most cases, the estate must create at least a part-time position for an archivist during its first years. The exact nature of archiving the documents and mementos is as different in each case as the materials that have been left behind. Despite their many contingencies, there are a variety of ways to structure an archive. The following list is just one way to organize archival materials, and it can be changed or augmented as necessary:

1. Documentation of the oeuvre (see above)[257]
2. Documentation of the creative and physical processes by which the oeuvre and the individual works within it came about; documented sources of inspiration and information

3. Catalogues and other publications about the artist and his or her work in all media (videos, CDs, print, photographs, etc.)
4. Bills for and correspondence regarding art-related materials and from related service providers such as foundries and framers
5. Correspondence with artist colleagues and artists' groups
6. Correspondence with advisors such as lawyers and tax professionals
7. Correspondence with museums and curators
8. Correspondence with collectors and buyers
9. Correspondence with family, friends, etc.
10. Correspondence with galleries and auction houses, or otherwise pertaining to the art market
11. Plans for curating and hanging exhibitions, as well as exhibition architecture
12. Press clippings, including articles about the artist, interviews, and other relevant newspaper and magazine publications about the artist or their work
13. The artist's library
14. Travel journals and notes
15. Personal documents such as birth certificates, identification and passports, will, etc.

(2) Internal and External Custody of the Archive

To small and medium-sized artists' estates archival materials such as boxes of letters and other musty documents often as a burden. Many archives therefore question whether they should not simply hand the archive over to professionals at a university or a museum, or to one of the growing number of independent archives. At first glance transferring the estate's materials to experienced archivists with up-to-date knowledge of conservation techniques and practices seems like a perfect solution. Yet by outsourcing its archive, an estate loses part of the groundwork for its primary activities. It is essential for the estate to understand the central significance of an archive. The estate can bring undiscovered archival

253 Jacques Derrida, *Dem Archiv verschrieben. Eine Freudsche Impression,* Berlin 1997, pp. 18, 27. English translation from Jacques Derrida and Eric Prenowitz: "Archive Fever: A Freudian Impression," in: *Diacritics,* 55, Summer 1995, pp. 5, 14.
254 https://de.wikipedia.org/wiki/Archivar.
255 http://www.archivschule.de/DE/ausbildung/.
256 http://www.skd.museum/de/museen-institutionen/institutionen/gerhard-richter-archiv/.
257 See Chapter II.2. on the assessment of art objects.

materials to light in order to spark scholarly interest in the artist and their work, make itself indispensable to researchers, engage in an ongoing dialogue with experts and thereby maintain an overview of what is going on with the artist and his or her oeuvre. In most cases, it is therefore strongly suggested that the archive remain in house, especially during the estate's early years, to the degree that it is financially feasible. When possible, the archive should also be expanded through further acquisitions. This is how the archives of Alexander Calder, Hans Arp, Donald Judd, Franz West, and Mark Rothko operate, for example.[258]

To decide whether the archive should be housed internally or externally, consider asking questions along these lines:

1. Can the archiving and the maintenance of the holdings be financed independently?
2. Is there any interest on the part of the estate's stewards in scholarship and opening the archive to research?
3. What goal would be achieved by keeping the archive in house?
4. Where should the archive be housed when it cannot or should not remain with the estate?
5. Do I want to obtain the best price for the archive or find it a home where it will be used to facilitate discourse? Or both?
6. If transferring the archive, should there be a personal and geographic connection or a contextual and thematic tie to the repository?

The answers to these questions may change over the course of an estate's "lifetime." There are many prominent examples of estates deciding that after overseeing their archives for years—and in some cases for decades—the time was right to transfer the materials to an institution. Such was the case with the Robert Mapplethorpe Archive. After twenty years of work, it was handed over to the Getty Research Institute in Los Angeles. Michael Ward Stout, the director of the Mapplethorpe Foundation, explains: "[I]n the nineties we worried about going out of business without having found a home for our tailored collection together with our archives, including negatives and contact sheets. We had tried to keep back one print of every image plus some unique works for this purpose. We spent fifteen years exploring the best home .... [The Getty Research Institute] is better equipped and has more scholar access than any other museum. The Getty does not regularly exhibit contemporary art and is not specialized in twentieth-century photography, but, after the joint venture with LACMA [the

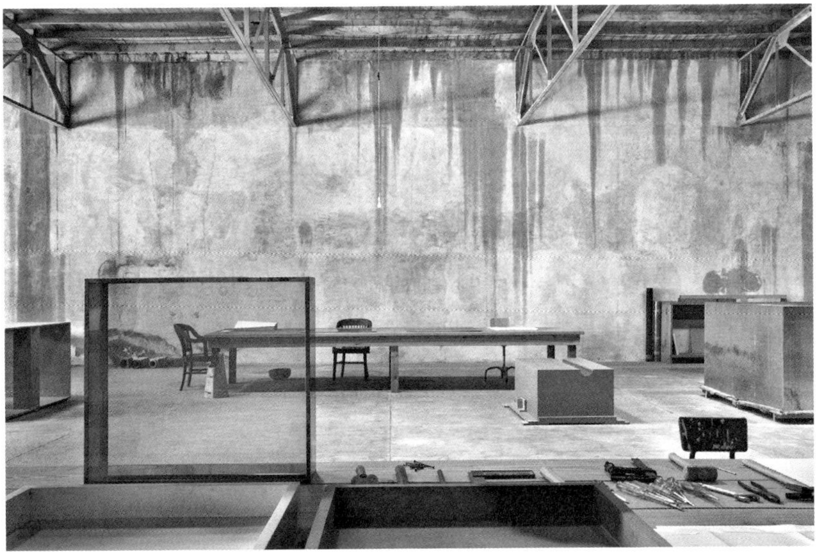

Donald Judd's studio in Marfa, Texas

Los Angeles County Museum of Art], one creates a fantastic package."[259] In this case, the Getty obtained not only Robert Mapplethorpe's archive through a gift-purchase program, but also a core collection of work, including negatives and contact sheets. A further example is the estate of Max Beckmann. After forty years, the Beckmann family is allowing its papers to be integrated into the holdings of the independent Max Beckmann Archive in Munich.

If the decision is made to give up the archive, regardless when, then all of the materials should be copied in full. Neglecting to do so can have severe consequences, as Barry Rosen describes with respect to the estate of Alan Kaprow: "Alan Kaprow sold his archive while he was still alive. Unfortunately, his studio did not copy the documents beforehand. This means that all researchers, including the estate itself, have to travel to Los Angeles to access the materials. Luckily the repository for Kaprow's archive is the Getty Research Institute, which does an amazing job supporting research and making Alan's work accessible!"[260] Alternately, the estate can require that the institution taking over the archive will

258 http://www.sigmar-polke.de/index.php?id=1&L=1; http://www.calder.org/about/archives; http://www.stiftungarp.de/; http://www.juddfoundation.org/archives; http://www.franzwest.at/.

259 See the interview with Michael Ward Stout in this volume.

260 Barry Rosen in conversation with the author.

digitize its holdings and make them available online. It should also be agreed that the family or stewards should have unhindered access to the materials and a voice in how they are handled.

Universities, museums, libraries, academies of science and the arts are all possible external partners for an artist's archive, as are specialized archival institutions. The following are just a few among many such institutions in Europe and the US:

1. Germany: Deutsches Kunstarchiv, Archiv für Künstlernachlässe der Stiftung Kunstfonds, Rheinisches Archiv für Künstlernachlässe, Künstlerarchiv des Berufsverbandes Bildender Künstler Berlin, Berlinische Galerie, Forum für Künstlernachlässe Hamburg, Deutsche Fotothek, Deutsche Gesellschaft für Photographie (DGPh)
2. Italy: FM Centro per l'Arte Contemporanea, Associazione Italiana Archivi d'Artista
3. Austria: Allgemeines Verwaltungsarchiv, Künstlerarchiv des Belvedere
4. Switzerland: Archiv Ostschweizer Kunstschaffende, Kunstarchiv des Schweizerischen Instituts für Kunstwissenschaft
5. France: Archives Nationales
6. Spain: Archivo Histórico National
7. United Kingdom: The National Archives, The British Council, Tate Britain Archive
8. United States: Archives of American Art (AAA) of Smithsonian Institution, Getty Research Institute (GRI), The Art Connection, the Senior Artists Initiative (sai), the Estate Project for Artists with AIDS, the Artists' Legacy Foundation

In the United States, artists' archives tend to find their way to university libraries or to thematically related collections, with interesting results. The University of Iowa in Iowa City has become the most significant archive for the Dada movement, although unexpected given its geographic location.[261] American museums often transfer their holdings to the Archives of American Art (AAA) at the Smithsonian Institution in Washington, D.C.[262] Rivaling the AAA is the Getty Research Institute in California, which is part of the J. Paul Getty Trust. With its generous endowment, it houses not only the archives of artists who worked in a range of media, including the visual arts and performance art, but also gallery archives such as that of the now shuttered Margo Leavin Gallery.[263] In contrast to the AAA, it does not limit itself to archives with an American connection.[264]

Central repositories for artists' archives in Germany are the German Art Archive at the German National Museum in Nuremberg, which houses the estates of Franz Marc and Ernst Wilhelm Nay for example. Similarly, the Academy of Arts of Berlin holds more than 1000 artists' estates.[265] In Europe, however, artists' archives are often transferred to a dedicated museum, usually on account of the personal motives of the artist or their heirs. For instance, Gerhard Richter was born in Dresden; the Bavarian State Painting Collections assembled the Max Beckmann Archive in Munich independently of the artist's family, but will absorb their private holdings. The Saxon State and University Library in Dresden has established the Archive of Photographers within its German Photographic Collection. Its goal in collecting and indexing this material is to provide comprehensive and vetted images for teaching and research, to the press, publishers, and to other interested parties.[266] Encompassing more than sixty estates, forty of which are physically housed in Dresden and twenty of which are digitized, the German Photographic Collection showcases and draws connections between German photographers and their legacies. At the same time, Sebastian Lux, the director of the F. C. Gundlach Foundation in Hamburg, who helped to found the project at the German Photographic Collection, emphasizes that the Archive of Photographers also aims to "retrieve the estates from the Internet (through exhibitions and publications)."[267]

b) The Catalogue Raisonné

After the archive has been put in order, the estate's next major task presents itself: assembling the catalogue raisonné. A catalogue raisonné gives a full overview of the artist's oeuvre. It categorizes his or her work, includes a complete exhibition history and provenance, and provides comprehensive references to publications, ranging from exhibition reviews to scholarly books and articles. When holding a published catalogue raisonné in one's hands, it is possible to literally grasp an artist's entire output and history. The information amassed in these essential

---

261 Mark Staff Brandl, "Künstlerarchive in den Vereinigten Staaten," in: visarte Berufsverband Visuelle Kunst Schweiz (ed.), *Künstlernachlässe*, Zürich 2007, p. 26.

262 Ibid.

263 http://www.getty.edu/research/special_collections/notable/index.html.

264 http://www.aaa.si.edu/aboutus.

265 http://www.adk.de/de/archiv/aufbau-aufgaben/.

266 http://www.deutschefotothek.de/cms/df.xml.

267 Sebastian Lux during the panel discussion "Photographic Estates and Premature Legacies" held by the Netzwerk Fotoarchive in Hamburg on March 17, 2016; http://www.netzwerk-fotoarchive.de/podiumsdiskussion-in-hamburg/.

resources helps determine the value of the oeuvre as a whole, as well as individual works within it. Moreover, by including lesser-known works, it often provides a more expansive and complete view of the oeuvre than was available during the artist's lifetime. Finally, it helps to guard against counterfeits: "The better you know the oeuvre, the easier it is to spot a fake,"[268] observes Eva Wiederkehr-Sladeczek, Head of the Archive and Documentation at the Zentrum Paul Klee in Bern. A catalogue raisonné is therefore an essential tool for researchers, collectors and art dealers.

Estates and catalogue raisonnés are inherently intertwined with one another. On the one hand, estates usually hold materials that are essential to compiling the catalogue raisonné, such as lists of works written down by the artist, documentation of sales, loan requests and approvals from his or her lifetime. On the other hand, reproductions are essential to a catalogue raisonné, and during the period that the works of art are under copyright, they cannot be reproduced without consent. Whenever possible, the estate should use its position as copyright holder to play an active role in the compilation of the catalogue raisonné. If the estate cannot or does not wish to take this on, it can request access to outside researchers' materials for providing documentation and image rights. In turn, these materials are veritable goldmines when it comes to future collaboration with universities, museums, and the art market.

(1) The Historical Development of Catalogues Raisonnés

A catalogue raisonné (CR) is the comprehensive index of an artist's work in various media, including painting, sculpture, printmaking, and works on paper.[269] It includes reproductions of and information about each and every piece in the artist's oeuvre. Because it is definitive, one refers to "the catalogue raisonné" of an artist, or to "the catalogue of works on paper" when there is a separate publication dedicated to an artist's work in a single medium. Each work has a separate entry that includes basic information such as title, period, signature, and date as well as medium, dimensions, and the history of ownership and provenance. In addition, it provides supporting documentation such as exhibition history and bibliographic references. This information may be augmented by commentary on individual works, interpretive essays, and additional texts. New discoveries about the works and the results of conservation research provide constant incentives to update the catalogue raisonné.

Early on, the catalogue raisonné was more of a biographical resource. This began to change in the nineteenth century, when the so-called Holbein Dispute irrevocably altered its conception.[270] At that time, cataloguing and authenticating the artist's work became a key component, and in this respect, concepts such as original, copy, and fake gained currency. The aforementioned dispute was over the authenticity over two paintings of the Madonna by Hans Holbein the Younger. One was in the former collection of the Elector of Saxony and hangs today in the Old Masters Picture Gallery in Dresden, while the other was in the Royal Collection of Hessen until 2011 and is now at the Museum Würth. In a symposium that accompanied an exhibition displaying both paintings in 1871, leading art historians used new methods for authenticating works based on style to deem the Hessian version, also known as the Darmstadt Madonna, the original. It was then that the modern understanding of a catalogue raisonné crystallized, in that it not only presented art through the lens of the artist's biography, but also brought in expert opinion.

As early as the seventeenth century, the painter Claude Lorraine sought to counter the rise of fakes by creating a register of his work. He entitled his portfolio of drawings the *Liber Veritatis (Book of Truth)*—it is housed in the British Museum in London today. The term "catalogue raisonné" (CR) was most likely coined by Adam von Bartsch, who wrote extensively about art. As a bibliographer at the royal library in Vienna, he was sent by his prefect Gottfried van Swieten to Paris to catalogue the most important print collections, including those in the Cabinet du Roi, and to acquire Johann Anton de Peters's collection of graphic work. He complained to van Swieten of the "want for order and the lack of comprehensive registers." Moreover, he elaborated upon the market value of a catalogue raisonné, arguing that it helped to bridge the gap between buyer and seller and to substantiate the goods at hand.[271] Paris art dealer Emde-François Gersaint went a step further in 1751 when he included questionable works in his catalogue of Rembrandt's prints.[272] He also wrote commentary on individual works in his auction catalogues, which he likewise referred to as catalogues raisonnés.

---

268 Eva Widerkehr-Sladeczek in a conference paper entitled "Vom handschriftlichen Œuvre-Katalog zum Online-Werkverzeichnis," at the International Symposium *Sammeln, Zuschreiben, Weitergeben: Zur Aktualität von Werkverzeichnissen,* held by the Alfried-Krupp-Wissenschaftskollegs at the University of Greifswald, September 17–19, 2015.

269 http://metro.org/media/files/files/0df1431c/Gabrielli.pdf.

270 https://eikones.ch/fileadmin/documents/ext/project/project/bader/bader.pdf.

271 Antoinette Friedenthal in the conference paper "Werkgeschichtliche Grundbegriffe: Œuvre und Catalogue raisonné im 18. Jahrhundert," at the International Symposium *Sammeln, Zuschreiben, Weitergeben: Zur Aktualität von Werkverzeichnissen,* held by the Alfried-Krupp-Wissenschaftskollegs at the University of Greifswald, September 17–19, 2015.

272 *Catalogue raisonné de toutes les pièces qui forment l'œuvre de Rembrandt,* Paris 1751; https://archive.org/details/touteslespieces00gers.

(2) Standards, Methods, and Costs

Whether it provides an overview of the artist's oeuvre in digital or print form, a catalogue raisonné establishes the fundamental categories of the art in the catalogue, as well as influences the way we discuss the art. Because it creates value, the originators and editors also carry a great ethical responsibility. In order to maintain the integrity of the artist and the authenticity of his or her work, the meticulous scholarly assessment must be carried out independent of any financial interests. "As a 'register of reason,' the work on the catalogue raisonné requires diligence more than intellectual brilliance," remarks the art historian Anette Tietenberg, who works in Braunschweig. Yet the catalogue raisonné also requires more than organizational abilities, as it must harness "the power of facts to ensure its future relevance."[273]

Although there are no official standards for compiling a catalogue raisonné, the work should always be carried out with great attentiveness and care. To achieve the highest quality possible, both scholars and artists have established useful guidelines. For instance, the New York archivist Caroline Gabrielli outlines the process for establishing an online catalogue raisonné.[274] More general guidelines are provided by the Authentication in Art foundation, which is based in the Netherlands.[275] Bildhauermuseen, a consortium of forty-one member museums in Germany and Austria, likewise establishes criteria for catalogues raisonnés of sculpture.[276]

Independent, professional scholarly assistance is required in the compilation of a catalogue raisonné, as the artist's oeuvre must be categorized and assessed objectively.[277] Generally, this process takes about five to ten years, and in some cases longer. The Cologne-based Ernst Wilhelm Nay Foundation, which is dedicated to the well-known proponent of modernism in post-war Germany, hired two art historians—one for eight years and the other for twelve—to complete the catalogue raisonné. The Foundation's management estimates the cost to have been between 600,000 and 700,000 euros.[278] In the mid-1990s, the Richard Diebenkorn Foundation began planning Richard Diebenkorn's catalogue raisonné, which will be published in 2016.[279] Robert Motherwell's catalogue raisonné took seven researchers working concurrently ten years to compile. These examples make it clear that costs can easily reach the millions, although location is certainly a mitigating factor. For example, rent and personnel cost less in Berlin than in London or New York.

Archivist and scholar Caroline Gabrielli observes that the personnel compiling the catalogue raisonné should cooperate in the following duties.[280] Note, however, that one person may assume more than one of these roles:

1. An editor / advisor who ensures that the catalogue raisonné is assembled according to established conventions.
2. An art restorer or another expert who examines the work and is responsible for correct technical terminology.
3. A project manager who oversees the project and manages the content of the catalogue raisonné.
4. A scholar who provides documentation and assesses the state of research on each work.
5. An archivist who manages the research findings and reproductions for later retrieval, publication, and preservation.
6. A database manager who records the research findings in a database.
7. Database developers / consultants who program the program or the database to best suit the project's needs.
8. Web developers or web design consultants who design the website's aesthetic and structure.

There are costs associated with travel and technology as well as personnel. Travel costs are contingent upon the comprehensiveness and quality of the archive. The

---

273 Annette Tietenberg in the conference paper "Das Werkverzeichnis als werkkonstituierender Faktor in der Kunst seit 1960," at the International Symposium *Sammeln, Zuschreiben, Weitergeben: Zur Aktualität von Werkverzeichnissen*, held by the Alfried-Krupp-Wissenschaftskollegs at the University of Greifswald, September 17–19, 2015.

274 Caroline Gabrielli, "Preparing the Catalogue Raisonné: A Guideline for Publishing Online," in: *Art Libraries Journal*, 40, January 2, 2015, pp. 42–49.

275 http://authenticationinart.org/pdf/Guidelines.pdf.

276 Astrid von Asten, Ursel Berger, Josephine Gabler and Arie Hartog, "Grundlagen zur Erstellung eines Bildhauer-Werkverzeichnisse," 2004; http://www.bildhauermuseen.de/cassetto/pdf-lago/Grundlagen%20WVZ.pdf.

277 This work becomes more complex when certain works are no longer extant, or when the oeuvre was ephemeral, as in performance art. Street art is a case in point, as it is constantly disappearing and it is not sanctioned by museums but rather catalogued by the anonymous masses that post their photographic documents online. Since street art is illegal, it is not possible to take a traditional approach to the catalogue raisonné," explains the art historian Ulrich Blanché, who directs the "Online-CR" of the most famous street artist, Banksy: Ulrich Blanché in a conference paper on "Banksys Street Art Werkverzeichnis—Crowdgesourced und Geogetagged," at the International Symposium *Sammeln, Zuschreiben, Weitergeben: Zur Aktualität von Werkverzeichnissen*, held by the Alfried-Krupp-Wissenschaftskollegs at the University of Greifswald, September 17–19, 2015.

278 Interview with Christian A. J. Klein, director of the Ernst Wilhelm Nay Foundation in Cologne, at the symposium *Management von Künstlernachlässen / Wie kann man das Œuvre eines Künstlers lebendig halten?*, Van Ham Fine Art Auctions, January 20, 2016.

279 http://crsaforum.org/2014/01/14/project-profile-the-richard-diebenkorn-catalogue-raisonne/.

280 Gabrielli, "Preparing the Catalogue Raisonné," 2015 (as in note 274), pp. 42–49.

earlier the archive is organized and augmented—ideally during the artist's lifetime—the more information there will be at hand about individual works of art, including photographic documentation and other relevant content. In the absence of such information, the research team must examine each and every work in person. When the oeuvre is scattered across the globe, this results in an immensely demanding and expensive travel schedule.

Today, catalogues raisonnés should be digitized and in English. It almost goes without saying that online databases can be expanded and updated easily and that there is a wide range of software solutions available. Moreover, the scope of the online catalogue raisonné should encompass the following:

1. Links to internal archival material
2. Links to documentation such as checklists and exhibition photographs
3. The integration of video and audio materials
4. The possibility of incorporating negative or inconclusive results, so that the limits of previous research are well understood
5. Links to external sources such as archival holdings and press articles or other publications, as well as public search engines and databases

Because software for inventory or for internal databases is usually based on flexible models, these functions are usually already included. Early on, it is also imperative to select a database that can be used internally but that also provides a module for web publishing.[281] Among other things, this module then helps determine which sets of information developed for internal use should be published online and for whom. Gabrielli recommends asking at the outset: Who should have full access to the catalogue raisonné? Should access only be local or should it be published on the web? Does the technology allow necessary information to be linked? How much does this particular solution cost? Does it necessitate ongoing technical support, or must separate IT providers be brought on? [282]

The aforementioned database for inventory management can suffice in the beginning and help build a basic version a catalogue raisonné. In order to reduce costs, it is possible to obtain third-party funds from foundations or organizations. Additionally, the estate may also choose to cede the task to an external party. Scholars and independently financed organizations come to mind: the SIK-ISEA Institute in Zurich,[283] Artifexpress in New York,[284] and the Berlin Institute for Artists' Estates.[285] Another possibility would be to collaborate with galleries, or to establish project groups that bring together professionals from different institutions.

(3) Catalogues Raisonnés Compiled during the Artist's Lifetime

Although catalogue raisonnés have traditionally been assembled after the artist's death and required decades of work, technical advances and the widespread professionalization of the art market have led may artists to begin the process during their lifetimes. In this way, they do not leave it up to scholars to define their work, but rather create their own *Gesamtkunstwerk,* which is often loosely translated as a total work of art.[286] The artist thereby becomes both documentarian and steward of his or her own work, "transforming what was originally an art historical task into a work of art."[287]

By actively cataloguing and categorizing his or her art, the artist can help shape their legacy and create an artistic testament. Depending on the artist, this compilation of their life's work can fill shelf upon shelf. The catalogue raisonné that the Paris art historian and publisher Christian Zervos began assembling with Picasso a full fifty years before the artist's death ultimately resulted in thirty-three volumes,[288] while Dieter Roth's personal archive spanned forty.[289] From the very early days of his career, Klee kept a meticulous catalogue of his oeuvre, which he transferred to binders in 1934, allotting one page to each work. He created a complicated numbering system that makes it exceedingly difficult to reinsert works that were not in his original list. In this case, the artist's painstaking preparatory work allowed the Klee Foundation to catalogue his work

281 For example, the database the Menil Collection developed for the catalogue raisonné of Jasper Johns's drawings (http://jasperjohnsdrawings.menil.org/about/the-project/) has five separate modules: an object module, a publication module, an exhibition module, a module for the technical description of the object, and a collection module. It will be published in 2016. Building these databases and linking the separate information modules always requires a similar process, as the core information for catalogues raisonnés remains the same. It is more expensive to start from scratch. However, doing so allows for the software to be fully customized. For example, new modules can be integrated into the system from the beginning and additional ones added as needed.

282 Gabrielli, "Preparing the Catalogue Raisonné," 2015 (as in note 274), pp. 42–49.

283 http://www.sik-isea.ch/de-ch/Dienstleistungen/Dienstleistungen/Publikationen.

284 https://artifexpress.com/posts/listen-the-future-of-art-book-publishing.

285 http://artists-estates.com/.

286 Refer, for example, to the cover design of Ilya Kabakov's catalogue raisonné.

287 Tietenberg's conference paper of 2015 (see note 273).

288 http://www.artnews.com/2014/06/03/zervos-picasso-catalogue-reprinted-and-priced-at-20-thousand-dollars/.

289 Tietenberg's conference paper of 2015 (see note 273).

thoroughly in the 1990s, resulting in a nine-volume catalogue raisonné that presents Klee's wide-ranging oeuvre in chronological order.

Gerhard Richter's catalogue raisonné is another prominent example that was begun during the artist's lifetime. Richter numbers his works consecutively and publishes them online at www.gerhard-richter.com, which is an exemplary website overall. In an interview with Hans Ulrich Obrist, Richter explained that his numbering system is in part a bureaucratic whim, but that there is also more to it than that because it allows him to maintain an overview of his practice. Other artists might draw upon certain themes to substantiate their work, but Richter evaluates his in terms of good and bad.[290] Thus, the artist's numbering system is unusual in that it does not include all of his work, but rather only those that he considers worthy of inclusion. Those works that he does not regard highly do not receive a number, even if they have already left his studio. For the most part, Richter has not given numbers to works produced before *Table* of 1962.[291] These include the murals from his early years in Dresden in the cafeteria of the Dresden Art Academy and at the German Hygiene Museum, as well as the later commission *Rheinhausen*, which he completed in the then West Germany.[292] Richter's approach raises a fundamental question that has both art historical and legal dimensions: What should and what must be included in a catalogue raisonné complied by the artist? As the art historian Gregor Wedekind asks: "Who has the right to decide if not the artist? He or she is the ultimate authority and art historians have to accept that."[293] Readers expect that the catalogue raisonné be truthful, even if the artist-author chooses to take liberties. Academics, on the other hand, aspire to objectivity and at some point will want to assemble a catalogue raisonné that also includes those works rejected by the artist. This happened with in Francis Bacon's first catalogue raisonné,[294] which was dedicated to his early work up to 1963 and had a section dedicated to "destroyed and abandoned works," which he also wanted to have included. It will be interesting to see how academic approaches to catalogues raisonnés complied by artists continue to develop, to say the very least.

c) Estates and Authentication

After the catalogue raisonné has been published, the estate should determine whether it will assume the task of authenticating the artist's work. Authentication is the confirmation that a work of art is original. In contrast to an attribution in its narrowest sense, where there is still some lingering doubt as to a work's authenticity, an authentication helps solidify that assumption as a definitive positive verdict.[295]

Authentication is more than a mere practicality in an art market flooded with fakes. Although forgeries are as old as the art market itself, this problem has expanded exponentially in the twenty-first century. According to estimates, more than forty percent of works sold annually are fakes,[296] with the percentage considerably higher for some artists. For instance, experts have estimated that more than ninety-five percent of the works by the avant-garde Russian artist Natalia Goncharova are counterfeits.[297] A full fifty percent of the Paris-based Fondation Giacometti's annual budget is dedicated to exposing fakes.[298]

It is understandable that owners want to differentiate between originals and counterfeits, and also that they will often use all available means—including legal ones—to overturn unfavorable authentications. One could say that estates are the natural entity for clearing up such matters, especially when they have already complied the catalogue raisonné. To that effect, Jack Flam of the Dedalus Foundation believes that authentication is necessary to preserving the integrity of an artist's oeuvre, which is to him one of the estate's primary obligations.[299] Richard Calvocoressi, the former director of the Henry Moore Foundation, shares Flam's view: "The catalogue raisonné and authentication committees go hand in hand, they are interrelated in my view. You can't have a catalogue raisonné without some kind of authentication committee because otherwise who is the authority?"[300]

---

290 Gregor Wedekind in the conference paper "Werkverzeichnisse durch Künstler am Beispiel Paul Klee (und Gerhard Richter)" at the International Symposium *Sammeln, Zuschreiben, Weitergeben: Zur Aktualität von Werkverzeichnissen,* held by the Alfried-Krupp-Wissenschaftskollegs at the University of Greifswald, September 17-19, 2015.

291 https://www.gerhard-richter.com/de/art/paintings/photo-paintings/household-icons-39/table-4954.

292 http://www.welt.de/print/die_welt/kultur/article111739673/Das-Bild-das-Gerhard-Richter-nicht-schaetzt.html.

293 Wedekind's conference paper of 2015 (see note 290).

294 John Rothenstein and Richard Alley, *Francis Bacon,* New York 1964.

295 Friederike Gräfin von Brühl, *Marktmacht von Kunstexperten als Rechtsproblem,* Baden-Baden 2010, p. 17.

296 https://www.law.columbia.edu/media_inquiries/news_events/2011/november2011/kernochan-art-authentication.

297 http://theartnewspaper.com/market/widespread-forgery-of-avant-garde-artist-exposed-at-russian-art-week/.

298 Tobias Timm, "Kunstfälschungen. Unter Verdacht: Ohne Schiedsrichter über die Frage Echt oder Falsch kann der Kunstmarkt nicht funktionieren. Doch jetzt wollen viele Künstlerstiftungen und Nachlassverwalter Fälschungen nicht mehr aussortieren. Schuld sind teure Prozesse," in: *Die ZEIT,* January 10, 2013.

299 See the interview with Jack Flam in this volume.

300 See the interview with Richard Calvocoressi in this volume.

Nevertheless, many estates shy away from authentication, especially in the US. The legal risks associated with authentication are high when a lot of money is at stake, and astronomical legal costs and unfavorable rulings can be devastating to an estate. Ultimately, authentication determines the value of another party's property, which is the heart of the issue.

Usually lawsuits are filed for breaking antitrust laws because the authenticator has abused his or her dominant market position. Additionally, an expert can be held accountable for a faulty appraisal that did not meet current standards or for overlooking other factors important in that instance—that is, in those cases that the authenticator was knowingly dishonest or negligent.

For estates, the costs of such claims and damages are high, and markedly more so in the United States than in Europe. In contrast to Europe, in the US each party carries its own costs, regardless of whether they win or lose the case. Moreover, the risk of punitive damages is far higher in the US, which is due to differences between American and European indemnity laws. In Europe, the primary purpose of indemnity law is to determine the occurrence of loss, and monetary compensation only comes into play when that loss is deemed irretrievable. Furthermore, the plaintiff is obligated to ask for the least compensation possible. By contrast, the American legal system defines damages in terms of capital and also covers hypothetical losses. Its laws also aim to punish guilty parties.

These tenets of American law have had considerable ramifications for artists' estates in the United States in recent years. For instance, the Richard Diebenkorn Foundation set aside millions of dollars before publishing the catalogue raisonné in anticipation that collectors whose works were not included would file lawsuits.[301] The Andy Warhol Foundation's authentication committee ceased its authentication activity after lawsuits cost more than seven million dollars—even though most of them were decided in its favor.[302] When a group of collectors accused the Keith Haring Foundation of an antitrust conspiracy, it faced millions in damages,[303] but the case collapsed. However, for its part, the Keith Haring Foundation sued the same collectors for holding an exhibition of the works in question, which it had deemed to be fakes in 2007.[304] On account of these events, the Keith Haring Foundation has stopped authenticating works. Further prominent examples are the Roy Lichtenstein Foundation and the Noguchi Museum, which have likewise ceased to authenticate art.[305] Christopher Rothko, son of Mark Rothko, recently demonstrated the tragi-comic consequences of these events before a New York court. When presented with a painting that the Knoedler Gallery had sold to Domenico de Sole, Chairman of Sotheby's, on the pretense that it was a Rothko, he simply uttered "nice" and praised its excellent condition. Was it real or not? He never comments on authenticity as a matter of principle.[306]

The state of New York responded in March 2014 by submitting a bill that aims to establish more security for authentication committees; it is currently being negotiated in the State Assembly.[307] If it is passed, the bill will require plaintiffs to carry a heavier burden of proof, and art experts will be able to recover their legal costs if the court decides in their favor.[308] Whether this initiative will lead American estates to resume authenticating works remains to be seen.

In some legal systems, estates can protect the authenticator by drawing up a contract with the owner of the work at hand. The latter must waive their right to sue if the work in their possession is deemed inauthentic. At the Zentrum Paul Klee in Bern, such contracts are crucial to the authentication committee's terms of business. Just how far these terms will go towards fending off lawsuits and the criteria for their efficacy must be considered in the context of any given country's laws. To that end, it is imperative to seek professional counsel in these matters.

For further reading on this complex legal topic in the United States, refer to Judith Prowda's *Visual Arts and the Law: A Handbook for Professional.* Friederike Gräfin von Brühl's *Die Marktmacht von Experten als Rechtsproblem* provides insight to the legal context in Germany and in Europe. Additionally, experts and estates providing authentication services or hope to do so in the future should follow the forum Authentication in Art.[309]

---

301 "Fear of litigation is hobbling the art market," in: *The Economist*, 24. November 2012; http://www.economist.com/news/business/21567074-fear-litigation-hobbling-art-market-collectors-artists-and-lawyers.

302 https://www.law.columbia.edu/media_inquiries/news_events/2011/november2011/kernochan-art-authentication.

303 http://www.courthousenews.com/2015/03/09/keith-haring-foundation-dodges-40m-lawsuit.htm.

304 http://www.widewalls.ch/no-case-against-keith-haring-foundation-03-2015/.

305 http://artlawjournal.com/authenticating-art/.

306 Elke Buhr, "Der chinesische Rothko," in: *Monopol*, March 2016.

307 http://www.lexology.com/library/detail.aspx?g=d7c5edab-e6eb-4045-be06-1b98c0d620cd.

308 http://artlawjournal.com/authenticating-art/.

309 http://authenticationinart.org/about-us/. The most recent working paper is from 2014; http://authenticationinart.org/pdf/Authentication-In-Art-Congress-May-2014_Recommendations-of-Art-and-Law-Work-Group_Official-Release.pdf.

d) The Artist's Estate as a Stimulus for Academic Research

In addition to supporting research for a catalogue raisonné and facilitating the authentication of works, there are many ways to promote academic research on an artist. In this respect, an open archive is invaluable since outside researchers will come the more you welcome them. Ursel Berger, former director of the Georg Kolbe Museum in Berlin sums up the point nicely: "Research on an artist is substantially impeded when their heirs refuse access to the estate. Oftentimes those overseeing the estate hold back materials that they perceive as too personal. However, a letter that sheds light on a marital crisis, for example, can provide clues as to the genesis of a work of art. The decision to restrict materials is usually made without regard to the consequences for academic research on the artist's work."[310] Ideally, the administrators of the estate know the archive well enough to guide researchers toward undiscovered materials. To facilitate scholarly research, access to the space in which the collection is stored should be quick and easy. The Vandenberg Estate is an example of how establishing a directly accessible storage space for large works of art can be done well without high costs. Upon request, it provides access to over one thousand canvases. Many artists leave behind vast libraries that are treasure troves for researchers because they provide insight into the artist's development and context. It is therefore important to make these collections also accessible to scholars. The Donald Judd Library is a stellar example: not only can scholars visit the collection in Marfa, Texas, but they can also peruse each and every volume online.[311]

Opening the archive to outside researchers is an important step, but the estate can go even further by actively promoting research. Estates can do this most effectively by offering research fellowships, the number and frequency of which depend on their finances. An annual fellowship, which might, depending on the final resources of the estate, only amount to a few thousand euros or dollars can go far when used to support groundbreaking research. Symposia on the artist take more time to organize, but are just as important since they bring together members of the research community to discuss current scholarship. It is not necessary to restrict the topic to the work's direct art historical context, as the exploration of broader themes can also shed new light on the oeuvre. Another effective yet less time-consuming approach is to make contact with relevant academic research groups and institutes and provide them with information on the estate's resources and endeavors.

Over the last five years, the Stiftung Arp e.V., which we advise, has aimed to become *the* center for research on the life and work of Hans Arp. In 2013 it unveiled its showrooms, which are open by appointment and provide a full overview of the artist's work. A comprehensive library on the work and influence of Hans and Sophie Taeuber-Arp includes a multitude of primary sources and exhibition catalogues as well as a wide range of secondary literature. It also encompasses scholarly literature on artists and movements related to Arp and Taeuber-Arp. The showroom and library welcome new approaches, a stance that is reinforced by the Stiftung Apr e.V.'s newly established fellowships, which are awarded on an annual basis to both senior and junior scholars and curators. Research topics have ranged from the analysis of Arp's plaster studies to a critical edition of the artist's literary oeuvre and an exploration of haptic perception and the role of touch in his art and theory.[312] The conference *Hans Arp and the USA*, which took place in Berlin in 2015, was dedicated to the widespread appreciation of Arp's work among museum professionals, art dealers, and collectors in America.

The Archipenko Foundation, The Jay DeFeo Trust, and the Keith Haring Foundation likewise have open archives and offer fellowships for study and research purposes. In collaboration with the Getty Conservation Institute, the Sam Francis Foundation analyzes painting techniques. The Morris Louis Conservation fund supports a similar research project on the best conservation practices for color field painting. The Henry Moore Foundation furthers research at its aforementioned institute in Leeds by offering a range of fellowships on the broad theme of sculpture.[313] Similarly, the Andy Warhol Foundation awards fellowships for curatorial research.

2. Active Collaboration with Museums

The boundaries between universities and museums are fluid, since museums also research for exhibitions and on their collections more generally. Exhibitions and museum collections are one of the most important sites for furthering the discourse on deceased artists. Collaboration with museums should therefore be a major focus of every estate.

---

310 Ursel Berger, "Wie erkennt man posthume Bronze? Zur Verantwortung von Nachlassverwaltungen," in: Ursel Berger, Klaus Gallwitz and Gottlieb Leinz (eds.), *Posthume Güsse. Bilanz und Perspektiven*, Berlin 2009, p. 34.

311 http://library.juddfoundation.org/JUDDlibbrowse/.

312 For more information, see: http://stiftungarp.de/forschungundprojekte/stipendien/.

313 See for example the summaries of the fellows' research projects in 2012: https://www.henry-moore.org/hmi/research/hmi-visiting-research-fellowships/fellowships-archive/201213-fellows/fellowship-reports-2012.

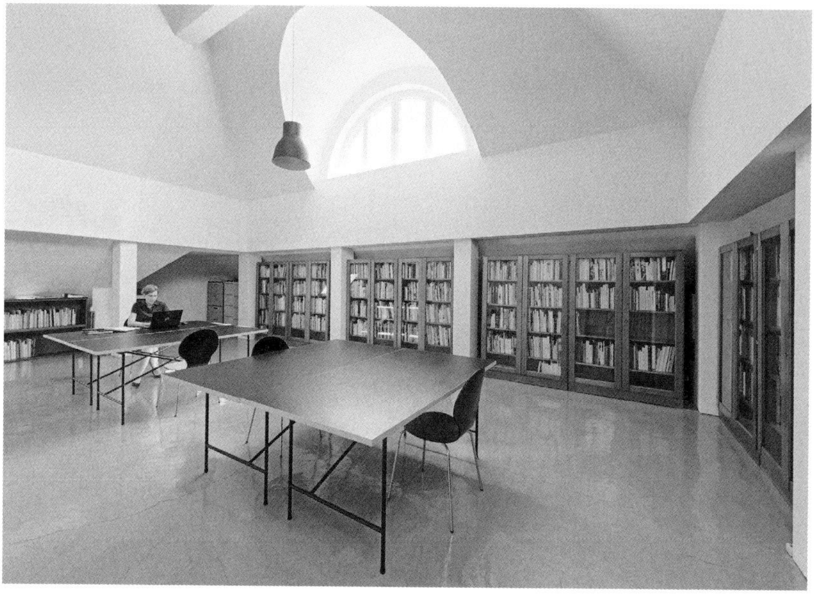

The Stiftung Arp e.V.'s galleries displaying works by Hans Arp and Sophie Taeuber-Arp, 2012

a) Initiating Exhibitions

It is very important to take on an active role here as well. Instead of passively waiting for loan requests, estates should establish contact with curators and museum directors and help to develop and further ideas for exhibitions. Mayen Beckmann, the granddaughter of Max Beckmann, has done just this. In order to disseminate knowledge about her grandfather's work throughout Europe and in Asia, she launched exhibitions in Spain, England, Scotland, and Korea. She attributes her success to the estate's large holdings, which are especially rich in works on paper, so much so that partner museums were able to obtain most of the loans for these exhibitions from this single source. By coordinating additional loans, Mayen Beckmann was able to offer museums more or less complete exhibitions, thereby sparing them from the time-consuming work of organizing loans from multiple institutions. For museums, the possibility of showing rarely exhibited works is also enticing. For estates, exhibiting these works is an opportunity to draw attention to lesser-known aspects of the artist's oeuvre.

Maintaining a presence in group exhibitions is important for estates both large and small, because they help to re-contextualize works and to place them within broader cultural and historical frameworks. Group exhibitions often lead to surprising revelations, which then spark ideas for future exhibitions. It is also exciting when historical work is shown in relation to contemporary art; this kind of exhibition can help introduce the current generation to the artist. For example, the 2015 exhibition *Stranger than Paradise* presented the English photographer Keith Arnatt's work from the 1980s as a point of departure for contemporary art and provided the occasion for a younger public in Germany to discover his work.[314] Philippe Vandenberg's estate is leading the way by inviting contemporary artists such as Berlinde de Bruyckere to engage with its collection or to curate museum exhibitions.[315] Another way to garner contemporary artists' attention is to collaborate with art schools and universities, so that art students can learn directly from the original works of art. A compelling example is the Robert Rauschenberg Foundation's Loan Bank, a pilot program that lends art to two university museums, which are then incorporated into course syllabi and lesson plans.[316] Over the next three to four years, the Foundation will cooperate with the museums, loaning them two to four works in various media selected by museum employees on a rotating six-month basis. In this way, the art is seen afresh within the context of the university museums' collections, and it also reinforces the institutions' educational programming each semester.[317] The Robert Rauschenberg Foundation has lent works to forty-six museums all over the world.

Regardless of the kinds of exhibitions it supports, the estate should ensure that they are accompanied by publications whenever possible. In this way, the work of the estate is preserved for posterity. Moreover, exhibition catalogues are an excellent means to disseminate new research to a broader public.

b) Targeted Donations

Many artists' estates are generous donors to museums. In contrast to the previous discussion, the present question is not so much whether museums can be dedicated stewards and how much of the estate should be bequeathed to them, but rather the targeted donation of individual works of art.

---

314 *Stranger than Paradise,* Sies + Hoeke, Düsseldorf, October 24 – November 25, 2015. The exhibition was curated by Gesine Borchardt, with works by Bas Jan Ader, Giovanni Anselmo, Keith Arnatt, Olga Balema, James Benning, Julius von Bismarck, Björn Braun, Vajiko Chachkhiani, Julian Charrière, Eli Cortiñas, Daniel Gustav Cramer, Owen Gump, Pierre Huyghe, Joan Jonas, Maria Loboda, Michael E. Smith, Wolfgang Tillmans, and Tobias Zielony.

315 Berlinde de Bruyckere curated an exhibition for the estate in Paris at La Maison Rouge and in the De Pont Museum in Tilburg.

316 http://www.rauschenbergfoundation.org/newsfeed/six-major-art-institutions-acquire-seminal-rauschenberg-works.

317 http://artmuseum.princeton.edu/story/rauschenberg-loan-bank-program.

Such gifts have positive ramifications for both the museum as well as the estate. Museums can fill gaps in their collections, while the artist's work is promoted and its visibility increased when accepted into a collection. Donating a work of art is a remarkably generous act, and the following considerations should be taken into account to help ensure that it provides the intended outcome:

1. In which collections is the artist not yet represented but should be?
2. Are there geographic regions where the artist's work has not yet been shown?
3. Which museum collections relate most strongly to the artist's oeuvre?
4. Are there aspects of the oeuvre that have been underrepresented in museums?
5. Which existing collections are relevant to the artist's biography and the historical and geographical contexts in which he or she worked?
6. Is the institution prepared to offer a gift in return, such as a publication or an exhibition?

Many estates use the gift-purchase program model. In this combination of a donation and a sale, either all of the works at hand are sold to the museum below market value or some are given while others are sold. In addition to the financial consequences for the estate, this model can also have a psychological effect on the perceived value of the remaining art, as Jack Flam makes clear with respect to Motherwell's Dedalus Foundation: "At the beginning, we had thought about giving works away, but we needed money for our programs, and we also realized that when you give things away they are valued less. If there is some skin in the game, it works better for everybody."[318] The Robert Rauschenberg Foundation's gift-purchase program for the artist's late work is a positive example of this model. It invited selected American museums to participate, offering them reduced pricing, and six accepted. As with comparative programs conducted by the estates of Andy Warhol and Georgia O'Keeffe, the offer was good for three years. Ultimately, the estate was able to place Rauschenberg's lesser-known works from the 1980s and 1990s in museums.[319] The program likely led to greater recognition of this aspect of the artist's oeuvre, and it would not be surprising if the market value of these works increased because of it as well.

A gift-purchase program allows the estate to be actively engaged with museums and to support the common good while meeting its financial obligations. In this manner, the Dedalus Foundation also placed works in institutions such as the Baltimore Museum of Art, the Fondation Beyeler, and the Museum Wiesbaden.[320] A similar program allowed the Robert Mapplethorpe Foundation to find a home for its core collection at the Getty Research Institute.[321] In Europe, the Ernst Wilhelm Nay Foundation was able to ensure that works by the German proponent of Art Informel landed at the Tate Modern, the Centre Pompidou, and the National Museum of Art, Architecture, and Design in Oslo, Norway. Nevertheless, according to estate manager Christian Klein, the museums were primarily motivated to acquire the works in order to fill gaps in their collections, as the Foundation did not offer them steep discounts.[322]

It can also be prudent to make gifts to more than one museum. This alleviates the financial burden on individual museums and helps promote broader engagement with the art, ultimately ensuring wider visibility of the oeuvre. Transferring a work to a museum implies that it will be lent to other institutions as well, but the estate should stipulate that the bequeathed work should be made available for loan to be safe. This helps ensure that the work remains part of a lively ongoing discourse.

3. Entering the Art Market: Branding and the Marketplace

The art market has always played a role in the art historical recognition of individual artists. And today the market is just as important as museums and scholarship in determining their value. At a time when gallery shows attain museum-level quality and museum exhibitions are co-financed by galleries, the borders between these arenas have become increasingly fluid. Since most artists' estates are dependent on the market, it is of the utmost importance to develop a concrete market strategy. The following questions can help get the ball rolling:

1. What is the current state of the market for the artist's work? Is that market regional, national, or international?
2. Can and should a wider market be reached?

---

318 See the interview with Jack Flam in this volume.

319 http://de.phaidon.com/agenda/art/articles/2014/march/04/the-rauschenberg-foundation-distributes-later-works/; http://www.rauschenbergfoundation.org/newsfeed/six-major-art-institutions-acquire-seminal-rauschenberg-works.

320 http://dedalusfoundation.org/foundation/programs/collections.

321 http://articles.latimes.com/2011/feb/08/entertainment/la-et-lacma-mapplethorpe-20110208.

322 Interview Klein (see note 278).

3. Is it possible to continue working with galleries who had a relationship with the artist during their lifetime or is it necessary to seek out new ones?
4. Which works should be sold?
5. What are the best venues for selling the art: galleries or auction houses?
6. Over what period of time?
7. Under which conditions?
8. What would be the advantages of purchasing works for my own collection?

a) Forming Active Relationships with Galleries

Before entering the art market, the estate must find the right gallery. It is helpful to consider whether the artists the gallery (currently) represents have thematic ties to the artist's oeuvre or if the artist influenced any of the living artists on its roster. The dealer's passion for the artist's work is decisive, as their gallery will become its most important representative on the art market.

Munich art dealer Fred Jahn asserts that for galleries, working with estates means "reassessing historical works of art through the filter of the present—a long-term endeavor."[323] When they discover and preserve artists' estates, galleries fulfill an important cultural role that is very different than the one they play when representing living artists. David Nash of the gallery Mitchell-Inness & Nash explains: "Working with an artist's estate you have to have a very clear objective. You are usually responsible to a legal advisor, some sort of executor or attorney of one kind or another. When you are dealing with living artists it is altogether a different business. You have to take into account his future, what is best for him, and all kind of other things you don't have to think of when you are dealing with an artist's estate."[324]

Once a gallery has been selected, it is important to consider what shape the relationship will take. Hardly anyone knows an artist's work better than his or her estate, and almost no one knows the art market better than a gallery. Regular communication between the two parties helps ensure what is best for the artist's oeuvre. To that end, the estate should support the gallery in its endeavors. It is also important to consider the market with respect to the estate's own collection and archive:

1. What could make an interesting gallery show?
2. Which aspects of the artist's oeuvre are underrepresented on the market?
3. Has the work been properly contextualized?
4. Which other artists can be shown alongside the artist? Which artists inspired him or her?

5. Which works should be offered exclusively to museums and select private collections, and which ones can be put on the wider art market?
6. Are there upcoming museum exhibitions that could be augmented by parallel gallery shows?

Although it might be hard to imagine, a gallery's artists and artists' estates will often compete with one another for the next show or to be featured at art fairs. For this reason, it is of the utmost importance that the estate continually presents the gallery with new ways to approach the artist's work within its broader focus. Consider offering the gallery new exhibition concepts and leads on interested buyers. Keep the dealer up to date on the estate's activities and whenever possible, try to include the gallery. Visits to the estate's archive and showrooms or other exhibition spaces can be great ways to facilitate more personal encounters with the art and to solidify the gallery's status as an ambassador for the artist, as can orchestrating direct contact between the estate's key personnel, family members, and important collectors.

Above all, the estate's activities on the secondary art market should be undertaken in close collaboration with the gallery. Absolute transparency between the estate and its gallery is necessary to the success of their mutual endeavors. The gallery can best determine how much of the oeuvre can be absorbed by the art market and how to maintain the delicate balance between supply and demand. When the gallery understands the estate's long-term goals, it will be able to act in its best interests and not compromise them for the sake of a quick profit. To maintain its end of the bargain, the estate should never sell work without first consulting with the gallery. Finally, it can be helpful for the estate to speak openly with the gallery about its budget and to make a timeline for the sale of specific works so that its financial needs are met.

All of this is even more critical when the estate is working with more than one gallery. It makes sense to have multiple galleries when a large number of works must be sold in a relatively short period of time, as was the case with Mapplethorpe, or when the estate wishes to diversify its geographical market, as the Robert Rauschenberg Foundation did. Nevertheless, this strategy should be carefully thought through. Particularly with respect to smaller and medium-sized

---

323 http://www.tagesspiegel.de/kultur/archive-und-kuenstlernachlaesse-gruss-vom-grossvater/12280126.html.
324 See the interview with David Nash in this volume.

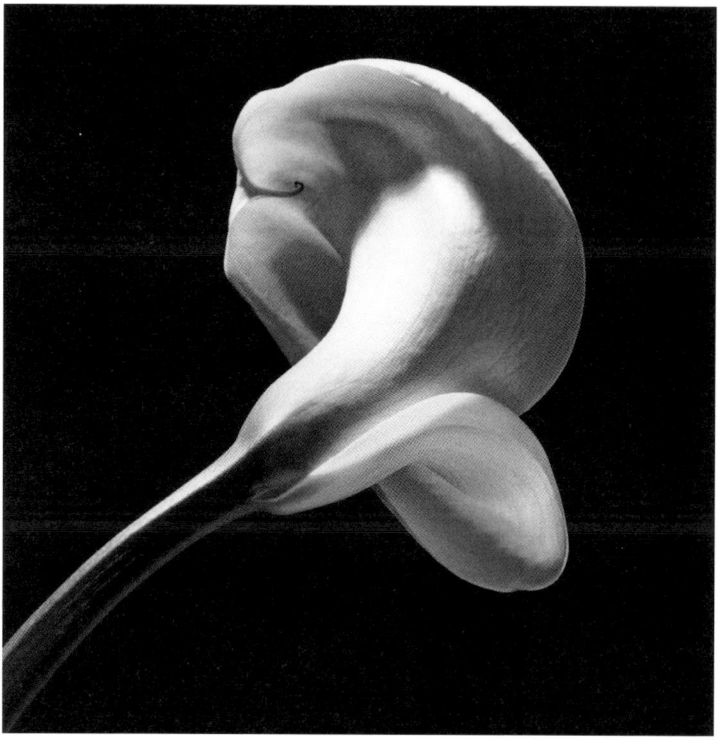

Robert Mapplethorpe, *Calla Lily*, 1984

estates, it can lead to neglect on the part of one or more galleries. There have also been unfortunate cases of galleries competing with one another for the best works in the estate. In my experience, this is both detrimental to the reputation of the artist as well as to the prices his or her works command. Open communication between all parties, mutual agreement to terms, and the fair distribution of works, however, can ensure that the estate benefits from having multiple galleries.

b) Market Strategy

The best sales strategy for an artist's estate is also the simplest: sell as little as possible and only as much as absolutely necessary. In order to meet its budget, an estate must continually weigh what should be sold when, but without compromising its holdings too severely.

In the period directly following the artist's death, it can be tempting to sell too much too fast. There are many reasons estates do this: inheritance taxes are looming, the heirs are making financial demands or the burden of expenditure and the death of a loved one is just too overwhelming. If possible, the sale of multiple works at once should only occur as part of a targeted market strategy or if the artist is already commanding such high prices that the proceeds can finance the estate's central endeavors. One such example is the aforementioned renovation of Donald Judd's home and studio in SoHo, which the Judd Foundation supported by auctioning off thirty-five works of art. It garnered twenty-eight million dollars for its new initiative in a single night.[325] In addition to finding the right time to put art on the market, it is also wise to hold on to the most significant pieces for as long as possible, even when it is clear that they would bring in a lot of money quickly. Estates would be well advised to consider placing works in the appropriate museums and private collections, as this will increase the value of its holdings over the long term.

In her book *Affairs of the Art*, Katrina Strickland provides a noteworthy example of how the right strategy can lead to success on the art market. When the Australian sculptor Robert Klippel died in 2001, his son Andrew Klippel, a successful musician who divided his time between Sydney and Los Angeles, assumed responsibility for the estate.[326] Andrew moved from one Australian gallery to another, but did not find the international public he had been hoping for at any of them. Then he tried offering twelve pieces for auction at Sotheby's, but only half of them were sold. Later, Andrew said that the auction floor had not been the best place to sell his father's work, and that the overall worth of his oeuvre suffered for it. Having resolved to transcend Australia's limited market, he shifted his focus to marketing his father's sculpture internationally. In 2012, Andrew moved his father's estate to the Swiss Galerie Gmurzynska. He learned in the process that in contrast to the music industry, repositioning art on the market takes a long time. "In music, you can get somewhere in nine or ten months, and in another ten months, it can all be over. In the art world, it takes a lot longer."[327] It takes time to reveal the full range of an artist's work. Exhibitions that highlight lesser-known phases help the public develop an appreciation for them. Such are the rewards for an estate that develops and implements long-term goals—with the help of a good gallerist.

---

325 http://www.nytimes.com/2006/04/24/arts/design/24judd.html?_r=0.

326 Strickland, *Affairs of the Art* (2013), p. 151.

327 Ibid., 157.

c) Participation in the Secondary Art Market

There are two good reasons for estates to participate directly in the secondary art market, which is defined as the purchase and sale of works of art that have been sold previously. Either the estate wishes to fill gaps in its own collection or it expects to resell the acquisition for a profit.

Filling gaps is a good approach for estates whose activities center upon their collections and who also have the necessary means. For instance, with the assistance of donors, the estate of the German sculptor Gerhard Marcks continually acquires major works for its Gerhard-Marcks Museum in Bremen. As the leading expert on the artist, the estate can recognize buying opportunities, given that it follows not only market prices but also the breadth and quality of its offerings. If a significant work comes onto the market but the estate does not have enough cash on hand, it can work with specialized financiers or partner with its gallery to offer the dealer an exchange.

Some estates use their market savvy to purchase works with the intent of reselling them for a profit. When skillfully employed, such activities can secure the means to carry out research and to protect the core collection, which would have to be disseminated bit by bit otherwise. However, if an estate is considering entering the secondary art market, it should only do so in cooperation with its dealer, not only to maintain this important relationship, but also to fully utilize both parties' knowledge. Estates should also remain aware of the moral responsibility that comes with participating in the art market, especially when they are involved in assembling a catalogue raisonné or authenticating works. In such cases, the estate must do everything in its power to maintain academic integrity and to ensure that it never mixes its scholarly and economic interests. To that end, all relevant information should be made public. Finally, in order for these economic activities to be carried out legally, proper council must be retained. American laws regarding insider trading for estates were discussed previously.[328]

---

328 See Chapter III.

Art Alone Isn't Enough! How Do You Finance Eternity, and Is it Even Necessary?

"What I'm interested in is money!" Salvador Dalí

VI. Should an Artist's Estate Live Forever? Investments, Returns, and the Future

Most artists' estates are "art rich and cash poor," meaning that they have assets in the form of art but few liquid resources. Even when some of the estate's work can be carried out without hiring personnel, other activities are unthinkable without significant financial resources. Only in rare cases do artists' estates receive outside financial support through grants or other means. Estates are therefore responsible for financing their own activities, and as a rule this usually means selling art, accompanied by additional earnings from copyright royalties and resale rights.

Heirs are generally not so well off that they can finance the estate independently. There are exceptions however. One such example is the Alfred Erhardt Foundation in Berlin. The Munich investor Jens Erhardt established the foundation in order to make the work of his father, the German photographer and documentary filmmaker Alfred Erhardt, available to the public. In addition to its archival work, the foundation promotes contemporary art and media art. To this end, it maintains the home of the artist's birth near the Thuringian city of Gera as well as an exhibition space in central Berlin.[329] Family members likewise support the foundation dedicated to Fausto Melozzi, who was a friend of Lucio Fontana in his student days.[330] Of course it is great when family resources coincide with a passion for the work, but even in these exceptional circumstances the estate must still define its goals and establish the means by which it will achieve them.

Financial planning is at the core of estate activity and must be tailored to each estate's goals. It is important to consider the balance of income and expenditures both in terms of an annual budget as well as long-term finances.

But before we address expenditures and income in detail, we should ask whether a given estate will exist in perpetuity or not. The alternative to a permanent estate is an estate that is dedicated to achieving certain goals before eventually dissolving. These two possibilities fundamentally alter financial planning.

1. Sunset and Eternity Models

What is the purpose of estate management after scholars have analyzed the work and it has achieved widespread public renown? What happens when the estate has reached its charitable goals? If there is no longer a studio or a museum to engage, and there are no direct family members left, what is the point of self-perpetuation? At a certain point, the estate may entrust the artist's legacy to art history. The Sunset Model[331] and the Eternity Model both raise the following fundamental questions:

1. Should the estate's work continue indefinitely? If so, why?
2. If not, how long would the foreseen work take?
3. Which tasks should the estate pursue?
4. Will the estate's scope of work change over time? What will these duties look like in 20, 30, 40 or 100 years?
5. Am I utilizing all possible sources of income for the planned life of the estate? Alternately, is it better to forfeit copyright income, so the work may be distributed more widely? If so, when?
6. If I choose to follow the Sunset Model, what kind of flexibility does the law allow for the legal entity I have chosen?
7. If I anticipate an end to the estate's work, what is the plan for its cessation and at what point in time will it come to an end?
8. If the estate's work should cease, how should its remaining assets be handled?

---

329 http://www.alfred-ehrhardt-stiftung.de/index.php?profil.

330 http://www.fondazionefaustomelotti.org/en/.

331 Francie Ostrower, "Sunsetting: A Framework for Foundation Life as well as Death," p. 5; http://www.aspeninstitute.org/sites/default/files/content/docs/pubs/Sunsetting2.pdf.

The so-called Sunset Model establishes the foreseen end of an estate. When the institution managing the estate has fulfilled its purpose or when its previously determined lifespan has expired, it ceases to exist. It is also possible to plan the estate's duration based on available funding.[332] A prominent example of this "expiration model" is the Georgia O'Keeffe Foundation. In 2006, it transferred its assets to the Georgia O'Keeffe Museum in Santa Fe.[333] If all goes to plan, the Judith Rothschild Foundation will cease its activities in 2018, while the Roy Lichtenstein Foundation will be dissolved thirty years after its founding, which would be in 2029. Nevertheless, an estate's planned closure is contingent upon whether there is someone who feels called to continue the work, perhaps because they knew the artist, and the extent to which family members remain engaged.[334]The original motive for the estate's work may change over time. It is therefore only when the estate's goals and milestones are crystal clear from the outset that its end should be determined in advance. However, having a set goal with an end in sight also eliminates the pressure of continually reinventing the estate. The trustee of an American foundation put it this way: "The prospect of a hanging does concentrate the mind."[335]

With a Sunset Model, finances can be maximized over a certain period of time, which can be a relief in periods of low interest rates or for estates with more limited means. It is possible to plan for a foundation to cease operations when its resources are expected to run out, and the plan may be flexible or set in stone. Or, a foundation may build capital for a certain time and then distribute it among one or more nonprofit organizations along with the rest of its assets.

Lawmakers in Germany made provisions for limited-term foundations in 2013, and according to the law they must operate for at least ten years and their end must be determined at the outset. It can also be combined with a non-consumable endowment. Additionally, a foundation's management may now obtain the authority to transform a foundation that was originally set up for eternity into a limited-term foundation. German foundation authorities recommend this option as an alternative to the traditional foundation model when resources amount to less than one million euros.[336] Examples of artist's estates that follow this model are not yet forthcoming, though several countries, including Belgium, Spain, France, Austria, Denmark, and Switzerland, have established such laws—albeit with differing conditions.[337] For example, an English trust must plan to dissolve after a specified event or on a set date.[338]

All estates following the Sunset Model share an obligation to determine exactly what to do with their remaining assets. Transferring an estate's remaining holdings to a museum is one option, and offering it the remaining liquid assets can be a great incentive as well.

The corollary to the Sunset Model is the Eternity Model, which requires more complex strategic and financial planning. Foundations that plan to exist in perpetuity, such as those dedicated to Rauschenberg, Motherwell, and Warhol, must continually reflect upon their reasons for existence. It is exciting to observe how such foundations redefine their purposes over the course of time. When the estate has fulfilled its mission with respect to the artist's work, a transformation takes place. It usually coincides with the completion of the catalogue raisonné or the expiration of the foundation's copyright. At that point, many foundations and estates shift their focus from the stewardship of the artist's oeuvre, which does indeed become exhausting at a certain point, to broadening their missions. This can include promoting young artists, funding art publications, supporting art historical research in general or nonprofits that represent a range of interests.

Since it was established in 1977, the Henry Moore Foundation has developed organically. For some time, Moore's work has been well represented in museums and private collections, it remains intriguing to art historians and curators, and the Foundation's authentication program is well established. Yet the work of the Foundation continues. The artist's oeuvre led the Foundation to embrace the wider theme of sculpture, and it now promotes all of the medium's rich and varied aspects through exhibitions and innovative programing, which ranges from children's workshops to dance performances. Other foundations have expanded their reach beyond the arts. The Robert Rauschenberg Foundation has established fellowships for political themes such as segregation,[339] and the Joan

332 The Artist-Endowed Foundations Initiative (AEFI) at The Aspen Institute has conducted comprehensive research on the Sunset Model for estates in the American nonprofit sector and also advises on the subject: http://www.aspeninstitute.org/publications/sunsetting-framework-foundation-life-well-death; http://www.aspeninstitute.org/policy-work/nonprofit-philanthropy/artist-endowed-foundations.

333 http://artdaily.com/news/13970/Georgia-O-Keeffe-Foundation-to-Transfer-Assets#.Vt2uPZPhBR0.

334 http://www.sharpeartfdn.org/supplement/2008-supplement.pdf, p. 79.

335 Ostrower, Sunsetting (see note 331), p. 3.

336 Melanie Jakobs, "Verbrauchsstiftung: Neue gesetzliche Regelungen": http://stifter-fuer-stifter.de/verbrauchsstiftung-neue-gesetzliche-regelungen/.

337 Annette Rebsch, *Die europäische Stiftung*, Berlin 2007, p. 60, notes 201–04.

338 Ibid., p. 60.

339 http://artforum.com/news/id=55144.

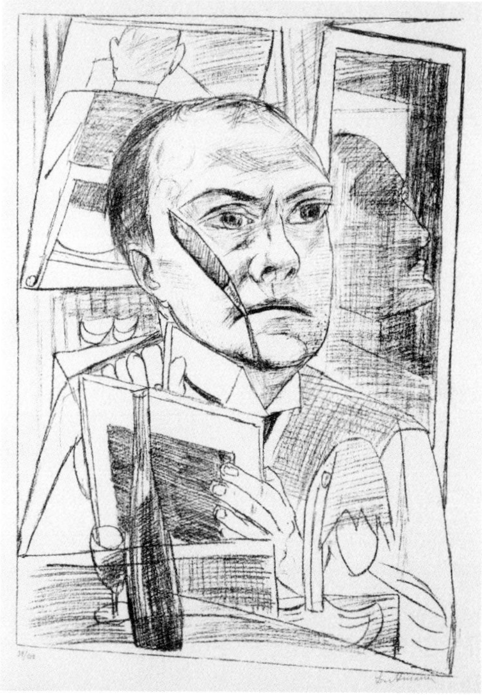

Max Beckmann, *Self Portrait in the Hotel*, 1922, from the print portfolio *Trip to Berlin*, Berlinische Galerie, loan from the State of Berlin

Mitchell Foundation awarded "Emergency Grants" for the arts in New Orleans after the devastating Hurricane Katrina.[340] And when an artist like Andy Warhol has achieved widespread recognition and fame, there is only one option left: wiping the slate clean. When the Andy Warhol Foundation had fulfilled its obligations to the artist's oeuvre, it liquidated its holdings and used the revenue to help finance nonprofit art projects and organizations. Joel Wachs, the president of the Andy Warhol Foundation observes: "the growing number of artist foundations will extend the sort of support that the Warhol provides to community-based and artist-centered organizations. ... Those communities are where the next Andy is going to come from."[341] Warhol will now go down in history not only as a great artist, but also as a great philanthropist, which he certainly would have appreciated.

Many estates consider whether they should proceed after their copyright has expired. This is often a double loss: at the same time that an important revenue stream evaporates, the estate also loses an important means to wield influence. Mayen Beckmann anticipates a turning point when the copyright to

Max Beckmann's work expires in 2020, since she "can decline requests or participate in projects only as long as the copyright is protected."[342] At that point, it is no longer possible to have control over diverse projects, and at the same time there are fewer ways to go about them. For privately managed estates that exist for the sole purpose of administering the artist's work, copyright would be a good reason to cease operations.

2. Estate Expenditures

Once the estate has determined whether it will adopt the Sunset or Eternity Model, it can then turn its attention to the details of financial planning. Sound financial planning begins with the analysis of income versus expenditures.

In most cases, estate expenses may be categorized as follows:

1. Personnel or external management
2. Travel and expenses
3. Rent (for the archive, storage, etc.)
4. Commissions for the sale of art
5. Publications
6. Legal and tax fees
7. Accounting
8. Additional administration costs

A wide variety of circumstances, including location and legal status, determine just how high these costs will be. Because the determining factors are so different in each case, it is difficult to estimate costs. We outline the costs and divergent financial plans of four different types of estates below, however, in order to provide an overview.

Mid-Size European Estates

A mid-size European estate, in the form of a business partnership, comprises of a team of nine individuals who volunteer or receive only a small compensation for their work. Scholarship and conservation is carried out in partnership with

---

340 http://www.artnews.com/2012/01/09/the-artist-as-philanthropist/.
341 http://www.blouinartinfo.com/news/story/1305536/predictions-for-2016-a-tale-of-two-art-worlds.
342 See the interview with Mayen Beckmann in this volume.

a university. When the family is also highly involved, this structure allows for a relatively lean expenditure structure:

1. Personnel costs
   - Research advisor (art history professor) 6,000.00 euros
   - Research staff and archivists (art historians): full-time, funded by the university
   - Conservator (student): full-time internship, provided by a university
   - Assistant (art history student): 1 day/week, internship, provided by a university
   - Researchers dedicated to works not in the estate's holdings: exchange program with other estates, 1 day/week, unpaid
   - Lead archivist (art historian): 2 days/week, lump-sum payment for cataloguing a specified number of works for the catalogue raisonné: 4,800.00 euros
   - Several family members with various responsibilities 6,000.000 euros

   Total: 16,800.00 euros
2. Real Estate (upkeep for the inherited studio) 3,000.00 euros
3. Administrative costs 6,000.00 euros
4. Travel and expenses 20,000.00 euros
5. Additional art-related costs (photography, framing, restoration and preservation) 10,000.00 euros

   Total expenditures: 55,800.00 euros

This mid-sized European estate's fixed costs amount to about 55,000.00 euros, including the maintenance costs for the studio as well as administrators' travel costs. Moreover, it has strong relationships with a conservator, a photographer, a framer, and a designer who are all hired as needed. There are additional costs associated with the catalogue raisonné, exhibitions, and other projects that add up to 25,000.00 to 50,000.00 euros annually, so that the total budget amounts to about 100,000.00 euros. Thus, it is possible for smaller estates to finance their core endeavors through their own dedication and smart collaborations with outside institutions such as universities.

The aforementioned Alfred Ehrhardt Foundation in Berlin has a similar cost structure.[343] Its yearly expenditures amount to 56,000.00 euros, which are allotted as follows:

1. Personnel	
– Research and business administration (2,500.00 euros/month for a part-time position)	30,000.00 euros
– Intern	1,500.00 euros
– Tax and legal counsel	2,000.00 euros
– Travel and expenses	2,000.00 euros
Total:	35,500.00 euros
2. Property Maintenance	
– Additional costs (1,000.00 euros/month)	12,000.00 euros
– Refurbishment of the interior (prorated annually)	500.00 euros
Total:	12,500.00 euros
3. Administration	
– IT	2,500.00 euros
– Office supplies	1,000.00 euros
– Archival supplies	500.00 euros
– Insurance	2,000.00 euros
– Other	2,000.00 euros
Total expenditures:	56,000.00 euros

Established European Foundation

Larger foundations have considerably higher costs, most of which goes toward personnel, administration, and counsel from lawyers and tax advisors. The estate of a modern French artist spent 312,000.00 euros in 2015 on the following:

1. Personnel	
– Research direction, full-time	
– Non-executive director, part-time	
– Accounting, part-time	
– Unskilled labor / storage personnel	
– Tax and legal counsel	
Total:	188,000.00 euros
2. Real Estate	
– Office and gallery space	

343 Christiane Stahl, "Zukunftsmodelle für die langfristige Finanzierung der Alfred Ehrhardt Stiftung," in: Christiane E. Fricke, *Der Gang der Dinge. Welche Zukunft haben photographische Archive und Nachlässe?*, Berlin 2013, p. 150.

– Storage	
Total:	60,000.00 euros
3. Administration	
– IT	11,000.00 euros
– Insurance	22,000.00 euros
Donations	13,000.00 euros
– Other	7,000.00 euros
4. Travel and expenses	11,000.00 euros
Total expenditures:	312,000.00 euros

Large Sunset Estate

The Roy Lichtenstein Foundation is a large estate that follows the Sunset Model.[344] Its central endeavor is maintaining Lichtenstein's studio in Greenwich Village and the adjacent building that houses the archive, a library, and offices.[345] In 2014, its expenditures amounted to approximately 2.7 million dollars,[346] most of which funded nine full-time positions and building maintenance. Its costs were divided along the following lines:[347]

1. Administrative and Personnel Costs	
– Executive Director	
– Exhibition Support Manger	
– Head of Archives and Associate Director Roy Lichtenstein Study Center Project	
– Archivist	
– Senior Administrator	
– Digital Data and Support	
– Assistant to Catalogue Raisonné Manager	
– Catalogue Raisonné Manager and Researcher	
– Registrar	
– Additional administrative costs	
Total:	$2,141,000.00
2. Pension funds	$84,000.00
3. Legal counsel	$196,000.00
4. Accounting	$84,000.00
5. Travel and entertainment	$154,000.00
6. Publications	$2,500.00
Total expenditures:	$2,625,500.00

Large Eternity Estate

The Robert Rauschenberg Foundation is a large estate that plans to exist in perpetuity. In 2014, its expenditures amounted to ca. 6 million dollars, which gives a sense of the amount of capital needed to continue operating and further develop nonprofit endeavors.[348]

1. Administrative and Personnel Costs
   - CEO
   - COO
   - Program Officer
   - Director of Philanthropy
   - Director of Archives and Scholarship
   - Senior Curator
   - Senior Registrar
   - Manager of Media and Special Projects
   - Finance Manager
   - Residency Coordinator Rauschenberg Residency
   - Studio Supervisor Rauschenberg Residency
   - Program Coordinator
   - Collections Manager
   - Facilities Supervisor Rauschenberg Residency
   - Assistant Curator
   - Associate Archivist

---

344 For more information, refer to *A Visual Artist's Guide* 2008 (as in note 45), p. 79; http://www.sharpeartfdn.org/supplement/2008-supplement.pdf.

345 In order to finance its long-term expenses without relying on external donations, capital was set aside at the beginning to generate income. Ten million dollars were invested in treasury notes and bonds to create a starter endowment, which covered half of the foundation's operational costs in 2008. That year, the estate subsidized the other half of its expenditures with copyright royalties, thereby providing the provisions for projects such as the catalogue raisonné.
The estate's beneficiary is Lichtenstein's family, including both of his wives and his sons from his first marriage, all of whom have served or still serve on the board. In the beginning, the estate was endowed with 15 works of art, which were to be followed by more; in 2007 the family also donated its archive to the estate. See Hoffman, "Reflections" 2008 (as in note 45), p. 79; http://www.sharpeartfdn.org/supplement/2008-supplement.pdf.

346 The Aspen Institute estimates annual costs for artists' estates in the United States at around 750 thousand dollars; http://www.aspeninstitute.org/sites/default/files/content/docs/psi/AEF_V1.pdf.

347 Ibid.

348 http://nonprofits.findthecompany.com/l/974671/Robert-Rauschenberg-Foundation.

– Administrative Assistant	
– Media Associate	
– Operations Manager	
– Warehouse Assistant	
Total:	$4,570,000.00
2. Pension funds	$410,000.00
3. Legal counsel	$720,000.00
4. Accounting	$135,000.00
5. Travel and entertainment	$112,000.00
6. Publications	$20,000.00
Total expenditures:	$5,970,000.00

3. Sources of Income for Artists' Estates

Selling art and copyright royalties are two ways estates can offset the expenditures discussed above.

a) Selling Art

An estate's collection is its primary asset. It is also a potential source of income. As discussed in Chapter 5, the best strategy for the primary and secondary art markets is to sell as much as necessary and as little as possible. It should also be determined which works constitute the core of the estate's holdings and therefore should remain in its collection. Because artists often exchange works with each other and collect art themselves, an estate's holdings often include work by other artists. If such works were not of major significance to the artist's development, then they should be sold to finance the estate's endeavors. Additionally, an estate may generate income by buying and selling the artist's work, but only in cooperation with its gallery.

b) Copyright

Artists' estates may also generate income through copyright and resale rights. In order to do so, the estate must have inherited those rights or otherwise become rightful owner.

Copyright law regulates and protects intellectual and cultural property[349] and allows the copyright holder to determine whether and how the work may be reproduced or altered, among other things. In some contexts, resale rights, or *droit de suite,* is an extension of copyright for visual artists. Resale rights ensure

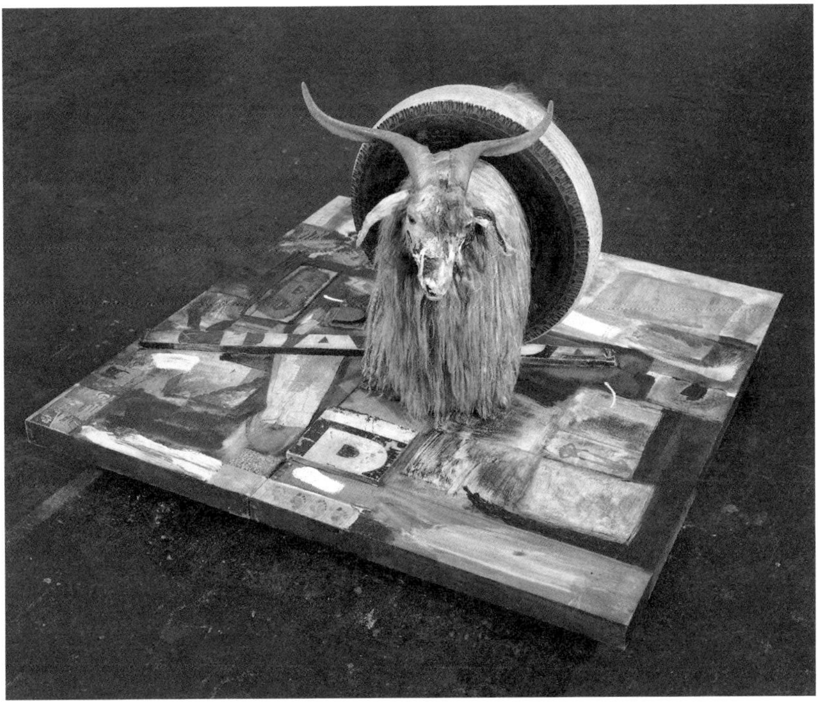

Robert Rauschenberg, *Monogram*, 1955–59, Moderna Museet, Stockholm

an artist's right to profit from the increasing value of his or her work on the secondary art market.[350] Moreover, copyright remains in effect post mortem. In most states, it does not expire for fifty to seventy years after the artist's death.[351]

As immaterial assets, copyright holdings have important value for estates in that they provide income without chipping away at substance. Moreover, copyright allows the estate to protect the integrity of the artist's oeuvre and to stay

349 http://www.ifb.uni-erlangen.de/fileadmin/ifb/doc/publikationen/gruendungsinfos/12_schutz_eigentum.pdf.

350 Liliane de Pierredon-Fawcett and John M. Kernochan, *The Droit de Suite in Literary and Artistic Property: A Comparative Law Study* (New York, 1991), p. 301.

351 At the Berne Convention for the Protection of Literary and Artistic Works, representatives from the international community agreed that copyright for intellectual property would not expire until at least fifty years after the creator's death, and the participants made a provision for extensions as well. Many countries have taken advantage of them. In the European Union, Switzerland and the United States, copyright lasts for 70 years after the artist's death, in Mexico it remains in effect for 100 years, while in Canada, China, and Japan the work is protected for 50 years, with the exception of film. Ancillary copyright usually expires sooner, although it varies according to each state, and in some cases may be extended.

informed about publications and research. In the broadest sense, an estate may harness its copyright to wield decisive influence.

(1) Reproduction and Distribution Rights

The creator of a given work holds the exclusive rights to their intellectual property. However, copyright may take very different forms. For estates, reproduction and distribution rights are significant.[352] These rights take the form of immaterial exploitation rights as opposed to bringing tangible goods onto the marketplace. Copyright royalties are therefore the most important streams of revenue for estates. In the art world, these rights extend to all reproductions of the artist's work, including each and every museum postcard, exhibition catalogue, or film shot or scene. In most countries, lawmakers make concessions for fair use under specific circumstances. In Germany for example, fair use applies to library books, because libraries pay fees to compensate for copyright royalties.[353]

It is difficult to protect all of the rights covered by copyright. In order to simplify their oversight, many countries have collecting societies that represent their artists. Through ties with similar organizations in other countries, they also help protect artists on international turf. The collecting society Bild-Kunst represents the visual arts in Germany, while the ADAGP (Société des auteurs dans les arts graphiques et plastiques) and the ACS (Artists' Collecting Society) and the DACS (Design and Artists Copyright Society) perform the same functions in France and the United Kingdom.[354] These organizations can be helpful partners for estates that do not wish to manage copyright on their own. However, in some countries, estates are required to become members of these institutions. This is why estates in Germany can only receive certain copyright royalties through VG-Bildkunst.

The Andy Warhol Foundation demonstrates how much estates can earn from copyright royalties. It has its own licensing department and allocates many different licenses for every imaginable product, ranging from T-shirts and umbrellas to designer strollers. In 2009 alone, licensing Warhol's work brought in 2.5 million dollars.[355] Such high numbers are, however, the absolute exception. In Germany, for example, there are only four artists whose annual royalties exceed 100 thousand euros.[356]

Copyright holds more than monetary significance for estates. When an estate grants usage rights strategically, it can influence the artist's reception. The copyright holder may decide to waive royalty fees, which would encourage art historians to write about the work. By contrast, they may withhold all reproduction rights, which can severely restrict research or even prevent it entirely. On a more positive note, copyright allows estates to play an active role in current research; since scholarly art historical publications include reproductions of the works at hand authors usually contact copyright holders early in the process. In this way, estates learn about new research and can offer archival material or other resources that would enrich the project. Jack Flam believes copyright is so important to the Dedalus Foundation because it ensures that only the best reproductions of Robert Motherwell's paintings are published, while simultaneously allowing the Foundation keep an eye on how those images are used.[357]

If the estate's aim is a wide distribution of the artist's work, it can take the bull by its horns and authorize free use. The Robert Rauschenberg Foundation took this bold step when it offered full image rights for scholarship, education, and the press. Chief Executive Officer Christy McLear makes a straightforward yet compelling argument for the Foundation's decision: "The people who are the best stewards are the scholars and the museums. ... Professors were making choices of images and teaching based on what images are available. That affects our history. What you teach should be the best pieces, not the free pieces."[358]

(2) Posthumous Editions

For the estates of sculptors, installation and video artists as well as photographers and printmakers, it is possible to generate income by commissioning posthumous casts, proofs, or editions of the work. The right to make such copies, however, must be inherent within the applicable copyright law.[359]

---

352 Refer to § 15 UrhG.

353 http://www.bildkunst.de/vg-bild-kunst/ueber-die-vg-bild-kunst/was-wir-tun.html.

354 The following website provides an overview of these organizations: http://www.bildkunst.de/urheberrecht/folgerecht/folgerecht-in-der-europaeischen-union.html. See also: http://www.bildkunst.de/en/vg-bild-kunst/sister-societies.html.

355 http://www.artnews.com/2009/11/01/warhol-inc/.

356 Interview with Dr. Urban Pappi, executive director of the VG Bild-Kunst, at the symposium *Management von Künstlernachlässen / Wie kann man das Œuvre eines Künstlers lebendig halten?*, Van Ham Kunstauktionen, Cologne, January 20, 2016.

357 http://www.nytimes.com/2016/02/27/arts/design/rauschenberg-foundation-eases-copyright-restrictions-on-art.html?_r=1.

358 http://www.latimes.com/entertainment/arts/miranda/la-et-cam-robert-rauschenberg-foundation-copyright-20160304-column.html. See also: http://www.latimes.com/entertainment/arts/miranda/la-et-cam-robert-rauschenberg-foundation-copyright-20160304-column.html.

359 On the legalities, see for example: Gerhard Pfenning, "Urheber- und Verwertungsrechte," in: Berger / Gallwitz / Leinz, *Posthume Güsse* 2009 (see note 310), p. 18 ff.

Before creating posthumous copies of the artist's work, the estate must ensure that its approach would have been in accordance with the artist's intentions. Moreover, it has to be utterly transparent about which works were created during the artist's lifetime and which ones were commissioned after his or her death.[360] Only under these conditions may museums and the art market recognize posthumous works. The artist's will supersedes any and all copyright allowances. For example, Henry Moore determined that his foundry in Berlin could complete any casts that were still in progress at the time of his death, but otherwise prohibited posthumous editions of his work.[361] By contrast, Rodin expressly articulated his intention for his work to be widely disseminated and therefore laid the foundation for many posthumous editions of his sculptures. Today, most of the Rodins on the market were cast after the artist's death, as is the case with the German sculptor Wilhelm Lehmbruck's sculpture. Edgar Degas's wax models were never cast during his lifetime, although his bronzes are now ubiquitous in museums. The Foundations of William Eggleston, Edward Weston, Diane Arbus, and Francesca Woodman allow posthumous editions of the photographers' work.

All of these foundations are forthright about the posthumous status of these editions and openly communicate the number thereof through proper identification. For example, it is imperative to clearly indicate not only the year the original work was produced, but also the year the cast or print was made. In other words, it should be clear at first glance that the work at hand is a posthumous edition. The following examples demonstrate just how important it is for the estate to oversee the quality of these editions and, when possible, to work with the same foundries or studios that the artist had during his or her lifetime.

Most posthumous editions will sell for about thirty percent less than originals. However, when the artist produced very few editions during their lifetime, the difference can be much greater. Frisch Brandt, Executive Director of the Fraenkel Gallery in San Francisco, which has represented Diane Arbus for more than thirty years, has observed that there are far more posthumous works than photographs developed by the artist herself.[362] For that reason, those works produced during the artist's lifetime are much more valuable on the market than those printed by Neil Selkirk after her death. According to Brandt, Arbus's original photographs begin at twenty-five thousand dollars and can exceed one million dollars, while Selkirk's range from five thousand to 100 thousand dollars.[363]

When the artist enjoyed market success, it can be especially tempting to turn to such reproductions as a source of income. Yet alongside the moral question of whether an artist's work should be produced in posthumous editions, one must be aware that the market is uncertain and reacts negatively to a proliferation of posthumous editions. Goods become more valuable when they are only available in limited quantities; this is why prices increase markedly after the artist's death. Thus, the estate's directorship should carefully consider whether and how they take advantage of this particular revenue stream, regardless of what copyright allows.

(3) Resale Rights

Resale rights ensure the artist's right to profit from the increasing value of his or her work when it is resold.[364] Also referred to as *droit de suite* due to their French origin, they can be a significant source of income for estates. Where applicable,[365] artist's resale rights ensure the heirs a percentage of the profits from each resale for fifty to seventy years post mortem.

---

360 Most legal systems do not restrict the number of how many editions can be produced. France, however, limits the number of posthumous casts that may be deemed "original" to twelve; further editions are considered copies. For more information, see: Régis Cusinbercher, "Edition orginales de bronzes du Musée Rodin. Reproductions des œuvres de Rodin. Réflexion au regard du droit," in: Antoinette Le Normand-Romain, *Rodin et le bronze. Catalogue des œuvres conservés au Musée Rodin*, 2 vols. (Paris, 2007), pp. 65–77.

361 In his last will and testament, Henry Moore decreed that no further casts of his sculptures should be made and that none of his works that remained unfinished were to be completed by others. The only exception would be works that his foundation, in agreement with his wife Irina and Professor Bernhard Meadows or their successors, deemed fully realized but that had not yet been cast. Moreover, if Hermann Noack had begun casting a sculpture at the time of his death, it could be completed. David Mitchinson, "Henry Moore – Die späte Bronzen," in: Berger / Gallwitz / Leinz, *Posthüme Güsse* 2009 (see note 310), p. 148.

362 http://crcrsaforum.org/2014/01/23/project-profile-smith-cr/.

363 http://observer.com/2014/09/double-negative-photographers-are-increasingly-printing-new-versions-of-vintage-pictures/.

364 Resale rights originated in France in the 1920s and for that reason are often referred to by the French term, *droit de suite*. Often discussed exclusively in terms of property law, *droit de suite* is actually a hybrid of property law and personal rights. It protects the inalienable rights of the copyright holder as well as the right to partake in future market earnings. According to legend, the French government granted its artists resale rights on account of the fate of Jean-François Millet's granddaughter: while his painting *The Angelus* appreciated in value from 70 thousand francs to one million over a few short years, she was selling flowers in the street. See Rita E. Hauser, "The French Droit de Suite: The Problem of Protection for the Underprivileged Artist Under the Copyright Law," in: *11 Copyright Law Symposium* (ASCAP), 1, 1962, p. 13f.; Jon D. Stanford, "Economic Analysis of the Droit de Suite – the Artist's Resale Royalty," in: *Australian Economic Papers*, 42, December 2003, pp. 386–98. Reproductions des œuvres de Rodin. Réflexion au regard du droit«, in: Antoinette Le Normand-Romain, *Rodin et le bronze. Catalogue des œuvres conservés au Musée Rodin*, 2 vols. (Paris, 2007), pp. 65–77.

365 More than 65 nations recognize resale rights; http://earights.org/visual-artists-resale-right/. These include Algeria, Belgium, Brasil, Chile, Costa Rica, Democratic Republic of the Congo, Ecuador, France, Germany, Guinea, Hungary, Italy, Ivory Coast, Luxemburg, Madagascar, Mali, Morocco, Peru, the Philippines, Portugal, Senegal, Spain, Tunisia, Turkey, Uruguay, and Vatican City.

The European Union's adoption of *droit de suite* laws in 2001 had major ramifications for the art market[366] because it was extended to the United Kingdom,[367] which has the most significant art market in Europe.[368] It obligated all member countries to comply with the new guidelines by 2006; those that had not previously recognized *droit de suite* had until 2010. The law now applies to all EU citizens as well as for non-EU residents whose countries likewise uphold resale rights.[369] Heirs may claim resale rights for seventy years after the artist's death, but the exact amount they receive is contingent upon the selling price and is limited to no more than 12.5 thousand euros per transaction.[370]

There are limits to resale rights in the EU that can be a burden for certain kinds of estates. Instead of merging resale rights with copyright, which would endow the copyright holder with resale rights, some EU countries have defined heirs separately in the context of resale rights. In France the definition is relatively narrow and only applies to legal heirs as individuals, not as legal entities.[371] Thus, the French law does not recognize the resale rights of the Fondación Dalí, which is categorically the exclusive beneficiary of all copyright royalties from Dalí's intellectual property, including copyright. In fact, the French collecting society refused its petition to receive resale profits.[372] Similarly, because the Stiftung Arp e.V. in Rolandseck, Germany, is a legal entity that holds the copyright to Hans Arp's work, but it does not meet the French law's definition of a legal heir and is therefore ineligible to receive royalties from sales on the secondary art market in France. Furthermore, the European Courts decided in 2015 that lawmakers in EU countries may determine whether the seller or the buyer must pay the beneficiary.

The United States, China, and Switzerland do not make national provisions for resale rights. In the US, most states[373] have determined that the *droit de suite* compromises property rights,[374] which in this case would be the collector's rights. Nevertheless, strides have been made towards establishing federal guidelines for resale rights. The Judiciary Committee introduced a bill to Congress in 2014 that would have provided for *droit de suite* for auction sales exceeding five thousand dollars with a cap of five percent of resale royalties and a limit of thirty-five thousand dollars.[375] China is also considering how it might institute resale rights.[376] By contrast, Switzerland passed a new copyright law in December 2015 that does not allow for resale rights, despite the fact that many voiced their support for them.[377]

c) Real Estate

Some estates also inherit further assets in addition to art and copyright. Most often these include real estate in the form of the artist's studio and/or residence, which may then be transformed into a gallery space or the estate's offices. Moreover, some inherited properties can provide rental income. It was in this manner that the foundation dedicated to the German painter Magda Bittner-Simmet secured its financial future.

Financing estate work through real estate is a model that estates that did not inherit property should also consider. Proceeds from the sale of art may be invested in buildings that can both house the estate's administration and show-

---

366 "Council Directive 2001/84 of 27 September 2001 on the Resale Right for the Benefit of the Author of an Original Work of Art," in: *Official Journal of the European Community*, L 272, 2001, p. 32.

367 In the beginning, the United Kingdom strongly resisted the EU directive, not only out of concern that it would have a negative effect on the British art market, but also because the law seemed so out of step with Common Law. For an overview, see David Heathcoat-Armory, *A Market Under Threat: How the European Union Could Destroy the British Art Market* (London, 1998).

368 Since resale rights expire 70 years after the artist's death, they are only applicable to modern and contemporary art. However, art from these periods makes up a large share of the art market, and more than 15% of global modern and contemporary art sales take place in London. Refer to the Tefaf Report, *The Global Art Market in 2013*, Table 2g, p. 37.

369 Council Directive 2001/84 (see note 366) Article 7, Paragraph 3.: "Authors who are nationals of non-EU countries enjoy the resale right if the legislation in their country permits resale right protection in that country for authors from the Member States. However, Member States may decide to apply this Directive to authors who are nationals of non-EU countries but whose habitual residence is in the Member State concerned."

370 Article 4 of the guidelines for rates in the European Union has established the following rates for resale rights: 4% for sales between 3,000.00 to 50,000.00 euros; 3% for sales between 50,000.00 to 200,000.00 euros; 1% for sales between 200,001.00 and 350,000.00 euros; 0.5% for sales between 350,000.00 and 500,000.00 euros and 0.25% for sales exceeding 500,000.00 euros—but with a maximum compensation of 12,500.00 euros. The base sum for sales varies according to individual countries within the European Union. For example, the law applies to sales of 400.00 euros in Germany and 750.00 euros in France. http://eur-lex.europa.eu/legal-content/DE/TXT/?uri=CELEX%3A32001L0084.

371 Judgment of the European Court of 24 February 2015, Az. C-41/14; http://curia.europa.eu/juris/celex.jsf?celex=62014CJ0041&lang1=en&type=TXT&ancre=.

372 Ibid.

373 California, Georgia, and Ohio recognize resale rights. However, due to New York's dominance of the art market, these state laws do not have significant economic ramifications.

374 Shira Perlmutter, "Resale Royalties for Artists: An Analysis of the Register of Copyrights' Report," in: *Journal of the Copyright Society*, 40, 1993, p. 313.

375 http://www.bildkunst.de/urheberrecht/folgerecht/folgerecht-in-usa-china-und-der-schweiz.html.

376 Ibid.

377 http://www.visarte.ch/sites/default/files/news_pdfs/MM_Folgerecht_11%2012%202015_d.pdf.

rooms as well as living or office spaces that generate rental income. In this way, assets in the form of art, which do not generate cash, are transformed into real estate assets, which provide a steady source of income while simultaneously diversifying the estate's financial portfolio. The foundation dedicated to the work of the German photographer Alfred Erhardt is currently contemplating such a model.[378]

d) Additional Sources of Income

In reviewing the options for financing an artist's estate—selling art, copyright royalties, and in some circumstances real estate—it becomes apparent that (public) third-party funds have not been discussed. In most countries that participate in the Western art market, there simply is no direct source for the ongoing funding of artists' estates. This is astounding because there are so many public funds dedicated to promoting the work of living artists. All the more so because, as we have seen, the ongoing engagement with an artist's oeuvre after their death is a significant and meaningful way to support their work.

To that end, all estates must be self-sufficient. Developing a sound financial strategy is just as important for nonprofit giants with several employees and assets in the hundreds of millions as it is for a small estate run by a single dedicated individual. The greatest challenge is to (slowly) sell off art to support the estate without forfeiting too much of the artistic and cultural content that form the basis of its work. Supreme discipline is required to protect and preserve a core group of works of the highest quality. At the same time, this is difficult to achieve, as the wide dissemination and visibility of the artist's oeuvre helps to ensure the estate's longevity. When the artist's name is disseminated in this manner, new advocates for the artist will take up the banner of his or her legacy.

378 Stahl, "Zukunftsmodelle" 2013 (as in note 343), p. 151.

"I want to die forever." David Ostrowski

Summary

An artist's estate is successful when it is able to keep the work alive: when subsequent generations of artists draw inspiration from it and when curators, researchers, and collectors continuously find new ways to approach it. This goal is achieved when the estate initiates dialogue and exhibitions, contextualizes the work, and makes it accessible to contemporary artists. Reaching it, however, requires a quantity of high-quality works as well as financial resources. Furthermore, a vast array of knowledge and skills, ranging from an art historical understanding of the work to managerial and business know-how, are crucial to the success of this endeavor. Thus, heirs often devote a significant portion of their lives to this work

There is extreme pressure to professionalize artists' estates today, perhaps more so than ever. The production of art in the twentieth century was vast, and it shows no signs of abating in the twenty-first: there are more art students, art schools, and museums,[379] and the already highly competitive globalized art market is becoming more so. This increased interest in art and its makers can only guarantee short-term visibility, not long-term survival. Accordingly, the question of how to set up an artist's estate has become pressing, and should ideally be addressed while an artist is still alive.

Good estate management can be learned. A clear understanding of the task at hand and a well-defined strategy are crucial components of this process. Estates ensure that the work doesn't fade away after an artist's death by continually inviting dialogue; it is also helpful if those in charge are on good terms with one another and have respected reputations. Even when they see their responsibilities as familial, family members and close friends of an artist should be committed to professional modes of operation. Their dedication to the oeuvre is long term, and is the cornerstone of their work.

Planning and/or working for an artist's estate is a constant reminder of an artist's eventual death, and can therefore be painful. This is true for both an artist who establishes an estate while alive as well as their loved ones. The artist must address fundamental questions and topics, however, if he or she wishes to set up the estate independently and pass it on in a fully realized form. An artist has to face questions pertaining to his or her life's work and its success, evaluate and organize the works on hand, and perhaps even destroy some of them. If he or she no longer possesses the required strength to do so, then it is wise to set the heirs on the right path. Spouses and children bear not only the burden of losing a loved one, but also the material burden of the estate. The great responsibility of managing an estate can quickly become overwhelming, as the to-do list can seem endless. For family members, working with the estate means an ongoing reassessment of their relationship with an artist. Moreover, the task poses great challenges to the direction of their own life. The confluence of these emotional circumstances makes it exceedingly difficult to maintain an objective point of view on an estate. It is therefore all the more important to develop those structures and strategies that will facilitate the estate's professionalization. It is also important that there be enough breathing room for the stakeholders to avoid arguments but not so much flexibility that they lose direction, as both are poison to successful estate work.

Estates today should present themselves as autonomous art institutions that are supported by the three pillars of scholarly research, museums, and the art market. There is no "one-size-fits-all" model. The possibilities are as varied as the artists' oeuvres and the interests of those involved in the estate. Solutions to the unique problems that arise with individual artists' estates arise when heirs and stewards pose the questions that have been explored in this volume.

The interviews in the second half of this book demonstrate just how varied these solutions can be. Over a period of three years, I consciously approached artists' estates that had arrived at very different solutions: from privately run estates to those managed by galleries or that had been integrated into museum collections, as well as nonprofits with several employees. I learned from all of

---

379 In the US alone the number of art students increased 25 percent between 2000 and 2009, while the number of museums has doubled since the 1990s: http://www.artmarketmonitor.com/2014/05/22/museum-growth-isnt-only-in-china-americas-museums-have-doubled-in-number-since-1990s/.

them, and it was only through my conversations with these varied estates that I was able to consolidate my own view on what it means to be responsible for an artist's oeuvre. Two important concerns unify all artists' estates, no matter how different they might be. They repeatedly ask themselves the following questions: What would the artist want if they were alive today? Do we have a solid art historical understanding of the work and are we acting on its behalf and not just for our own personal gain? These questions help establish the guidelines for each and every artist's estate. Only when they are addressed can Andy Warhol's take on the meaning of death for an artist really come true: "Death can really make you look like a star!"

Interviews

Michael Baumgartner
Zentrum Paul Klee

The Zentrum Paul Klee was established in Bern in 2005, sixty-five years after the death of Paul Klee (1879–1940); the artist's estate, which had been managed up to that time by the Paul-Klee-Stiftung (Paul Klee Foundation), based at the Kunstmuseum Bern, became part of the collection of the new institution. The Zentrum Paul Klee opened in a new museum building the same year. This was made possible by the financial support of the Swiss benefactors Maurice Edmond Müller (1918–2009) and Martha Müller-Lüthi (1924–2007) at an amount of 110 million Swiss Francs, whereby they also brought in their friend of many years, the star architect Renzo Piano, as the architect responsible. With around 4,000 paintings and works on paper, the Zentrum Paul Klee today has the largest collection of Klee's works in the world. The Swiss art historian Michael Baumgartner is the head of the collection as well as exhibitions and research at the Zentrum Paul Klee.

Klee was born in Bern in 1879 as the son of a German man and a Swiss woman. Following teaching activities at the Bauhaus in Weimar and Dessau and at the Kunstakademie (art academy) in Düsseldorf in the nineteen-twenties and thirties, he returned to Bern as an emigrant in 1933, but passed away before the City of Bern was able to approve his naturalization. His estate was initially managed by his widow, Lily Klee (1876–1946), and after the war was then transferred in part to the Paul-Klee-Stiftung. Felix Klee (1907–1990), the artist's only son, received another part in 1952; he also managed his father's entire written estate and began cooperating with the Paul-Klee-Stiftung around the mid-nineteen-fifties. The idea of establishing a museum took concrete form following Felix Klee's death in 1990.

The Paul Klee Zentrum is responsible for conservation measures to preserve the works of the artist in its collection and presents them in exhibitions with changing thematic focuses. One of the Zentrum's very important research projects is inventorying Klee's handwritten notes on his theory of pictorial form in an online database. It is also responsible for authenticating works by Klee. The foundation board currently includes Ulrich Sinzig as president and Peter Tschanz as vice-president as well as Janine Aebi-Müller, Ulrich Aebi, Dieter Baumann, Alexander Klee, Susanne Landolf Wild, Andreas Marti, Lorenz Meyer, Heinz Röthlisberger, Veronica Schaller, and Mariangela Wallimann-Bornatico. In 2013, the Zentrum Paul Klee's total budget was twelve million Swiss Francs. Forty percent of this sum is financed using its own resources, while the rest comprises subsidies from the City and the Canton of Bern as well as the Burgergemeinde Bern (Citizens' Community of Bern).

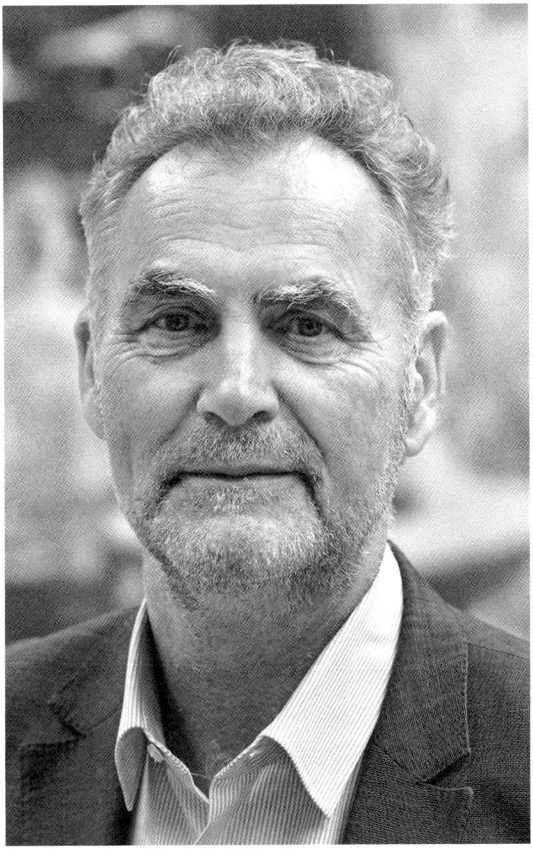

Michael Baumgartner

Loretta Würtenberger: The Zentrum Paul Klee opened in Bern in 2005 and manages the estate of Paul Klee. How exactly did that come about?

Michael Baumgartner: A large part of the estate was originally supervised by the Paul-Klee-Stiftung, which was established in 1947 and was based at the Kunstmuseum Bern from 1948 to 2004. The other part of the estate remained in the family for around fifty years. After the end of World War II, and shortly before the death of the artist's widow, Lily Klee, it was possible to save the estate from being seized by the Allies. Later, Klee's son, Felix, and after his death in 1990, Felix's second wife, Livia Klee-Meyer, as well as his son, Alexander Klee, took over parts of the estate.

In 2004, the holdings of the Paul-Klee-Stiftung were transferred from the Kunstmuseum Bern along with a donation from Livia Klee-Meyer to the Zentrum Paul Klee, which today possesses nearly 4,000 works as well as additional archival materials relating to the artist.

To understand the different backgrounds for the dividing up of the estate, one has to go back to 1946, when Lily Klee died in Bern on September 22 as a German national. In May 1946, Felix Klee, Paul and Lily Klee's only son, who had been called up for military service in Germany in 1944, returned to Germany from captivity in Russia as a prisoner of war. And Paul Klee, who died in 1940 as a German national as well, had lived in Germany as an artist until 1933. Two days prior to Lily Klee's death, the Bern collectors Hans Meyer-Benteli and Hermann Rupf purchased the artist's entire estate from her in order to save it from the liquidation that threatened under the terms of the treaty with Washington. This was concluded between the Allies, the victorious powers after World War II, and Switzerland in May 1946; the treaty regulated the recovery of assets in Switzerland that belonged to Germans living in Germany to the benefit of the Allies. On September 24, 1946, Meyer-Benteli and Rupf established the Klee-Gesellschaft (Klee Association) along with the Bern collectors Rolf Bürgi and Werner Allenbach, and transferred Paul Klee's estate into its possession. The aim of the Klee-Gesellschaft was to manage Paul Klee's legacy as effectively as possible. For this reason, the members of the association founded the Paul-Klee-Stiftung on September 30, 1947, and furnished the foundation with around half of the works in the estate as its inalienable property.

When Felix moved with his wife, Efrossina, and his son, Alexander, from Germany to Switzerland in 1948, as sole heir, he asserted a claim to Paul Klee's entire estate. After four years of litigation, an extrajudicial settlement was finally reached in 1952: Felix Klee recognized the legitimacy of the Paul-Klee-Stiftung; from the Klee-Gesellschaft he received ownership of the works in its possession as well as part of the holdings of the Paul-Klee-Stiftung; the Klee-Gesellschaft dissolved on December 31, 1952. Paul Klee's written estate was divided up between the Paul-Klee-Stiftung and Felix Klee. The Paul-Klee-Stiftung received Paul Klee's complete oeuvre catalogue, his journals, and writings on art theory, while Felix Klee took over his father's correspondence, his library, and a collection of documentary photographs. The oeuvre catalogue became an important instrument for ascertaining the authenticity of Klee's works.

In the years directly after the conflict over Klee's legacy, the Paul-Klee-Stiftung and Felix Klee were at first quite antagonistic. Felix began lending works by his father for exhibitions and was very active at this time. He oriented his life toward making his father's work better known. He also worked here in Bern as a director and radio play editor at Swiss radio. The Paul-Klee-Stiftung, in contrast, worked in a somewhat more restrained way in the nineteen-fifties.

After the war had ended, Felix Klee managed the written estate of his father and, starting in the nineteen-fifties, continuously expanded the archive. In 1953 he became a member of the foundation board of the Paul-Klee-Stiftung, and was its president from 1963 until his death. The foundation received prints from his photo archive and books from his special library on Paul Klee. Felix Klee also worked as a director at the Stadttheater (municipal theater) in Basel as well as for the Swiss national radio broadcaster Beromünster at its studio in Bern. He published numerous books on his father's work, including the *Tagebücher von Paul Klee 1898–1918* (Journals of Paul Klee 1898–1918).

LW: But both parties were truly concerned about safeguarding the estate.
MB: Yes. Felix Klee began cataloguing the estate as a whole and, for example, compiled all the photographs of works that he was able to procure in files. He was very active, documenting the Klee holdings in public and private collections, preparing expert reports, and bringing together information on Paul Klee's life and work from other archives. He rescued his father's correspondence and cultivated contact with other estates such as the Kandinsky archive. He knew Nina Kandinsky quite well. Felix Klee did a lot to develop the first archive on his father's entire oeuvre. In 1957 he published the first edition of Klee's journals and, in 1979, Klee's correspondence with his family—his wife, Lily, his son, Felix, and his parents—in two volumes.

LW: How did Felix Klee finance his activities?
MB: He had a regular income as an employee of Swiss radio. But he was quite restrained when it came to selling works from his collection, which he stored in a modest five-room apartment in Bern.

LW: Did he also lend works to exhibitions?
MB: Yes, he liked lending works, and the big Klee exhibitions of the nineteen-fifties to seventies largely consisted of loans by Felix Klee.

LW: What was the cooperation between Felix Klee and the foundation like at the time?
MB: The Paul-Klee-Stiftung and Felix Klee operated relatively separately up to the beginning of the nineteen-seventies. Even though Felix Klee became a member of the foundation board of the Paul-Klee-Stiftung in 1953 and was its president from 1963 until his death in 1990, and the Paul-Klee-Stiftung organized a

number of big Klee exhibitions in Switzerland and abroad with Felix Klee's active support, Felix Klee nonetheless largely developed the archive of his father's artistic work on his own. That first changed in the nineteen-seventies, when a paradigm shift took place in the Klee-Stiftung. Jürgen Glaesemer, who was selected as the foundation's first conservator in 1971, then emphasized scientific standards to a great extent. As a result, the Klee-Stiftung became more and more of a research institution and was developed further. At that point in time, Felix was also prepared to provide insights into the extensive correspondence between Paul and Lily Klee that he possessed. A rapprochement occurred. Felix Klee got along well with Glaesemer and there was no antipathy between them; they instead knew how to take advantage of the synergies of the two estate archives. Many documents were naturally still in boxes in Felix Klee's apartment, and the letters had to be photocopied, but Glaesemer was nonetheless able to publish the Paul-Klee-Stiftung's holdings of works in three volumes—two on Klee's hand drawings and one on the colored works—and already integrated a lot of sources in doing so. At the time, he already had the catalogue raisonné on Klee's oeuvre in the back of his mind as a project. This project was then tackled in the nineteen-eighties. Felix Klee supported the creation of the catalogue raisonné. In the nineteen-eighties there was therefore already a tendency toward the two archives becoming cooperative and exchanging information; they were simply only still separated in physical terms.

LW: How has the Klee foundation financed itself since the nineteen-fifties?
MB: The Paul-Klee-Stiftung based at the Kunstmuseum Bern was a public-law foundation. The Kunstmuseum covered the costs connected with taking care of the works and the personnel. The foundation did, however, also generate income itself, since it held the copyright on the foundation's collection. If works from the collection were reproduced, the foundation then received copyright fees. Since Klee's works enjoyed great popularity and were frequently reproduced, a sizeable sum came together each year. For two decades, the foundation only had one single research associate. It was only after Jürgen Glaesemer assumed office in 1971 that the foundation employed a conservator and a research assistant. After Glaesemer's early death in 1988, his employee of many years, Stefan Frey, managed the "Catalogue Raisonné Paul Klee" project until 1995. He systematically copied not only the documents kept by Felix Klee, but also documented works by Klee in public and private collections around the world and searched in archives for documents relating to Klee. When I started working as a research assistant at the Paul-Klee-Stiftung in 1995, there were therefore already a lot of

copies of outside correspondence with artists with which I was able to work. Added to that was the fact that, in 1995, thus five years after the death of her spouse, Livia Klee-Meyer, the daughter of the architect Hannes Meyer and second wife of Felix Klee, held out the prospect of donating her part of the inheritance as a gift to the City and Canton of Bern; although on the condition that a museum dedicated to Paul Klee would be built. The initiative for this came from Alexander Klee, Felix Klee's son from his first marriage, in 1992. From the very beginning, both of them, Livia and Alexander Klee, firmly intended to make the parts of Felix Klee's collection that they had inherited available to a Klee museum.

LW: Klee's heirs managed again and again to put public responsibility before private gain from the estate. Did this also correspond to Felix Klee's intentions in his will?

MB: When Felix Klee died quite unexpectedly of a heart attack in 1990, he did not leave a will. It was first on the initiative of Alexander Klee that the idea arose of donating parts of the Felix Klee Collection to the public sector, which Livia Klee-Meyer did in 1997 with the transfer of the artworks that she had inherited to the City and Canton of Bern. In 2008, Livia Klee-Meyer and Alexander Klee then also gave the entire archive of the Klee family, with thousands of documents and photographs, to the Zentrum Paul Klee.

For the family, it was important that something wise be done with Felix Klee's estate. As a result, we were "forced" to procure the funds to systematically document the entire estate, meaning the letters, the photographs, as well as the studio utensils. Each object was recorded, digitized, and inventoried. By 2007, we had gained an overview of more than 10,000 objects. In 2008, with a team of three people, we began systematically creating data sets for these objects. Within five years, the estate had therefore been catalogued to such an extent that we could work with it professionally. External researchers also have the opportunity to access this database and the digital assets.

LW: Did Livia Klee-Meyer and Alexander Klee have children who might be able to raise a claim to Paul Klee's estate? Difficulties could indeed arise if the children lay claim to the inheritance at a later point in time.

MB: That's true. Livia had no children and donated all of her part of the estate to the museum. A second part of the family estate is available to the Zentrum Paul Klee as a long-term loan. The Klee family has always been conscious of its responsibility for Klee's legacy.

LW: If you compare the current situation at the Zentrum Paul Klee with the time when Klee's estate was kept at the Kunstmuseum Bern, how would you evaluate the situation then and today?

MB: It was a quantum leap. Previously, the Klee-Stiftung at the Kunstmuseum was financed by the city and canton and special exhibitions with Klee's works were presented. The Zentrum Paul Klee created a completely new dimension, and for a long time there was criticism that the foundation was completely separate from the Kunstmuseum. There's a different tendency today and we have already been working actively with the Kunstmuseum for a longer period of time. The solution that we have now found is that, as of 2016, we have a joint foundation board, but remain in two separate institutions. By doing so, we have established the prerequisite for being even more present on an international level.

In 1998, the surgeon Maurice E. Müller gave the City and Canton of Bern a large donation to build a museum. A building in the center of the city was originally planned, but, as the benefactor family, the Müllers made it a condition that the museum be erected on the eastern edge of Bern, and offered the Schöngrün parcel of land, directly near their home, for it. Plans to establish a joint museum for contemporary art along with a Klee museum were not realized. Thanks to the great dedication of the benefactor, it then became possible to realize the Zentrum Paul Klee over a seven-year construction phase.

LW: The Zentrum Paul Klee has its home in a building by Renzo Piano. How did that come about?

MB: The building was privately financed. It would have been very difficult for the public sector to finance a new museum building. The Bern orthopedic surgeon and pioneer of osteosynthesis, Professor Maurice E. Müller, expressed his readiness to finance the building as a patron of the arts.

LW: How did the relationship between the Klee foundation and Maurice Edmond Müller arise?

MB: Above all his wife, Martha, was very interested in art. Müller was prepared to make a substantial share of his assets available for the construction of a museum dedicated to Paul Klee. He had the vision to make something big possible. He was then already relatively old, around eighty. He called Josef Helfenstein, who was the curator of the Paul-Klee-Stiftung then, and said that he would really like to help. The museum question was naturally already under discussion at the time, since Livia Klee-Meyer had declared her intention to donate her inheritance to the City and Canton of Bern. It was indeed public knowledge that the city and canton were short of cash.

LW: How big was the sum that Maurice Edmond Müller donated for the construction of the Zentrum Paul Klee?
MB: A total of 110 million Swiss Francs.

LW: That was virtually a Deus ex machine that appeared there.
MB: Yes. Maurice Edmond Müller said he was willing to finance the construction, but demanded in exchange that he be allowed to choose the architect himself. That was already quite controversial. We would have preferred to hold a competition. But Müller chose Renzo Piano as the architect and said, he'll build it, he'll make a project, and I'll finance it. So, everything ran its course. Piano created his design, which naturally cost much more to realize than originally planned. It was at first forty million Francs, but kept on increasing. Müller nonetheless always kept pace.

He did not, however, want to finance the costs of running the Zentrum Paul Klee, so the city and canton subsidize this institution, which is itself a public-law foundation, along with the so-called Vorortsgemeinde (outlying municipality). The Paul-Klee-Stiftung merged with the Stiftung Zentrum Paul Klee in 2004. The building belonged to the Maurice and Martha Müller Foundation, which was initially responsible for its upkeep, until 2015. The museum opened in 2005. A lot of visitors came the first two years. The third and forth years, however, the number of visitors sank and it became clear that the financial means that the Zentrum Paul Klee had at its disposal would not suffice. At the outset, there were 250,000 visitors, and in 2008 the number fell to just under 100,000. Our total budget was around twelve million Francs. The Zentrum Paul Klee therefore had to generate around forty percent of that, or nearly five million Francs, itself. We take in a part of the sum as an event and congress location—something that Maurice Müller already initiated. Lots of companies and institutions hold their conferences here. We have an auditorium that seats 300 and a forum whose technology is state-of-the-art. Visitor numbers naturally continue to play a role. Peter Fischer, who began managing the Zentrum as its director in 2011, realized higher visitor figures by means of an aggressive strategy. But the Zentrum Paul Klee was in debt and the Burgergemeinde Bern ultimately had to help the museum and clear its debts. Fortunately, we had that support. But it was really a big issue. There was a lot of discussion in the press about why the museum did not finance itself and taxpayers had to intervene. There was a new awareness of this situation, and with the new director, Peter Fischer, the Zentrum Paul Klee has now been in the black for three years. The budgets have been kept and we have clearly met our targets.

LW: Where did the other seven million Swiss Francs of the total budget come from?
MB: Up to that point, we received around six million Francs as a subsidy from the city, the canton, and the Regionale Kulturkonferenz (RKK, regional cultural conference). Since 2015, we have been financed solely by the Canton of Bern. That is the basis of our financing, and it has been promised to us long term.

LW: I find it interesting that meanwhile, even in the case of first-class artists, it is generally no longer sufficient when only works are left behind as an estate. Funding also has to be made available, for instance, to evaluate the estate in-depth and develop the archive.
MB: That is a crucial point. Interest in the estate can only first arise when such foundations are already in place.

LW: There are many examples of estates that have been donated to museums, and then disappeared into storage after only a couple of exhibitions. The Zentrum Paul Klee has proceeded in a completely different direction and made one estate the focus of its activities. I can imagine that Livia Klee-Meyer and Alexander Klee had a lot of influence in 2005. Because Paul Klee's work is so interesting financially, they were able to demand that a Paul Klee museum be created in exchange for the works.
MB: The reason for that can probably already be found in 1952, when both Felix Klee and the Paul-Klee-Stiftung made it their goal to make Klee's estate accessible to the public, and also recognized its potential. There's no other estate like Klee's.

LW: What makes Klee's estate so special?
MB: It is incredibly rich, also intellectually, biographically, and with respect to art theory. There's Klee's correspondence with his family, which gives so much information about the artist's life. Added to it are his autobiographical texts, which he wrote until 1920, and the notes on his teaching at the Bauhaus. There are also Klee's personal lists of work, in which he recorded and numbered his oeuvre—in 1911, he began inventorying his work up to that point retroactively.

He also, for example, included his childhood drawings of landscapes in the list of works.

Furthermore, as of 1911, he consistently mentions his technique in these lists and, up to 1919, even sales prices. He continued this inventorying of his production until three weeks prior to his death. That's why we are in a very good position with this catalogue of works with reference to clarifying authenticity and the catalogue raisonné, which is structured in exactly the same way as Klee's handwritten oeuvre catalogue. In terms of art history, Klee's estate is absolutely extraordinary.

The artist kept an extremely accurate catalogue of works, which formed the basis for the later oeuvre catalogue. He began systematically recording his paintings and drawings in a handwritten catalogue in the spring of 1911. The nine-volume catalogue raisonné on Klee's oeuvre, which was published between 1998 and 2004 and records 9,600 drawings, watercolors, paintings, and prints (edited by the Paul-Klee-Stiftung, the Kunstmuseum Bern, Josef Helfenstein, and Christian Rümelin) then developed from it. Paul Klee also preserved the manuscripts of his teaching activities at the Bauhaus in Weimar and Dessau. The book *Beiträge zur bildnerischen Formlehre (Contributions to a Pictorial Theory of Form)* along with around 3,900 pages of teaching notes forms Klee's pedagogical estate.

The Zentrum Paul Klee preserves the different parts of Paul Klee's estate and makes them available for research in various ways. The museum's scientific archive comprises original biographical documents—in addition to Klee's journals and teaching notes, these comprise above all his private correspondence with his family, friends, art dealers, and museums—as well as a special library with a collection of every publication on Klee since 1900. All known works and documents on Klee are inventoried in a database of his works (supported by the documentation software MuseumPlus). The catalogue raisonné, completed in 2004, is continuously updated based on this online database.

LW: You have come quite far in processing Klee's estate. What do you see the tasks of the Zentrum Paul Klee as being in the future?

MB: We have already expanded the focus of our work beyond Paul Klee, therefore, for example, to the subject of the Bauhaus, and have a lot of correspondence that goes beyond Klee. The library of the Zentrum Paul Klee is very wide-ranging, and I can easily imagine that there will be more collaboration with other institutions in connection with future research projects. Other topics include the theater of the Bauhaus or music in Klee's work. We have a music archive with over 600 compositions on and for Klee. No other artist has inspired so many composers. The archive collects works by modern composers as of 1930 who refer to Paul Klee in their compositions, including Pierre Boulez, Vinko Globokar, Krzysztof Penderecki, Francis Poulenc, or Tan Dun. We have scores and recordings of nearly 260 composers. Such projects contribute to a sense of continuity, and it's fascinating that Klee's oeuvre fans out into so many areas.

LW: Do you already notice the effect that access to the archive has been having on research?
MB: Yes. One example is the exhibition *Paul Klee—Special Class, Not for Sale* (2014/15), which we organized in cooperation with the Museum der bildenden Künste Leipzig (Museum of Fine Arts) and the University of Zurich, along with the accompanying catalogue with its some 600 pages. What became clear in the process is that it would not be possible to research the works that Paul Klee assigned to this "special class" at all if Paul Klee had not also clearly recorded the lists with the corresponding price classes. This is what makes it possible to work with the works in the first place. Did you have the chance to see the exhibition?

LW: Yes, and I found it extraordinary how Klee structured his own work and prepared his estate. He classified some 300 of his works with the abbreviations "SKl" or "Scl," the label for works in this special class. They were works to which he assigned special significance and that he envisioned for his estate collection. He therefore kept them off the art market and differentiated them from the works for sale, which were grouped into eight price classes. He therefore assigned the sales status and made a curatorial selection himself.
MB: Klee's approach is unique in its consistency. It is interesting from the perspective of the art market and also arouses great interest in young researchers, which we naturally support. It was first possible to realize this research project at all because of the indexing of the archival material, and there will be further such examples. We have also inventoried the pictorial theory of form—therefore Klee's pedagogical estate. We managed to get the project financed by the Schweizerischer Nationalfond (Swiss National Science Foundation); two members of staff wrote a dissertation on the pictorial theory of form and, for it, indexed all the documents on this topic, meaning a total of 2,500 sheets. The material was digitized and transcribed and is now accessible as open source. It can be accessed via the Zentrum Paul Klee's homepage.

LW: How big is the staff of the Zentrum Paul Klee?
MB: We have two and a half curator positions and three to four research assistants. There are also numerous part-time positions. Occasionally, there are also project-related employees, but we do not have any completely external staff.

LW: Does the museum have an authentication committee?
MB: Yes, we are the only place in the world where works by Paul Klee are authenticated. This has a long history, which began with Felix Klee. He discussed such questions with the Klee-Stiftung in the nineteen-sixties and seventies; since Felix Klee's death in 1990, only the Klee foundation and, since 2005, the Zentrum Paul Klee has issued official certificates.

We introduced the fact that an advance payment of a processing fee of 150 Francs has to be made prior to an authentication process. It's then that we take a look at the work, and if it's genuine, we issue a certificate, which costs 800 Francs. We review seventy to eighty works per year—around sixty-five of them fake.

LW: Does the committee meet at regular intervals?
MB: Distances here are short. We work according to a clear catalogue of parameters: first, I review a work, and then my two colleagues. We mostly work from photos and only look at the originals themselves when we have doubts. We have a collection of some 700 file cards with information on counterfeits. In eighty percent of all cases, I look at a work and know whether it's real or not. But all the parameters are carefully reviewed nevertheless. One time, all three of us had our doubts about the authenticity of a work. We put the case aside for a bit and then started all over again. Complex investigations were able to prove that the work was real. There are lots of parameters: Klee's signature is, for instance, very characteristic as well as the materiality of his works, and most of the time the work is artistically so strong that it is also even difficult to counterfeit the drawings.

LW: More and more estates are deciding to stop dealing with authentication questions. How do you see this?
MB: I can understand that quite well. Klee is a special case because we have the archive, the documentation, and the experience. With our know-how, we see clarifying the authenticity of works as our responsibility. I also hope that the committee at the Société Kandinsky, which has taken on this responsibility in connection with Kandinsky up to now, will continue to make this service

available after the dissolution of the Société Kandinsky. Many foundations are worried about legal disputes. But we stipulate in our conditions of business that we cannot be held legally accountable. Everyone who brings a work to be reviewed has to sign this document in advance. Nonetheless, today, it simply isn't possible to be sure that you won't be sued. In the case of Klee, difficulties relating to authenticity have fortunately rarely arisen up to now. We've never been sued.

The Zentrum Paul Klee is also very active as an international lender. In 2013, for example, works by Paul Klee went to the following museums and institutions: Kunstsammlungen und Museen Augsburg, Martin-Gropius-Bau, Berlin, Museum Berggruen, Berlin, Kunst- und Ausstellungshalle der Bundesrepublik Deutschland, Bonn, Kunsthalle Emden, Museum Folkwang, Essen, Hamburger Kunsthalle, Franz Marc Museum, Kochel am See, Fondation de l'Hermitage, Lausanne, Tate Modern, London, Museo d'Arte della Svizzera italiana, Lugano, Fundación Juan March, Madrid, Museo Nacional Centro de Arte Reina Sofía, Madrid, Centre Pompidou-Metz, Centre Dürrenmatt Neuchâtel, Gallery Dickinson Roundell, New York, Moeller Fine Art, New York, Musée du Louvre, Paris, Kunstmuseum Thun.[1]

LW: Do you propose exhibitions with particular themes to international museums?
MB: Yes, one good example is the current exhibition *Klee & Kandinsky*, for which we came up with the concept and where we knew that it could only be realized with a strong partner. There was first contact with the Guggenheim Museum in New York, and we were then able to obtain the Städtische Galerie im Lenbachhaus in Munich as a cooperation partner. In the case of the exhibition *Klee et la musique* at the Centre Pompidou in Paris in 2016, we also provided inspiration through encouraging this interest in Klee. The curators there have greatly benefited from the know-how of our institution. Then there are naturally exhibitions in which commercial interests also come into play: There's, for instance, a big interest in Klee's work in Japan. That was already the case when Felix Klee was managing the estate. A Klee exhibition takes place there every three years.

At the moment, organizing a Klee exhibition in China is currently being considered. We haven't had an exhibition there yet. For this project, we do, however, have to find sponsors. We would support such an exhibition, but, on the other hand, we also have to limit our commitments since we can't constantly overexploit our collection.

Our holdings comprise around 4,000 works, including many drawings, nearly 200 paintings, and around 800 watercolors—and of these watercolors, the same 250 are always requested. This makes things difficult for us, since we also want to present our collection ourselves at the same time.

LW: It's challenging to present the entire spectrum of an artist's estate after his death and again and again develop new concepts that do not reduce the artist to one perspective.

MB: Exactly. We are trying to do that, for instance, with the exhibition on Henry Moore that we developed along with the Tate Modern and which opened at the Zentrum Paul Klee in January 2015. And in cooperation with the Centre Pompidou, I am doing an exhibition on Paul Klee and the Surrealists at the ZPK in 2016. This also has positive effects on the making of loans between the institutions. Contemporary art is also a fixed component of our program. Thus, in 2014, we presented the exhibition *Taking a Line for a Walk* with works by Cy Twombly, Brice Marden, Henri Michaux, and others, and, in the winter of 2015/16, had Anthony Gormley as a guest in the big exhibition space with the work *Expansion Field.*

The foundation board also naturally stipulates how the museum should be used economically. But profitability is only one factor. It's just as important to recognize that projects that bring us money such as external exhibitions and the lending of works, generally also limit us. The optimal technical conditions are often lacking at other exhibition venues. At the Zentrum Paul Klee, in contrast, we have ideal conditions—no UV light, filtered glass, etc. These factors also have to be taken into account when we lend works. It is naturally our duty to present Klee's work. On the other hand, preserving it is also our responsibility. This presents a big challenge for an institution where the focus is only on one single artist.

LW: If Klee managed the institution today, would he be satisfied?

MB: That's a difficult question. I think he would be satisfied. It was his wish that his oeuvre remain together. That's why he also explicitly designated works for an estate collection. He himself wanted his artistic estate to endure; he believed that it was something that went far beyond him. One can also see this in how he composed his journal. He redacted it as an autobiography. The Zentrum Paul Klee is not just a machine for exhibitions, but instead also pursues the goal of

1 Zentrum Paul Klee (ed.), *Geschäftsbericht 2013. Stiftung Zentrum Paul Klee* (Bern, 2013), p. 13.

making Klee's thinking as an artist productive—entirely in the sense of the artist. I think that the fact that this has been dealt with very productively for sixty years would give him satisfaction.

LW: What advice would you give to living artists who want to plan their estate in advance?

MB: I think the most important thing is that artists already try to create clear conditions for their estate during their lifetime—as far as this is possible. Inheritance law regulates many things. But artists can still develop an estate collection and an archive. How the estate is handed down and whether there is a written estate is also important. Artists who are interested in art theory will most likely tend to bear this in mind. Dieter Roth is an example of an artist who already had an estate archive, but the work with his estate has nevertheless gotten quite out of hand. It's also helpful, of course, when an artist leaves behind money for estate purposes. A lot of things can be achieved when you have money. The artist Otto Nebel, for instance, left behind foundation capital, and this money is still so well invested that the Otto-Nebel-Stiftung has the financial means to actively manage the collection.

Mayen Beckmann
Max Beckmann Estate

Max Beckmann (1884–1950) was one of the titans of modernism, but considered himself the last of the Old Masters. While he never joined any of the avant-garde movements of twentieth-century art, traces of the experiences of Impressionism, Expressionism, New Objectivity, and abstraction can be found in his work. All the same, he kept to the classic genres of figuration, creating portraits, mythological tableaus, nudes, still lifes, and landscapes. In 1937, he emigrated along with his second wife, Mathilde "Quappi" Beckmann, to Amsterdam. Two years after the war ended the artist and his wife moved to the United States.

Beckmann's granddaughter Mayen Beckmann has been managing the estate since the death of her father, Peter Beckmann (1908–1990), the artist's son from his first marriage to Minna Beckmann-Tube (1881–1964). Mayen Beckmann works in Germany and internationally as an exhibition curator (including *Max Beckmann: Watercolors and Pastels,* Schirn Kunsthalle Frankfurt, 2006) and edited the catalogue raisonné of Beckmann's works on paper in cooperation with the art historian Siegfried Gohr. Mayen Beckmann never got to know her famous grandfather, but he was nevertheless always present for her in the hanging works of his in her parents' home.

The first Max Beckmann Gesellschaft (May Beckmann Society) was established in 1953 and existed until 1984. Peter Beckmann was also one of its members. The Freundeskreis Max Beckmann Archiv e.V. (Circle of Friends of the Max Beckmann Archive) was founded in 1996, but changed its name to the Max Beckmann Gesellschaft e.V. in 2005.[1] The society supports the Max Beckmann Archiv, which has its home at the Bayerische Staatsgemäldesammlungen (Bavarian State Painting Collections) in Munich, and makes materials available for exhibitions and research. The members of the board of the society are Mayen Beckmann, Christian Lenz (chairman), Hans-Paul Ottmann, Jeanette Scholz, Klaus Schrenk, Kai Werner, and Kuno Wilhelm. Another part of Beckmann's estate is found in the Archives of American Art of the Smithsonian Institute in New York. As a result of Mayen Beckmann's dedication, the Max Beckmann grant was brought into being in 2012. The American Academy in Berlin awards it each year to support the stay of outstanding American artists in Berlin.

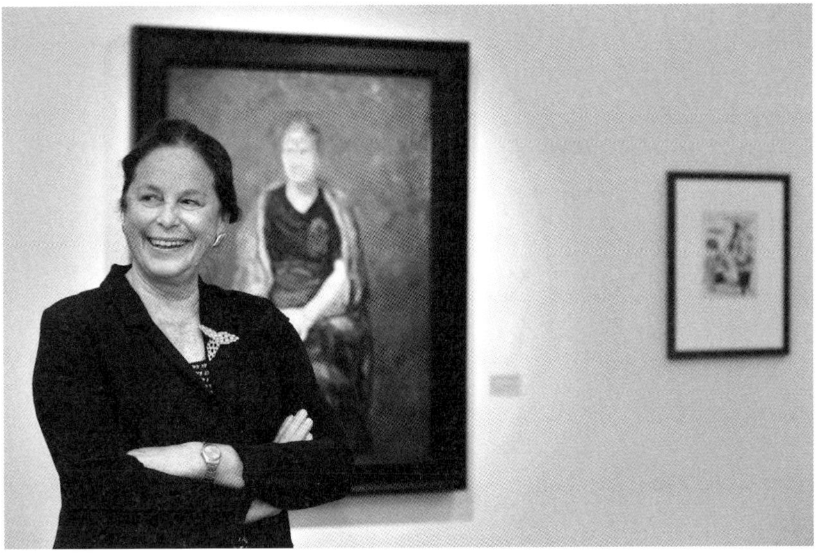

Mayen Beckmann

Loretta Würtenberger: What role in managing the estate did the family assume after Max Beckmann's death in 1950?

Mayen Beckmann: Max Beckmann was married two times, and after his death, both of his widows possessed different parts of his oeuvre. He was married to my grandmother, Minna Beckmann-Tube, from 1906 to 1925. She had a large number of his early works. He lived with his second wife, Mathilde Beckmann, née Kaulbach, from 1924 to 1950. She held a part of the estate of which half, according to Max Beckmann's last will and testament, was supposed to go to my father, Peter Beckmann. That was not possible at the time, since Max Beckmann lived in the United States, and, in 1950, a German who died in America was still considered a hostile foreigner, which meant that the estate was supposed to go the American state as a matter of principle.

It's also necessary to differentiate between the estate and works privately owned by Mathilde Beckmann. The pictures that Max Beckmann gave to his second wife as gifts are not part of the estate. My father ultimately relinquished his claim to his inheritance so that this part of the estate could remain self-contained in the United States.

1 http://www.max-beckmann-archive.org (accessed February 20, 2016).

As a result of a special arrangement that was reached based on the initiative of some American politicians, it was possible to have the entire estate remain with Mathilde "Quappi" Beckmann through her becoming an American citizen. It was also stipulated that Quappi could dispose of her private property with complete freedom, and that the estate would only go to my father at the end of her life. Quappi had no children of her own.

Shortly after Quappi's death, a prolonged legal dispute also arose in the United States, since her caregivers had persuaded her to sign the entire estate over to them. My father and Quappi's sister no longer wanted or were able to have anything to do with it at that point in time. I was the one who finally took legal action against the caregivers. That was around twenty years ago.

In addition to the legal proceedings against the caregivers, I also had to take legal actions against the executors of the estate, who were trying to bamboozle Quappi's sister, Hedda Schoonderbeeck von Kaulbach. They wanted Hedda to donate her inheritance and convert it into a foundation that would solely benefit the executors of the estate and an acquaintance of Quappi Beckmann. That acquaintance kept trying to get Hedda to give him an important painting as a gift even after the litigation was over. The legal proceedings as a whole cost a total of around ten million US dollars—and I learned a lot.

After Quappi's death, her sister and my father owned the rights to the estate. The copyrights are valid until 2020. I would very much like to try to achieve a few things during this time, such as the catalogue raisonné of Beckmann's drawings and publishing an annotated edition of his journals. As I see it, one of the main tasks of maintaining an estate is documenting the work of the artist from direct proximity—also because of all the counterfeits. Beckmann was fortunate because his family and the people he knew already looked after the corresponding documentation very early on and published a catalogue raisonné of the paintings at an early point in time.

The first catalogue raisonné of the paintings of Max Beckmann (Hans Martin Freiherr von Erffa [ed.], Barbara Göpel and Erhard Göpel, *Max Beckmann. Katalog der Gemälde,* 2 volumes, Bern 1976) was published in 1976. The catalogue raisonné published in 2006, in contrast, focuses on an aspect of Beckmann's oeuvre that had been underappreciated until this time: the watercolors and pastels. Mayen Beckmann also published Beckmann's correspondence with the art dealer I. B. Neumann (Mayen Beckmann and Michael Semler [eds.], *Briefe an I. B. Neumann,* Berlin 1997).

LW: You link both tasks, the catalogue raisonné of the works on paper and the annotated edition of the journals, with the expiration of the copyrights. Both tasks could theoretically also still be continued afterward.

MB: That's true, but I can only reject requests or intervene in projects as long as the copyright protection still applies. Afterwards, everything is open.

Special requests come again and again and it then suddenly appears in a text that Beckmann was, for instance, an alcoholic. He did drink, but the statement is specious. How is alcohol and drug consumption connected with the artistic work? Does an artist only work when he's drunk or stoned? Beckmann, in any case, never worked when he'd been drinking. Times when he had a hangover were lost days for him. He drank alcohol to relax after working. Such statements therefore have to be differentiated. But I can only intervene as long as the copyrights are still valid. I make use of my right of veto relatively rarely, but, in some cases, it's good to be able to say, "no," when you have the feeling that something is going in a very wrong direction in terms of the facts.

LW: You were in your mid-forties when you took over the management of the estate. How did you deal with this great responsibility? The decision to supervise such an estate oneself also certainly means that it dominates your own life.

MB: That's true. But Beckmann was already a really big focus in my life anyway. When you grow up with his paintings, you've been "brainwashed" by the time you're twenty in any case, so that you're basically only able to see by means of the pictures. But I was always also interested in other artists and, in the mid-nineteen-seventies, with my husband at the time, started collecting works by Georg Baselitz and German Expressionism, among others. I never thought that I'd have to take care of Beckmann's estate at such an early point in time, because I always thought that my mother would assume that responsibility after my father's death. Neither of us thought that my father would pass over her in his will. On the other hand, he made a wise decision, since my mother doesn't speak any English or other foreign languages. My mother is a wonderful person and achieved a lot at my father's side, but, at the same time, my father probably didn't want that claim to absoluteness. He didn't want her to regulate the estate on her own. He probably thought that I would be able to represent the estate better on an international level, which, at that point, was surely also important. Since my mother also had very clear ideas how things should be, there would also surely have been more power struggles in connection with the estate—something that my father wanted to avoid. In any case, we were all pretty flabbergasted when we saw the will.

For my mother, it was a serious crisis in her relationship with my father, which occurred, so to say, post mortem. She'd known as little about the will as I had. She found it by accident and was fair enough not to destroy it. That shows that she's a big person, since she also could've thrown it away. But I think she occasionally lay awake at night shaking her head.

LW: It often seems to me as if the generation of grandchildren have a greater emotional distance to the oeuvre and the individual who bequeathed the estate, which gives them a clearer view of things and enables them to manage the estate more objectively. If you compare how you manage the estate with the way your father did, would you say this is also true in your case?

MB: No, my father had a lot of distance since he didn't grow up with his father. He actually first got to know him a bit better again in Amsterdam, after Max Beckmann emigrated there in 1937. The first correspondence between the two of them also began at the time. But they didn't write or see each other on a daily basis. That's also why I think my father did a very good job.

While my father was still a practicing doctor, he dealt with the estate less creatively. But after he retired, he occupied himself very intensively with his father's oeuvre and wrote about the themes that he connected with it, for instance, the apocalyptic and religious aspects in Max Beckmann's oeuvre. In his work as a therapist he also worked repeatedly with Max Beckmann's pictures and confronted his patients with them, with the hope of triggering something, of treating fears through doing so.

LW: You haven't institutionalized the estate; you haven't made a foundation from it, for example.

MB: No, that wouldn't have worked with my mother. I've tried to regulate things in consultation with her in order to show consideration for her feelings. If it weren't for my mother, I would have institutionalized the estate much earlier because I was afraid that things wouldn't continue after me. I would've established a clear structure much earlier on.

LW: How would you have institutionalized the estate? Have you, for instance, observed things in connection with other estates that worked well there and that you would have liked to do as well?

MB: The problem is that there's no magic formula, since an estate always depends on the people involved. For example, you institutionalize an estate with another individual with whom you have a good working relationship. But when this person dies, you have to find somebody new, and the cards are then already reshuffled in an unforeseeable way. Things can then either go well again, or simply become arduous.

The same applies to cooperation with museums. The question in each case is whether you and the director understand each other well, and then the next one comes and you don't get along well with him or her and can only hope that things will go better again with the next one. Since directors change, it's ultimately about the museum and not about the particular person, but you do have to collaborate with people.

LW: Did Max Beckmann build an archive during his lifetime?
MB: He started keeping lists of pictures in 1905/06. He didn't keep them meticulously and they aren't really complete, but they do provide a good foundation. Beckmann also recorded the details of sales in the lists of pictures in part, and they then later served as a good basis for the catalogue raisonné. There were also inventory listings of Beckmann's prints, the watercolors, and the early drawings. His journals were also published quite early on, but today it's difficult to confirm the people and details mentioned in them. Good documentation is important, and we've just submitted an application to the Deutsche Forschungsgemeinschaft (German Research Foundation) in order to be able publish an annotated version of the journals. It's hard to get the foundation to award money for a project if the material to be worked on isn't owned by the state. In the end, we might have to finance the edition of the letters ourselves.

LW: Do you sometimes ask yourself how Max Beckmann would have managed his own estate?
MB: He wouldn't have managed it; he would've preferred to paint. But, at the same time, Beckmann was the sort of artists who always dealt with his dealers very assertively and purposefully. For example, he never shied away from power games with his two art dealers, Israel Ber Neumann and Alfred Flechtheim. He played them off each other a couple of times and consequently drove up the price of his works. When he emigrated to New York in 1947, he also dealt with Curt Valentin, his dealer there, very resolutely.

The fact that Beckmann had a clear stance regarding the monetary value of his works can be seen in the lists of his prints, in which he specified the price for which he sold them to the respective dealer. For me, Beckmann had very clear ideas about the connection between creativity and trade. There was never anything chaotic or uncontrolled about it.

Based on Beckmann's accounts, it's also possible to see that he probably worked on them when he had a creative block, when his nerves were bad, and he couldn't continue painting. You can comprehend how he created structure through organizing, which then ended again when he found his way back to painting.

LW: Where are Max Beckmann's documents stored today?
MB: There's the private archive located in my father's house; there are parts of Quappi's archive that I still have; and then there's the independently established Beckmann archive in Munich, which continues to grow with our support. It belongs to the Bayerische Staatsgemäldesammlungen in Munich and is managed in part by volunteers and in part by employees. These archives shall be brought together in the foreseeable future.

The exact date for that, however, is still unclear. I can first engineer this only after my mother's death. She's ninety-one years old and I can't simply start taking her household apart. We tried to do so ten years ago, but she then decided otherwise and couldn't bear to part from the work.

The Max Beckmann Archive currently holds around 5,000 letters, including nearly 300 written by Max Beckmann as well as letters from Thomas Mann, Walter Benjamin, Sigmund Freud, and other people. It also comprises approximately 6,000 photographs, some 60,000 newspaper articles, and 1,400 special publications.[2] Additions to these extensive holdings are continuously being made. Among the archive's tasks is also regularly updating the catalogue raisonnés of Beckmann's paintings, drawings, prints, and sculptures as well as his bibliography.

LW: How do the three archives currently work together? What will change when they are merged?
MB: The archives consult each other. Everybody who submits a scholarly request receives access to either the Beckmann archive in Munich or the private archive. It actually works quite well. But the archives nevertheless have to be merged at some point, since I can't simply say to my sons: "You will now continue to do this."

Part of Beckmann's written estate is unfortunately missing. In 1940, when the National Socialists marched into in Amsterdam, both Beckmann and his wife burned a lot of things. We have letters and texts and a couple of letters by

Quappi and her sisters that haven't been evaluated yet. That's not a lot, and I would ideally like to bring everything together. But that won't really be possible, since Quappi gave a large portion of the documents in her possession to the Archives of American Art in 1977.

Today I envision that the documents will no longer be shifted from here to there, but instead be digitized so that all of them are accessible.

LW: The Beckmann Archive is managed by the Bayerische Staatsgemäldesammlungen. Is it digitalizing it as well?
MB: No, they're not doing that, but they do at least provide a basis for further processing.

LW: Does the Bayerische Staatsgemäldesammlungen fund the Beckmann estate?
MB: Yes and no. Currently, Professor Christian Lenz, former curator for the nineteenth century at the Neue Pinakothek and the Schack-Galerie, supervises the archive, which was established on his initiative. The Staatsgemäldesammlungen finance the rooms and the technology. The supporting association covers everything else. The association also lacks a budget for acquisitions. In the case of more extensive projects, we hope for the support of the Kulturstiftung der Länder (Cultural Foundation of the German States) and other sponsors.

LW: Has the management of the estate and archive been mostly privately financed in the last twenty years?
MB: Yes, I've financed most of the work through income from copyrights. Various things can be done with the profit that's generated.

LW: Besides the archive, are works still held in the estate?
MB: Yes, there are a couple of works. I myself have lots of drawings. I have given the portion at my disposal to the Museum der bildenden Künste (Museum of Fine Arts) in Leipzig as a permanent loan. It should also remain there, since who else other than a museum can deal with 400 drawings?

LW: What persuaded you to choose the Museum der bildenden Künste in Leipzig?

---

2 http://www.max-beckmann-archive.org (accessed February 16, 2016).

MB: I simply thought about who still didn't have anything and who already had quite a lot. The Staatsgemäldesammlungen in Munich has a lot, and there have been loads of exhibitions on Beckmann in Munich, Hamburg, Frankfurt, and Cologne. But there hadn't been any exhibitions in the eastern part of Germany, and Beckmann was born in Leipzig. The museum in Leipzig is a very good museum, and the director was very interested. They also definitely wanted to create a Beckmann room. So, some of the pictures from my possession as well as sculptures and drawings went there. And they are also well taken care of there. Since, as a private individual, I wouldn't have been able to make the works accessible to scholars in the long run.

Beckmann's works are found in important museums and private collections around the world, including the Guggenheim Museum, New York, Hirshhorn Museum and Sculpture Garden, Washington, D.C., Museum of Modern Art, New York, National Galleries of Scotland, Edinburgh, San Francisco Museum of Modern Art, Städel Museum, Frankfurt am Main, Centre Georges Pompidou, Paris, Folkwang Museum, Essen, Kunstmuseum Basel, Kunstsammlung Nordrhein-Westfalen, Düsseldorf, Österreichische Galerie Belvedere, Vienna, Tate London, and Walker Art Center, Minneapolis. Extensive exhibitions on Beckmann's work have been presented, for example, at the Hamburger Kunsthalle (2014), the Kunsthalle Mannheim (2013), the Museum der bildenden Künste, Leipzig (2011), the Pinakothek der Moderne, Munich (2007), the Schirn Kunsthalle, Frankfurt (2006), the Museum of Modern Art, New York (2007), the Tate Modern, London (2006), and the Guggenheim Museum, New York (1997).

LW: Did you lend works to museums while they were still in your possession?
MB: Yes, again and again. I also personally organized exhibitions of the drawings in Korea, Spain, and so on. For the museums, that was naturally very convenient, since they didn't have to ask anyone else for loans.

In Spain, I also found a contact that has also done four other interesting and extensive exhibitions and catalogues. Things went pretty much the same in England and Scotland. An exhibition in Norway, where Beckmann has never been shown, is currently under consideration. I'm very thankful that Beckmann, even if he's also a very special German artist, has an international reputation.

With exhibitions, I always try to provide inspiration and to establish new viewpoints. Today, the museum in Leipzig takes care of the lending activities.

They perform this task very well. We often consult each other, and I get asked whether I agree to a particular loan. The cooperation is very good.

LW: How else do you collaborate with museums?

MB: I always try to interest museums in specific themes that haven't been worked on yet. For example, the Hamburger Kunsthalle is currently[3] showing an exhibition of Max Beckmann's still lifes. That's a part of his work with which hardly anybody is familiar. I try to ask: "Why don't you deal in terms of content with this or that area?" There are some things that still interest me, and I address them now and then. With some luck, the people I'm talking to take up the idea and new exhibitions and doctoral theses are created. Just a short time ago, for example, a very good master's thesis was done on the relationship between Henri Rousseau and Max Beckmann. That's a special topic that was important to me for a long period of time.

What's interesting about exhibitions on Beckmann is the fact that visitors stay a really long time. During the *Max Beckmann. Un peintre dans l'histoire* exhibition in Paris in 2002, it was calculated that each visit lasted an average of two and a half hours. That's a long time for a visit to an exhibition. And now in Hamburg, I'm again hearing from the curators that people spend quite a long time in the exhibition and talk to each other. That shows that the visitors at Beckmann exhibitions are a very specific group and differ from other museum visitors. It's otherwise assumed that nobody spends more than half a minute in front of a picture.

LW: How is the market for works by Max Beckmann? Is this an area in which you've played an active role?

MB: There's also only a small circle of relevant actors there as well. It differs from the case of Klee or Picasso, for whose work there are hundreds of trade routes, opportunities, and collectors. Beckmann's work is a case for specialists, which applies both to trade and to museums and collectors, for readers and for exhibition visitors.

Masterpieces of modernism are especially not exempt from doubt regarding the authenticity of artworks. For example, before a newly discovered painting by Beckmann, *Stillleben mit Gladiolen* (Still Life with Gladiolas), was sold for

---

3 *Max Beckmann. Die Stillleben,* Hamburger Kunsthalle, September 5, 2014–January 18, 2015.

270,000 Euros at auction by the Lehr auction house in Berlin in 2007, the auctioneer, Irene Lehr, had the painting examined by the Doerner-Institut in Munich and by Mayen Beckmann, who were confident that the painting was genuine. Barbara Goepel, coauthor of the catalogue raisonné published in 1976, in contrast, questioned its authenticity.[4] The scientific examination of the painting technique as well as the expert opinion by Mayen Beckmann ultimately confirmed the authenticity of the work.

LW: How do you deal with authentication?

MB: I don't process such requests by myself. There are several Beckmann experts, including Professor Uwe M. Schneede in Hamburg, Professor Christian Lenz in Munich, Professor Siegfried Gohr in Cologne, and Christiane Zeiller or Stephan von Wiese in Berlin. We basically all work together.

In most cases, we forward a request to everyone, and it's often immediately clear that something's not right, which means that it's not even necessary to look at the original. But there are again and again cases of doubt such as in connection with a group of four drawings that someone from the Netherlands purchased at a small auction and were supposed to go to the Lempertz auction house. I still believe that the drawings are authentic, because it was the original paper and there was also lettering on the reverse side that can always be seen on the real watercolors and drawings. The drawings aren't top-quality works, but they also aren't bad works. In this case, four specialists thought they were genuine, while the drawing experts thought they were counterfeits. The only option for such a case is to very openly disclose the opinions of the specialists. If the provenance is lacking, the auction house or the buyer has to bear the risk themselves. We were able to verify several details that point to the authenticity of the drawings, but we were unable to reconstruct the path the drawings had taken. There was also one oil painting that was a borderline case, because it wasn't included in the lists of pictures and had no known provenance. There was, however, a margin of discretion and good reasons for deeming it authentic.

LW: In the last twenty years, have you brought in external consultants, for example, in connection with legal questions?

MB: Yes, that's been necessary every once in a while. For example, there was a dispute with the foundry that cast Beckmann's bronzes. They were almost all cast posthumously in the United States. Only three bronzes were cast during Max Beckmann's lifetime. That was connected to the wartime period, and also for historical reasons. Quappi commissioned the posthumous bronzes in an edition of five.

But, in the early nineteen-eighties, when Quappi still had one more casting left within these editions, the foundry produced three more castings for itself. These works were then sold to collectors relatively inexpensively, who then donated them expensively to museums—a kind of tax-saving scheme. As a result, a museum in the Midwest of the United States suddenly possessed three identical bronzes by Beckmann. We therefore spent a long time talking to external attorneys in America and in Germany about what could be done. It would have been overtaxing for us to find all the sculptures and have them melted down, and to initiate legal proceedings against all those involved in the United States. We then found a solution in consultation with the individuals involved and marked the unauthorized castings as "non-estate casts" with a stamp. They were also documented.

LW: Are there posthumous editions of Beckmann's prints?
MB: In the nineteen-sixties, a large number of unscratched printing plates from Beckmann's *Jahrmarkt* (Carnival) series as well as individual plates were discovered in the cellar of the Hanfstaengl publishing house in Munich, where many editions were created during Beckmann's lifetime. At my father's instigation, they were then printed again in the sixties. The works are signed, which means that my father signed the backside, and they bear a stamp of the estate. They were also included in James Hofmaier's catalogue raisonné.

The intention behind this was to supplement the expensive originals with posthumous editions and hence facilitate wider dissemination. My father later had two plates that had not been printed during Max Beckmann's lifetime printed as well.

LW: Was there an edition size that he adhered to?
MB: He got together with the gallerist Günter Franke and they decided to print sixty sheets of each work. At the time, the original printer that had already taken care of the first edition still existed. This all took place during the postwar period, and not all the sheets from that edition were sold at the time.

4 Camilla Blechen, "Rekordzuschlag für Neuentdeckung," in *Frankfurter Allgemeine*, November 2, 2007; http://www.faz.net/auktion-rekordzuschlag-fuer-neuentdeckung-1488607.html (accessed February 16, 2016).

LW: And were the plates x-ed afterward?

MB: The plates are still not x-ed, but I had the steeling removed. They are very beautiful and are occasionally shown in exhibitions in order to document the printing process. It's also fascinating to see how a plate gradually gets worn down. The prints of Rembrandt and Dürer are re-etched again and again, touched up, and printed again. Plates get badly worn down by the printing process when the steeling is gone. At some point, the plates have to be archived in the museum to preserve them.

LW: Do artists or other estates sometimes ask you for advice?

MB: Yes, I'm asked for advice by artists and by collectors' estates—ones who are sometimes relatively helpless or even disinterested as far as dealing with the estate is concerned. It's difficult to give general advice, because each case is different. It makes a difference whether or not there are children. If an artist was really successful, everything is pretty much settled by lawyers. If there's no money, things become more difficult. There are then often masses of paper or poorly stored works, and no one wants to assume responsibility for that. It's terrible when a whole life's works are destroyed. It's even worse when an estate ends up in the wrong hands and consequently decays, although it could have been preserved.

LW: Do you have friendly relationships with the estates of other artists?

MB: No, not really. That has to do with the fact that Max Beckmann had hardly any close contact to other artists. I do, however, communicate with the estates of Max Pechstein and Erich Heckel as well as of Ernst Ludwig Kirchner. After World War I, Max Beckmann isolated himself and maintained friendships for the most part with poets, novelists, journalists, and musicians. He pretty much avoided friendships with artist colleagues except in Amsterdam. He would, however, have liked to have met Picasso.

LW: Would your grandfather have been proud of you?

MB: I can't answer that question. But I think that we would have understood each other quite well—once I'd grown up. He wasn't all that good with children.

LW: What aspects of the estate management do you find it important to pass on?

MB: For me, the need for dialogue in dealing with an artist's estate: it's not about issuing orders. That's especially true for artists' estates that are managed privately and in which several generations are involved. But the exchange with museums, galleries, collections, artist colleagues, historians, and friends is also crucial to managing the estate. That's the only way the artist's intention can be preserved, and the only way that important questions can be clarified.

Richard Calvocoressi
Henry Moore Foundation

Richard Calvocoressi was the Director of the Henry Moore Foundation from 2007 to June 2015. Under his leadership, Henry Moore's (1898–1986) former home and studio in Perry Green, Hertfordshire, were opened to the public and the Foundation expanded its international exhibition and support program. Calvocoressi had previously been the Director of the Scottish National Gallery of Modern Art in Edinburgh for ten years. He began his career in 1979 as a curator at the Tate Gallery in London, for which he developed the collection of European art of the pre- and postwar period.

The Henry Moore Foundation is one of the largest nonprofit artist's foundations in Europe. It supports numerous projects as well as cultural institutions and exhibitions in England and abroad, and awards grants to young artists and scholars. The emphasis is on the artistic genres for which Moore himself stood: sculpture, drawing, and printmaking. The Foundation has its headquarters in Perry Green, where an extensive collection of Moore's works is also found. Main works by the artist such as *Woman* (1957–58) and *Large Reclining Figure* (1984) are presented in a permanent exhibition along with works by other contemporary British sculptors in the associated 17.5-hectare-large sculpture garden. The Henry Moore Institute in Leeds, one part of the Henry Moore Foundation, has been in existence since 1977 and is one of the most important research and educational facilities for sculpture in the world. It comprises spaces for exhibitions and events, a research center and a library as well as a sculpture archive. Lisa Le Feuvre has led the Institute since 2010 as Head of Sculpture Studies.

The Henry Moore Foundation awards grants amounting to a total of £500,000 per year in the following fields: exhibitions, catalogues, and commissioned works, collections, research and development, artist work and residency fellowships as well as conferences, publications, and presentations. It also initiates exhibitions worldwide such as the Henry Moore retrospective at the Tate Britain (2010) and *Henry Moore in Spain*, in cooperation with the Fundación la Caixa in Barcelona (2013–14).

The Board of Trustees of the Henry Moore Foundation currently includes Nigel Carrington (Chairman), as well as the members David Wilson, Charles Asprey, Henry Channon, Celia Clear, William Thomas Edgerley, Laure Genillard, Antony Griffiths, Anne Wagner, and Peter Wienand. In 2014, the Henry Moore Foundation distributed around £4.5 million for nonprofit purposes (grants, research, exhibition projects, et al.).[1]

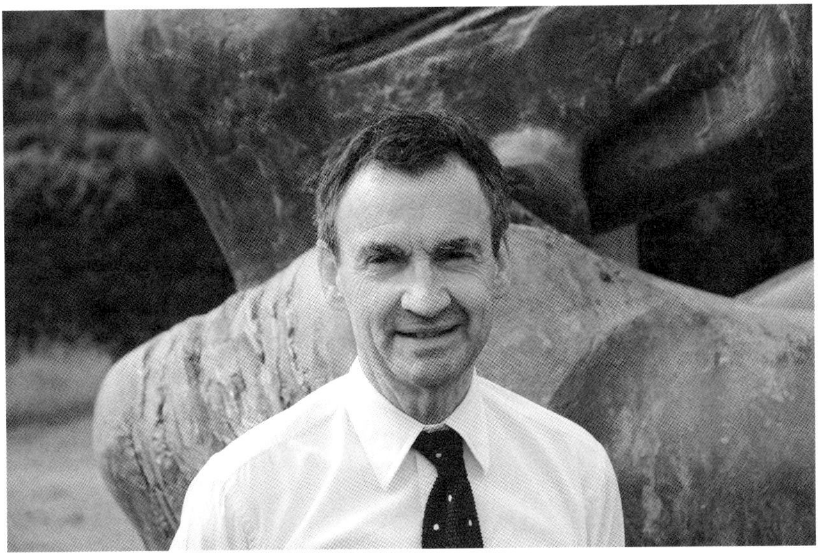

Richard Calvocoressi

Loretta Würtenberger: When was the Henry Moore Foundation set up and what was the original intention of it?

Richard Calvocoressi: The Henry Moore Foundation was set up in 1977 by Moore himself during his lifetime. He was one of those artists who had foresight, including for the time after his death. Originally the Foundation was tax-motivated since higher-rate taxation in Britain in the 1970s was very high.

Next to the charitable foundation Henry Moore set up an enterprise company. Everything he made after 1977 went into the enterprise company now called Henry Moore Foundation Enterprises. He became an employee of the enterprise company in his last nine years; he was on a salary for the first time in his life.

Before his death he had made sure that his wife Irina Moore and daughter Mary were well looked after, having left to Irina a collection of sculptures as well as their house in Perry Green which in turn went to Mary when Irina died. Before he set up the Foundation he additionally had done two things: he made a big gift of plasters, drawings, and sculptures to the Art Gallery of Ontario, Toronto. A second gift of a wonderful collection of thirty-five bronzes was made to the Tate Gallery (now Tate Britain) in 1978. Everything else went into the Foundation, including investments, property, and all his other assets on his death. Later, in

1 Henry Moore Foundation, *Trustees' Report and Financial Statements* 2014, p. 20.

2004, the Foundation bought his house, Hoglands, which was originally in the possession of the Moore family, and converted it to open it to the public. So everything was done in stages, but more or less all had been planned before Henry Moore died.

LW: It is not often the case that an artist oversees accounting, tax issues etc. in such a professional manner.
RC: Henry Moore was a very well organized man and he was well advised by his lawyer Lord Goodman. During Moore's lifetime whenever property became available—like a cottage or agricultural building or field around his house—he would buy it to protect it from development. So he bought around fifty to sixty acres of land around his house, which today are the headquarters of the Foundation, the library, and the studios. It also meant that he could offer the people who were working for him a place to live because it's quite isolated there. The Foundation today owns about ten or eleven domestic properties; nothing grand, but it protects the place.

LW: One of the unique characteristics of the Henry Moore Foundation is that it has built a structure whose impact goes beyond taking care of Henry Moore's legacy. Could you explain the main focus of the Foundation today?
RC: I think nowadays you cannot just look after an artist's estate as part of your Foundation. You have to go beyond that. The Henry Moore Foundation is the largest grant-giving artist foundation outside of the United States. We give away money for all sorts of projects that have to do with sculpture, interpreted as broadly as possible. Additionally, it remains our core responsibility to look after Henry Moore's work.

We have this huge collection of Henry Moore's work placed in Perry Green in Hertfordshire where he lived and worked until his death in 1986. Moore's sculptures have influenced artists of all generations. In 2013, for the first time ever, our *Moore/Rodin* exhibition was the first where we paired Moore with another great master. In the exhibition *Body & Void: Echoes of Moore in Contemporary Art* last year (2014) we looked at Henry Moore's impact on sculptors from Joseph Beuys and Bruce Naumann down to artists such as Tony Cragg, Anish Kapoor, Antony Gormley, and Richard Deacon.

LW: Henry Moore Foundation is already today one of the perfect foundation models. What motivates you now for the coming years, what are your upcoming projects?

RC: Our next big project is trying to improve the relationship between our Henry Moore Institute in Leeds, where Moore studied as a young man, and Leeds Art Gallery next door. Leeds Art Gallery has a very a good collection of twentieth-century British sculpture and it has a great archive. The ideal would be some kind of private / public partnership. It could attract gifts, works of art, bequests—you could really make it a center of excellence for sculpture. It could be a model for others.

LW: The Henry Moore Institute in Leeds is a world-recognized center for the study of sculpture with an important archive of British sculpture. Which of Moore's documents do you archive at the Foundation?

RC: At Perry Green, we have a very important collection of everything that has to do with Henry Moore: documentary material, correspondence, photographs, books, catalogues etc. If you want to research on Henry Moore's work, the Henry Moore Foundation is the best place to come.

LW: Many other estates give away or sell their archives to museums. What is your view on that?

RC: It may have something to do with the costs of setting up an archive and running it. You need a building; you ideally also need technical things such as special climate control. If you have to make it accessible to scholars you need a reading room; you need security. All that is quite expensive. There is an understandable attraction to giving an archive to an existing institution with an existing infrastructure. And there are big archives in Britain like the Tate Gallery that are actively—and quite successfully—trying to attract gifts from estates.

LW: Do you have an authentication committee?

RC: We have an authentication committee that's inside the Foundation. I'm the chair of the authentication committee, we have one or two experts from the staff, the curators, and then we have two outside experts. I suppose it's as independent as it can possibly be. The catalogue raisonné and authentication committees go hand in hand, they are interrelated in my view. You can't have a catalogue raisonné without some kind of authentication committee because otherwise who is the authority? In the case of Moore the catalogue raisonné already exists: The first catalogue raisonné on Moore's complete sculptural works was edited by Herbert Read, David Sylvester, and Alan Bowness and was published in six volumes between 1944 and 1988. It was followed by catalogues raisonnés on Moore's graphic works and drawings. Now it's a question of updating them.

LW: There are two different models for an artist's estate: the eternity model of an estate and the sunset model of an estate. What are your thoughts on that?
RC: That's what I periodically ask my trustees. They regard the Foundation as being in perpetuity. My point is that if that is the case we may have to take some very difficult decisions. Because in fifteen or twenty years there might come a point when we will run out of money. When I took over during the summer of 2007, about six months before the beginning of the financial crisis, the capital value of the endowment was around £100 million. Today the Foundation's capital value of investments stands at around eighty-five million pounds.

In the current financial environment, we have to look at our costs. There are grants that have to be looked after, buildings, security, gardening, and properties. There is a real danger in getting too big. At the beginning the Foundation was employing only four or five people and today there are forty. We did not have the Institute in Leeds, Perry Green was not open to the public, and we did not do big exhibitions. When I took over there was very much an attitude that money is not a problem and we can do what we like. That led to a culture of spending, not earning.

LW: How do you generate revenue?
RC: At Perry Green, we don't have a huge number of visitors because we are only open from April to October. When I took over we were attracting around 12,000 to 13,000 visitors a year, today we have around 30,000. In 2013 the *Moore/Rodin* exhibition was a huge success and we had 31,747 visitors. This success helped us to implement some improvements, such as a better ticket office and a coffee shop.

I am constantly trying to find alternative sources of income for the Foundation, such as publications and charging for copyright. Originally, we were hardly charging for copyright. That condition dates back to the time when Henry Moore set up the Foundation and decided not to charge for copyright. At that stage this was an interesting decision, because his work was out of fashion in the nineteen-seventies, with the rise of Conceptual Art and so on. Today licensing and copyright bring in a small but constant amount for the Foundation. Additionally, there is retail, merchandise, a shop, cafés, and we do weddings at Perry Green (maximum once a month). We started a Friends group about two or three years ago. That brings in a certain amount and we charge for our work on big international exhibitions of Henry Moore. Really successful exhibitions, like the *Moore/Rodin* show, we ended up with a surplus, and in that case of about £100,000, which was really satisfying.

LW: What would you do if your endowment shrank further and you would not be able to stop that through additional revenue?

RC: If there was, for example, a worldwide financial catastrophe, the one thing we would have to preserve would be the legacy of Henry Moore. We would probably not stay open to the public. We would have to say goodbye to the Institute in Leeds and we would have to stop giving money away through the grants.

LW: Can you produce works by Henry Moore posthumously in order to support the Foundation financially?

RC: Coming to the business of posthumous casts, Moore was a bit of a romantic. He stipulated in his will that after his death there should be no further casts with one exception: if there was a bronze cast already in the foundry that had not yet been finished and patinated, that could be finished under the supervision of Irina, his wife, and Bernard Meadows, his very trusted assistant. He worked with the Fine Art Foundry Hermann Noack in Berlin for larger casts and Hermann senior was a good friend of his. If there was a small edition of maybe three or four casts which had not yet been finished and there was a demand for one more, again that could be done after his death, but only at Noack under the supervision of Irina and Bernard. That was the case for probably half a dozen works.

In his will, drafted in 1985, Henry Moore stipulated that no castings of his sculptures were to be produced posthumously:

I DIRECT that after my death:

(a) No further cast or casts should be made in any material whatsoever of my sculptures

(b) No work of mine which is not completed should be completed by anyone but subject thereto my Trustees may with the consent of my wife Irina and Professor Bernard Meadows or the survivor of them permit finishing touches to be made to any work of mine which is for all practical purposes completed at the date of my death

(c) Notwithstanding the provisions of this Clause where a sculpture or a model of a sculpture has been delivered to Hermann Noack then:

(i) If he has begun any cast of that sculpture he may complete that cast

(ii) My wife Irina and Bernard Meadows may authorise him to make all or any cast or casts as are required to complete the edition of that sculpture.

LW: Do you sometimes regret this decision?
RC: No, because when it comes to authentication it makes it so much easier. But it would be lovely in a way to be able to make new casts and to sell them for the benefit of the Foundation; to do the projects we want to do.

LW: So also in the case of Henry Moore the question about posthumous casts with good reason boils down to what the artist's will dictates.
RC: Yes, and the hand of the artist is also so important. In fact, we recently did an exhibition of Henry Moore's plasters because up until relatively recently the plasters were considered as irrelevant. They don't appear in the catalogue raisonné for example. The catalogue raisonné is of the carvings and the bronzes, but it's quite clear that these plasters were works of art in their own right. You really see the touch of the artist on the plasters, the way he scratched them, drew on them, colored them …

LW: Did you have any problems with forgery?
RC: Yes we get fakes, very often with the maquettes, because in the nineteen-fifties the bronze maquettes were not always signed or numbered by Moore. Often he didn't get round to doing the stamping or signing and numbering, so that's an area where you get fakes.

LW: Do living artists or their heirs consult you about how to set up a Foundation? Or how to deal with their legacy?
RC: I organized a conference here in London in October 2013 called "The Artist as a Philanthropist" and invited a wide range of British artists. I expected that some might send their representatives, their managers or assistants, and quite a few did. There was someone from Tracey Emin's studio, from Antony Gormley's studio, from Damien Hirst. Anselm Kiefer sent his main assistant, Waltraud Forelli, from Paris who is very interested in the subject. The artist Richard Wentworth came and then a number of dealers and galleries and artists' families.

LW: You have been the Director of the Henry Moore Foundation for eight years. Is there any advice or conclusion you would like to share?
RC: I think any Foundation needs to get a good lawyer, specialized in the field of working with artists' foundations. Another recommendation is not to underestimate the financial burden of running an estate. Finally, I would say, choose your trustees very carefully. They should be people with different skills and experiences.

Jerry Gorovoy
Easton Foundation / Louise Bourgeois

Louise Bourgeois (1911–2010) was one of the most influential sculptors of the twentieth century. She became known for her unique, archetypal language of forms. In 2011, her sculpture *Spider* (1996) was sold at auction by Christie's for the price of $10.7 million[1]—at the time the highest price ever achieved for the work of a living woman artist.

Bourgeois met her assistant, Jerry Gorovoy, for the first time in 1980 at a gallery in SoHo, New York, where he, as curator, was presenting one of her works in a group exhibition. From this encounter developed a working relationship of many years that was characterized by deep trust. Bourgeois concentrated entirely on her creative work and left the work of preparing her exhibitions and managing her affairs to Gorovoy. He dedicated his life to her: for thirty years, he accompanied all her work processes and was simultaneously also responsible for presenting the work of the artist to the world. Besides Jerry Gorovoy, her two sons, Jean-Louis and Alain were the people closest to Bourgeois, but they were not part of the creative process in the same way.

Along with the children of the deceased artist, Gorovoy today manages a non-profit foundation that Bourgeois established in 1984. Since her death, the Foundation has managed the estate and also supports cultural projects and exhibitions.

Loretta Würtenberger: How was the Louise Bourgeois Foundation founded?
Jerry Govoroy: Louise Bourgeois's foundation is called The Easton Foundation, after the town in Connecticut where the family had acquired a country home in the nineteen-forties. The Foundation was created during Louise's lifetime, but upon her death it became the recipient of a large collection of her work, copyright for her art, and a vast archive of her documents. She also bequeathed her home, which had served as her studio, and an adjacent brownstone. Louise's sons, Jean-Louis and Alain Bourgeois, and I are on the Foundation's board. Louise set up the Foundation in a way that allowed me to continue working with her art in the same manner that I had during her lifetime.

LW: Which part of Louise Bourgeois's work is still left at the Foundation?
JG: All of Louise's artist's proofs from the editioned works made during her lifetime were kept off the market, and now belong to the Foundation. These

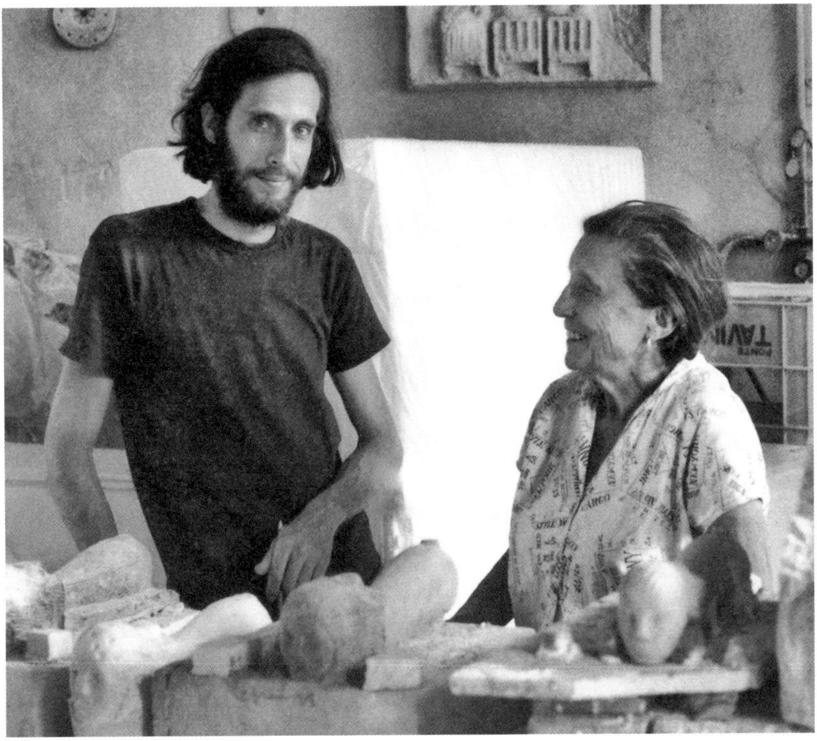

Jerry Gorovoy und Louise Bourgeois

works form the core of the Foundation's collection, and will not be for sale. The Foundation also has a selection of unique works from all periods of Louise's career. These important holdings have made it easier and more cost-effective for curators and museums to organize shows. The collection is also a great resource for scholarly research.

One part of Bourgeois's artistic works and designs is still today located in her house in Chelsea, New York City, where the artist lived and worked for nearly fifty years. After the death of her husband, the art historian Robert Goldwater, in the nineteen-seventies, part of the living space was converted into an office and studio space in which a wide, great number of work materials accumu-

1 "Louise Bourgeois (1911–2010) Spider," Sale 2480 / Lot 29, Christie's Inc., http://www.christies.com/lotfinder/sculptures-statues-figures/louise-bourgeois-spider-5496701-details.aspx?from=searchresults&intObjectID=5496701&sid=529053a2-ddb2-40d6-a687-cb910c92e592 (accessed January 18, 2016).

lated—including paints, pens, newspaper clippings, photographs as well as books and pieces of furniture from flea markets accumulated. Like an artistic signature, the environment that Bourgeois designed reflects her creative working process. To be able to preserve all the material in the estate and present it to the public, the Easton Foundation purchased the neighboring building for 4.5 million dollars in 2009 as an additional exhibition space.[2]

LW: In 2016 you are planning to open the townhouse in which Louise Bourgeois lived since 1962 to the public. How do you feel about opening up this very private space?
JG: The Foundation feels comfortable opening the building to the public, especially since it provides insight to who she was and the way she lived, and how this influenced what she created. Louise stated that she was "a woman without secrets." Many of her works were made in her Chelsea home and garden studio up to and even after the nineteen-eighties, when she acquired a large industrial studio space in Brooklyn. We are preserving Louise's house the way it was because it's so close in feeling and form to her sculpture. Her art and life were totally merged, and I think visitors feel this immediately. Having two adjacent properties has allowed us to set up the archives, a residency program, and a research center, while still keeping the house intact. We have also combined the two backyards to create an intimate sculpture garden.

LW: Was Louise involved in the future of the townhouse?
JG: After Louise was forced to abandon her studio in Brooklyn, she bought the adjacent townhouse in anticipation of the Foundation's needs. However, she left the organization and practical details for the board to work out.

To be honest, Louise was more focused on her new work than thinking about her legacy. After all, this was a person that generally did not go to any of her exhibitions, and left the organization of the installations to me. When people told Louise that they liked a show of hers, she often asked: "What was in it?"

LW: What further plans do you have for the Foundation?
JG: We have created an endowment for the Foundation to continue its activities in perpetuity. We have a vast archive that is in the process of being catalogued, and are building a comprehensive library, including films, voice recordings, and interviews with Louise. At some point in the future we may want to make shows with small exhibitions of her work. Right now we have so many museum shows

planned for all over the world that it doesn't make sense. Presently we have various materials from the archive on view.

LW: Can you talk more about the archive of Louise Bourgeois's papers?
JG: During her lifetime, Louise gave a few of documents to the Smithsonian Institution's Archives of American Art, as well as those of her husband, the art historian Robert Goldwater, but the Foundation inherited the bulk of her papers. It is an incredible collection. We have all of Louise's diaries, beginning in 1923, as well as a huge assortment of writings, documents, letters, agendas, exhibition announcements etc., as well as audiotapes and videotapes of interviews and films. There are also many photographs of Louise from all periods of her life. The long-term goal of the Foundation is to make all of this accessible to the public.

The Smithsonian Archives of American Art in New York have a collection of around 700 drawings, sketches, and letters by the artist from the years 1922 to 1994.

In 1990, Louise Bourgeois also decided to hand over the entire archive of her graphic prints—some 3,500 graphic sheets—to the Museum of Modern Art in New York City. The museum organized the first large retrospective of the artist in 1982, and Bourgeois had been friends with its curator, Deborah Wye, for many years. In collaboration with the Louise Bourgeois Studio, MoMA is working on a research project to inventory and digitize the graphic works. A website making all the material, including Bourgeois's artist's books, accessible went online in 2013.[3]

LW: What are your ideas for supporting research on Louise Bourgeois?
JG: We are facilitating and promoting research on Louise's works by scholars, inviting them to come and stay at the Foundation while they have access to the Archive. Further, the Foundation is supporting a catalogue raisonné of Louise's prints, organized by Deborah Wye for the Museum of Modern Art, here in New York. Eventually, the Foundation would like to see catalogues raisonné of her

---

2 Lucy Davies, "Inside Artist Louise Bourgeois' New York Home," in *The Telegraph* (June 15, 2014), http://www.telegraph.co.uk/culture/art/10890373/Inside-artist-Louise-Bourgeois-New-York-home.html (accessed December 15, 2015).

3 Louise Bourgeois, *The Complete Prints and Books*, http://www.moma.org/explore/collection/lb/index (accessed December 16, 2015).

entire oeuvre. These publications take a long time, and are expensive. Hopefully the Foundation can work with a university press. We have very good records.

We are currently beginning an oral history project in which people who have personal experiences with Louise or with her work are being interviewed.

LW: The opening of Louise Bourgeois's private house and studio is wonderful but it will also be quite a challenge to maintain it for another couple of decades.
JG: That's why we are setting up an endowment, so we can carry out long-term projects.

LW: Is the will published?
JG: No.

LW: Do you think that outside advisors were helpful?
JG: The lawyers were helpful from the legal point of view in carrying out Louise's wishes. If you are a successful artist in the United States, and you still have a lot of artwork, there are major tax consequences that have to be dealt with. So the idea of setting up a foundation becomes almost a necessity for an artist.

LW: The board of trustees consists of you and Louise Bourgeois's two sons, right?
JG: Correct.

LW: Do you think family involvement is helpful for an artist foundation?
JG: It depends. Lots of times artists don't make good parents, and there can be consequences. Some children of artists were never involved with the careers or artistic output of their parents, and have no real knowledge or experience of the art world. However, some family members are good shepherds of the artist's work and have a deep connection and devotion to it.

LW: Will you sell some of the works to create an endowment?
JG: Yes, creating an endowment is one of our important projects. In certain cases we have duplicate works that we can sell for the benefit of the Foundation. We would also like to place key works in the Foundation's collection with great museums. A lot of museums have one work, but I'm also interested in institutions like MoMA, the Tate, and the Pompidou having a larger concentration of Louise's works. This will provide a fuller picture of her artistic output, particularly given that her work varied over the decades in terms of material, form, and scale.

Louise Bourgeois is represented with her works in the most important international collections. Her main works are found in the Guggenheim Bilbao, the Tate Modern in London, the Jardin des Tuileries, and the Centre Georges Pompidou in Paris, the Hermitage in St. Petersburg as well as the MoMA, New York. Retrospectives of her have been presented in the following museums: the Hirshhorn Museum, Washington D.C. (2009); Tate Modern, London; Solomon R. Guggenheim Museum, New York; and the Museum of Contemporary Art, Los Angeles (2008); Centre Georges Pompidou, Paris, (2007); Kunstmuseum Bern, and the Kröller-Müller Museum Otterlo, Netherlands (1991); Fundació Antoni Tàpies, Barcelona; Städtische Galerie im Lenbachhaus, Munich: and the Musée d'Art Contemporain, Lyon (1990); Contemporary Arts Museum, Houston; Museum of Contemporary Art, Chicago; and the Akron Art Museum, Akron, Ohio (1983); and the MoMA, New York City (1982). The Hauser & Wirth gallery has been representing the work of the artist since 2010. Since her death, the gallery has realized exhibitions in close cooperation with the Easton Foundation and Jerry Gorovoy.

LW: Are you doing this with Louise's galleries?
JG: We are doing this in collaboration with the dealers. The market, for better or for worse, plays a large role in the reception of an artist's work. It can be a factor in what exhibitions museums do, and this, consequently, can affect the nature of scholarship. But the market also has a logic of its own, which doesn't always have to do with quality. Certain artists have periods in their careers where their output is quite uneven, not as original. Louise is an exception because her work continually changed and remained inventive at a very high level throughout her career.

LW: I agree that the market is often the determining force of what is in the limelight but I think one cannot underestimate that as a foundation you also have the power to shift that limelight by actively exhibiting and encouraging research on certain not yet totally discovered or appreciated aspects.
JG: Yes, you are right. History is continually being rewritten. Exhibitions and scholarship change our understanding and add to our knowledge of the artist. They can shed light on certain aspects of works or bodies of work, repositioning them historically, and this can have reverberations in the market. Louise's work is strong across all periods, and there is interest in all phases of her career. But still there are pieces of Louise's that have been problematic for the market to

absorb. It may be the subject matter, but it could also simply be their scale or weight. With our strong, in-depth collection of Louise's work, the Foundation has the opportunity to shape exhibitions through dialogue with the curators, pointing to less-seen or understood phases of her work.

LW: From your experience, what advice would you give a living artist concerning the planning of his or her estate?
JG: At a certain point in Louise's artistic career, when she was less known, we had to sell key works in order to build up her reputation and market. I think my advice would be for an artist to try and keep important works in their collection, saving them for museums or for their foundation. Of course there will always be pieces that need to be sold, but one thing that served us well is that we still have many of Louise's significant works in the Foundation. Now we can share these with a broader public, either through exhibitions or long-term loan.

Another point of caution has to do with the setting up of a foundation with lawyers and accountants as trustees. This may have to be the case when the artist has no children, but in general I've seen cases where it's problematic and detrimental. I think the mission of an artist's foundation is to preserve and promote artistic legacy. This requires a deep knowledge of the artist and their work. Sensitivity and creativity are necessary. For the most part, lawyers and tax accountants don't have a deep understanding of art. Rather than being appointed as a trustee with voting privileges, they should be hired and paid for their knowledge and time on an hourly basis. They should not be the driving force in shaping an artist's legacy. I think historians, curators, or artistic colleagues can better serve the main tasks of a foundation. They have a better sense of how to maintain scholarly research and museum activity, keeping interest in the work alive. The foundation also has a responsibility to make sure that the works are installed correctly and placed in the right context, as the artist would have wanted. You need this insight into what the artist's intentions were, what they believed in, and what the work meant to them. Context is important. Then there are also the issues of restoration and preservation of works. The essence of all these things has nothing to do with legal or accounting issues.

LW: Your work must have changed quite a lot after Louise passed away. You had such a close relationship to her. How was that for you?
JG: It was an adjustment. She definitely was and still is a big part of my life. Organizing the exhibitions and the installations of her works keeps her close to me.

David Nash
Gallerist of the Roy Lichtenstein and the Willem de Kooning Estate

The gallerist and former Sotheby's director David Nash is one of the leading dealers of contemporary art and classic modernism. He and his wife, Lucy Mitchell-Innes, established the Mitchell-Innes & Nash gallery in New York in 1996, which has since then represented artists such as Alberto Burri, Leon Kossoff, Tom Wesselmann, and Hans Arp. He was also a member of the Fine Art Committee of the Internal Revenue Service (IRS) for fourteen years and is today a member of the Board of Directors of the International Foundation for Art Research (IFAR). In 2014, along with the art historians Walter Feilchenfeldt and Jayne Warman, he published the online catalogue raisonné of the painting oeuvre of the artist Paul Cézanne,[1] which reproduces all of Cézanne's paintings in color for the first time and allows researchers quick access to all the related details of the works.

In 1999, nearly two years after the artist's death, his widow Dorothy established the Roy Lichtenstein Foundation. The Foundation, with its headquarters in New York, manages the estate and supports research projects and exhibitions with the aim of deepening the public's understanding of the work of Roy Lichtenstein (1923–1997) and the artists of his time. The Foundation further represents the copyrights for most of the works of the Pop Art artist and is preparing the catalogue raisonné of the paintings in a long-term project. In addition to Dorothy Lichtenstein as President, the members of the board also currently include the two sons of the artist, David Hoyt Lichtenstein and Mitchell Wilson Lichtenstein, as well as Elisabeth C. Baker, Jack Cowart (Executive Director), Ruth Fine (Chair of the Board), Maria Morris Hambourg, Michael Lobel, Leslie B. Samuels, and John W. Smith. In 2013, the assets of the Roy Lichtenstein Foundation totaled around sixty million dollars.[2]

Loretta Würtenberger: How did your relationship with the Lichtenstein Estate begin? Did you represent Roy Lichtenstein as a living artist as well?
David Nash: No. Until the day he died the Leo Castelli Gallery represented him. The question of how we came to represent him is probably a matter of personal connection. We knew his widow, Dorothy Lichtenstein, and the director of the Foundation, Jack Cowart very well. There were a few other dealers who were equally friendly with Roy; they expected to represent the estate and I think they

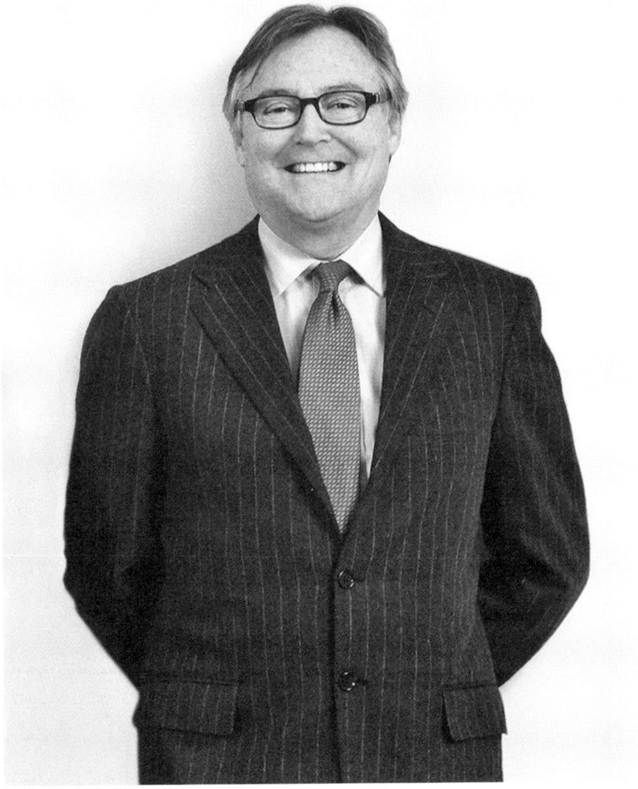

David Nash

had been lobbying massively to get it. I think the fact that we were relatively neutral and that we had the experience of representing the de Kooning Estate made us a good choice.

After Roy died, Dorothy told me that he had carefully set up everything in his lifetime, so they were not forced to sell any works. Roy left a clear will and Dorothy, obviously, had a clear idea of what he wanted to be done and how it should be done.

---

1 http://www.cezannecatalogue.com/.

2 Roy Lichtenstein Foundation, Form 990, 2013, Department of the Treasury, Internal Revenue Service.

LW: How did it feel being responsible for managing the estates of such great artists?

DN: Well at the time I did not think about it so much. In retrospect I realize it was an enormous responsibility, but we felt completely competent to carry it out. From our time at Sotheby's, Lucy and I had all the necessary qualifications. We had considerable experience in doing appraisals of artists' estates and in justifying the valuations with comparable data and we had a very long history of selling works, not just by de Kooning, but also by artists of that era. And a third advantage, we had long experience in dealing with the IRS because both Lucy and myself had been on the IRS art advisory panel which consists of a group of dealers, museum curators, and other experts who meet twice a year to give advice to the IRS on the valuations of paintings which have been submitted by tax payers for one reason or another—estate appraisals, gifts, and so on. So we knew not just how to do an appraisal, but how to do it in a way that the IRS would accept.

LW: Do you feel different about working with an estate than working with living artists?

DN: Oh, it is completely different. Working with an artist's estate you have to have a very clear objective. You are usually responsible to a legal advisor, some sort of executor or attorney of one kind or another. When you are dealing with living artists it is altogether a different business. You have to take into account his future, what is best for him, and all kind of other things you don't have to think of when you are dealing with an artist's estate.

LW: What is the status of the Lichtenstein catalogue raisonné? Are you working on it together with the Foundation?

DN: No, our job was and is to do the appraisals and to sell works if necessary. Everything else, such as the catalogue raisonné, is being done by the Foundation.

LW: Many authentication committees in the US were disbanded in the last few years. Are authentication committees still needed today?

DN: My view is that authentication committees are still very vital. Obviously the situation differs from country to country because the law differs. At the moment in the United States the committees or individuals who issue opinions are opening themselves up to the liability of a lawsuit if they give an unfavorable opinion. For this reason many of the artist's foundations have ceased to authenticate works. The Warhol Foundation has stopped, the Lichtenstein Foundation no longer does, and de Kooning never did. Basquiat no longer authenticates works. I think it is a real setback, not only for the artist, but also for the art world as a whole.

It's interesting that there have been a number of cases where unhappy or dissatisfied owners have sued a body of experts to reverse the decision. There was the famous Warhol case where Joe Simon-Whelan sued the foundation about a self-portrait. It cost the Warhol Foundation almost seven million dollars in legal fees to defend themselves, and in the end the case was actually dropped because the plaintiff had run out of money. Incidentally, in none of these cases has the plaintiff actually ever won.

As opposed to that, the law protects experts who give authentications in France. French heirs of artist's estates also have a slightly different attitude to keeping the market clean of forgeries and misattributions. I think this is to the benefit of the artist's reputation. The American legal system is not really for the benefit of the artist.

In 2011, the Roy Lichtenstein Foundation dissolved the authentication committee that it had established six years earlier. Although the Foundation was not entangled in any legal disputes at this point in time, the Executive Director, Jack Cowart, made the decision as a result of the growing concern over lawsuits. The Foundation preferred to invest its money in sensible projects rather than on the anticipated costs of litigation: "When it came time to renew our very large insurance premium, we began to ask ourselves, 'Is this a wise use of assets to protect the core purpose of the foundation?'"[3] The Roy Lichtenstein Foundation has an extensive archive and collaborates with external experts who take a position regarding questions of authenticity.

LW: If foundations are drawing back from the field of authentication, should other people take over this responsibility?

DN: I don't think that there is any substitute for the knowledge that the foundation can bring to this problem. Outside experts yes, they can be very knowledgeable and very helpful. Technical analysis can be very useful up to a certain point, but technical analysis cannot tell if Lichtenstein painted a work. The

3 Eileen Kinsella, "A Matter Of Opinion," in *ARTnews* (February 28, 2012), http://www.artnews.com/2012/02/28/a-matter-of-opinion/ (accessed December 16, 2015).

foundations have all the records, photographs, documents, notebooks, sketchpads, exhibition catalogues, etc. and are much more qualified to give an opinion than anybody else.

LW: You also represented the Estate of Willem de Kooning. How did that evolve?
DN: In the case of de Kooning, we were involved with the estate right from the beginning. Towards the end of his life, de Kooning was incapacitated by dementia and a court appointed conservancy handled his affairs. The trustees of the conservancy had already explored with us the possibility of what was going to happen after his death. In 1997, when de Kooning died, the trustees were faced with the responsibility of having all of his approved paintings, drawings, sculptures, and prints inventoried and appraised. Next, they had to have the appraisal by the IRS. On the basis of that appraisal they determined how much estate tax would be owed to the US government and then form a strategy for sales of the work over a period of years in order to realize the funds needed to pay this tax bill.

The Willem de Kooning Foundation, which was established in 2001, concentrates its activities entirely on research projects, exhibitions, and education programs dedicated to the remembrance of the Dutch-American painter Willem de Kooning (1904–1997). The private, operative Foundation is led by Amy Schichtel as Executive Director ,and the attorneys John A. Silberman, John L. Eastman, and Donn Zaretsky. Mitchell-Innes & Nash represented Willem de Kooning's estate until 2003.[4]

LW: Did de Kooning have any plans for where his work should go or what should happen with it?
DN: He had given a dozen pictures to his daughter Lisa but he had not left clear instructions on what had to be done with his other unsold works. After de Kooning's death, Lisa de Kooning and John Eastman—whom is a lawyer specializing in artist's estates—became co-executors of the estate. They instructed us to put most of the later works, which were in a very different style, into a separate group from the works that were going to be kept in the estate. Those works that would go into the foundation would be free of estate tax, but the works that remained in the estate would have to be valued and then a number were going to have to be sold to meet the tax obligations. At the end of all this, the residue would go to Lisa. There were lots of works in all media and once we had finished the appraisal, we had to work on the concept of a blockage discount.

John Silberman, an attorney who represented Lisa and Eastman and the Estate, did the final negotiations with the IRS. He decided on an across-the-board fifty percent discount, which is unusually broad. We had made the strategic decision that only a handful of de Kooning's very best works would come on the market. The challenge for the dealer, if you have a large body of work and you have got to sell it, is not to sell to people who will put it back on the market and then compete against you. We divided the works into three groups: The first group would be the handful of best works and we recommended no discount for them. We felt that they all probably could be sold within a short space of time at full market value. The second group would be the less good paintings, which was obviously a much larger group. We recommended a twenty-five or thirty percent discount for them. The balance of the works, which were mostly drawings, would constitute the third group and we recommended a sixty percent discount.

The next step, after coming up with the calculation of the tax bill, was to raise the money by selling enough works to pay the tax bill. The objective was to sell enough works over five years to pay the tax and leave as many of the good paintings in the estate as possible. However, even after the blockage discount, there was about $100 million owed to the US government. The appraisal of the remainder came to over $300 million after a deduction of the works going into the Foundation. Following the negotiations to apply a blockage discount, the estate was left with a tax bill of over $100,000,000.

LW: What was your strategy when putting the first works from the Estate on the market?

DN: Our strategy was to get off to a running start and we sold a couple of really good and expensive works right away. We wanted to sell some of the early pictures by de Kooning. One of them was a portrait from around 1944, which we sold to a major collector, and then we sold a major sculpture to the Nasher Museum. These sales brought in quite a lot of money. That made it possible for us to be a little bit more selective about what we sold after that.

LW: How closely did you work with other galleries? And do you think it is good to have an estate working with more than one gallery?

---

4 Kelly Devine Thomas, "Shaping De Kooning's Legacy," in *ARTnews* (August 9, 2011), http://www.artnews.com/2011/09/08/shaping-de-koonings-legacy/ (accessed December 16, 2015).

DN: In the case of the de Kooning Estate we shared representation with the Matthew Marks Gallery and this worked extremely well. We shared the commissions and the expenses. Despite the fact that both our galleries are New York based and both of us handle the work of artists who were working in the second half of the twentieth century, our partnership and our different client lists proved to be very successful.

Interview with Jack Flam
Dedalus Foundation / Robert Motherwell

Robert Motherwell (1915–1991) was among the most important protagonists of Abstract Expressionism in the United States. In the postwar period he created large-format paintings such as the well-known series *Elegy to the Spanish Republic* (1948–67), which are defined by black color fields and light-dark contrasts. The symbolism of the unconscious is reflected in them just as is Motherwell's examination of the great poets of the twentieth century, like James Joyce or Stéphane Mallarmé.

The artist established the Dedalus Foundation—named for a character from James Joyce's novel *Ulysses*—in 1981, ten years before his death. At the time, the Foundation's main objective was promoting public understanding and appreciation of the work of Motherwell and his contemporaries. From there, it developed into one of the largest artist's foundations in the United States, with an endowment today of fifty-five million dollars.[1] Motherwell selected Jack Flam as joint editor of the series of publications that he founded, *The Documents of Twentieth-Century Art,* in 1981. Flam has been a member of the board of the Dedalus Foundation in New York since 1991, and was elected as President and CEO of the Foundation in 2002. He is a professor of art and art history at Brooklyn College as well as at the City University of New York and is the author or editor of numerous publications on the art of the nineteenth and twentieth century.

Loretta Würtenberger: Set up in 1981 by the artist himself, the Dedalus Foundation is an operating foundation, whose main charitable activity is educating the public about modern art and modernism and about the legacy of Robert Motherwell. Over the years it has created a wide range of programs that support art projects, institutions, and individuals. What is the main focus of the Foundation today?

Jack Flam: Although it was founded in 1981, the Foundation became active upon Motherwell's death in 1991. During the first twenty years of its active existence, the Foundation worked to promote understanding of Motherwell's work by organizing exhibitions, placing works in museum collections, and most especially by preparing the catalogue raisonné of his paintings and collages (published by Yale University Press in 2012). During that same period, we also wanted to enhance public understanding of modern art and modernism generally, which Motherwell meant to be central to the mission of the Foundation. In order to

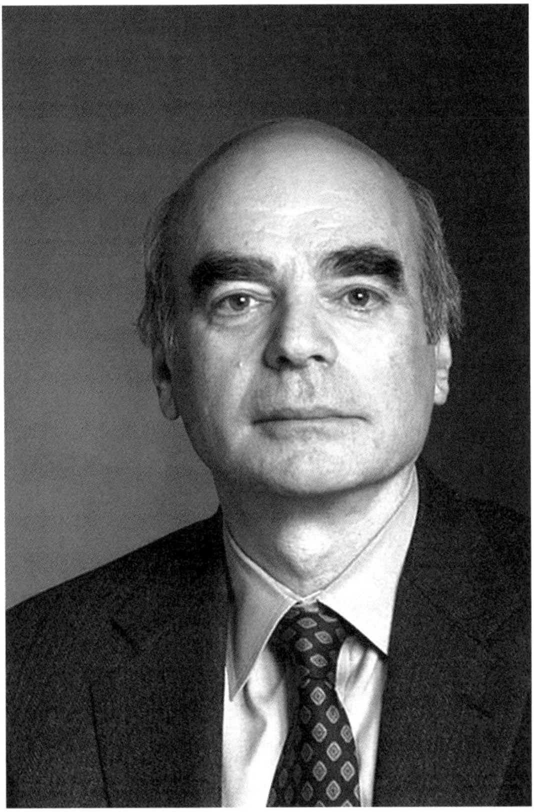

Jack Flam

do so, we started a grants program, which mainly supported exhibitions, educational programs, and scholarship about modern art. Since Motherwell's own wish for the Foundation was to promote the public understanding of modern art and modernism more broadly, with particular attention to his art and that of his peers, we supported a wide range of projects. They ranged from an exhibition of David Smith's sculpture to a book on Édouard Manet to projects involving art by living artists.

The grants program grew gradually but steadily. Our primary focus was on areas where we perceived needs within the art community. For example, we realized that there was a need to support PhD dissertations in art history, and also MFA (Master of Fine Arts) candidates in painting and sculpture, who often

---

1 Dedalus Foundation, Form 990, 2013, Department of the Treasury, Internal Revenue Service.

find the transition from student to professional artist difficult, because after graduation getting studio space and feedback from peers becomes so difficult. In response to these needs, we set up a program of Dedalus Dissertation and MFA Fellowships in those areas. In order to support significant research by more mature scholars of modern art, we also established a Senior Fellowship. We also were—and remain—deeply concerned about issues related to archives and to the conservation of art works. These are not "glamorous" fields of study, and so they are often overlooked by people and institutions seeking highly visible projects. Following Motherwell's own belief that priority should be given to support of projects on their merits, we created fellowships at the Museum of Modern Art archives and at the Conservation Center of the Institute of Fine Arts.

At the time, we were giving cash grants of about $700,000 each year. But all along, our plan had been that after the catalogue raisonné of Motherwell's paintings and collages was published, we would expand our programs in the domains of educational exhibitions and arts education, areas with which Motherwell was deeply engaged during most of his life. And instead of just giving money to organizations that applied for it, we would become more proactive in term of the kinds of programs we really wanted to focus on.

Coincidentally, about a year ago, just when we were looking for ways to expand our educational and curatorial outreach, a space at Industry City, in the Sunset Park area of Brooklyn, became available. Having this space allowed us to expand our educational programs in a number of ways. For example, in addition to the award of a $20,000 stipend for graduate MFA Fellows, we were now able to give the Fellows free studio space. Initially, the stipend for the MFA Fellowships had been meant to help the Fellows pay their studio rent. Now we were able to provide free studio space in addition to the stipend. The results were impressive, and last year we were able for the first time to exhibit their works at the end of the Fellowship period.

LW: It was the artist's wish to dedicate the Foundation not only to his work, but also to modern art and modernism conceived in the broadest possible way. Was this wide purpose given to you by Motherwell a burden or a gift of freedom?

JF: It gave us freedom. Or perhaps more accurately, it opened possibilities. And that was very exciting. Motherwell was not only interested in the visual arts, but also in poetry, dance, and music. For example, a few years ago, the Robert Motherwell Book Award was given to a scholar for a book on T. S. Eliot's *The Wasteland*, and a recent Senior Fellowship went to a scholar writing a book on Dmitri Shostakovich's string quartets.

As you know, in the United States there have been severe cutbacks in funding for education in the arts. In response to these cuts, we have greatly expanded our art education programs for young people, from art classes for kindergarten children to art and art history scholarships for graduating high school seniors. In particular, we are trying to establish a kind of dialogue between the students and those aspects of modernism that were so dear to Motherwell: the idea of modernism as a manifestation of an independence of mind and freedom of action that could be explored and expressed by art. When we started out, our main goal was to serve the arts community in the United States as a whole. We continue to do that today, but we now have given a greater emphasis on the education of the very young, and for the time being at least our main focus is more local. Today, we would characterize our main goal as wanting to change people's lives for the better through art. And we find that the best way to do so is to work with young people. In some cases, this is a continuation of our past programs. For example, we are giving scholarships to a dozen graduating seniors in New York City public high schools, and this is a program that has been going on for sixteen or seventeen years now. (We stay in touch with many of them and it has been very gratifying to see how well they are doing; some of them have become artists, some of them are teachers—seeing the fruit of the program is very exciting.) Having the space at Industry City has also allowed us to develop new kinds of programs, which introduce modern art and modernism—and art itself—to a broad range of people, from elementary school children to adult learners. This broadening of our perspective has been very exciting and rewarding for all of us at the Foundation, as well as for the people we serve.

The Foundation offers a broad spectrum of education and grant programs to support and assist art students, graduates, and curators. Each year, it also awards the Robert Motherwell Book Award for publications in the fields of the "history and criticism of modernism in the arts," and an Exhibition Catalogue Award as a distinction for outstanding exhibition publications. In recent years, the Dedalus Foundation has also supported numerous exhibitions, among others in the following museums: the Denver Art Museum; the Los Angeles County Museum of Art; the Modern Art Museum of Fort Worth; the Menil Collection; the Montclair Art Museum; the Solomon R. Guggenheim Museum; Japan Society; the Rubin Museum of Art; the National Academy; and the Jewish Museum.

LW: What have been the greatest challenges in expanding the Foundation's programs?

JF: To be honest, we didn't realize at the beginning the degree to which we would become involved in what are now are dynamic educational programs. In particular, the exhibition *Come Together: Surviving Sandy, Year 1* (2013) was a very ambitious project that generated an enormous amount of energy (it is memorialized on the website: cometogethersandy.com). After the show opened, we thought it could provide a forum for all sorts of other educational programs: poetry readings, dance performances, symposia about conservation, oral history sessions with artists who had been severely hit by the storm, and educational programs for school children. This was a turning point in broadening our programs. At the beginning you want to serve the art community, then there comes a moment when you begin to look outside and realize there is a great amount to be done in educating the public about modern art, especially in the United States, where there tends to be very little government support for arts education. So we started doing after-school programs last year, as well as programs within schools, and programs for adult learners. More recently, we've become interested in professional development in art and art history for public school teachers. Our concern about young people's understanding and reception of modern art is very much an extension of Motherwell's own concerns, which he wrote about several times.

LW: Coming back to Motherwell's oeuvre, how do you see the role of a catalogue raisonné for an artist's estate?

JF: I think it is extremely important for a number of reasons. First of all, it establishes the oeuvre. When the artist has had a broad historical impact and a firm presence in the market, as with Motherwell, you have to be especially cautious about fakes. When we started to work on the catalogue raisonné, we wanted to make sure that only authentic works by the artist would be represented. But we also quickly became aware of the ways in which a catalogue raisonné gives you the opportunity to interpret an artist's work, in ways that the artist himself might not have conceived. Because a catalogue raisonné includes everything the artist has done, it inherently holds within it a vast array of interpretive possibilities, simply because everything is there and fully documented. In the Motherwell catalogue, we did not emphasize the interpretation of individual works, but rather provided a point of departure for future writing about him and his work.

In 2012, after ten years of preparation, the three-volume catalogue raisonné *Robert Motherwell Paintings and Collages: A Catalogue Raisonné 1941–1991*, edited by Jack Flam, Katy Rogers, and Tim Clifford, was published in three volumes and comprises around 2,800 of Motherwell's works. The publication also contains essays on key themes in his oeuvre, such as the charged relationship between figuration and abstraction. The Foundation is currently preparing the catalogue raisonné of his drawings.

LW: When did you start working on Motherwell's catalogue raisonné?
JF: We started to work on the catalogue raisonné in 2001–02, ten years after Motherwell's death. For the next ten years, the catalogue raisonné was our main project, until it was published in 2012. At one time we had as many as seven full-time researchers.

LW: Were there files and documents that Motherwell had already prepared during his lifetime? What have been your main challenges in the context of the catalogue raisonné?
JF: Motherwell started to keep track of his work only in 1977, when an inventory system was created for the works in his studio, which was eventually extended to all of his works that could be located, in anticipation of a catalogue raisonné. As a result, some of his oeuvre was well documented, and some required a good deal of work to track down, document, and photograph. Especially in European collections, we had to track down a lot of undocumented works. We tried to see every work we knew of, and also the back of every work we could, especially the paintings, where there were often meaningful inscriptions on the versos. As we progressed, we photographed all the works and gathered all the documentation we could find about them. This allowed us to set up an archive in which there was a file for every work, in which there were photocopies of everything that had been written about that work, along with any relevant visual materials.

In order to track down undocumented works, we placed advertisements in general publications and most especially in the main art magazines. On our website there was a list of works that had not been located yet. We were also helped by our colleagues at other artists' foundations, who helped us track down works. Colleagues who were working on their own catalogues raisonnés, or who were going just to look at works, would come across a Motherwell at the home of a collector and would let us know about it. For example, if someone was going to look at a Richard Diebenkorn and came across a Motherwell, that person would call us and tell us what they saw so we could check to see if we had it in our files.

The catalogue raisonné of Motherwell's paintings and collages was published in 2012. Every six months we're doing an online supplement with new works we have discovered. The book has roughly three thousand works in it. It includes paintings on canvas and panel, paintings on paper, and collages. Since publication in the fall of 2012, we've found around a dozen works that were not in the book that we did not know about.

The first volume contains an overview of Motherwell's work. It contains essays by Katy Rogers and me, about Motherwell's life and artistic development, and a very detailed chronology, which was researched and written by Tim Clifford, as well as a bibliography and exhibition history. The second volume is the catalogue raisonné of the paintings on canvas and panel, and the third volume is the catalogue raisonné of the paintings on paper and collages.

LW: More and more artist foundations in the United States have withdrawn from the field of authentication and have closed their authentication committees. What is your view on that?

JF: I strongly believe in the necessity of giving opinions about authenticity, either through an authentication committee or through a catalogue raisonné. These are the two main ways of protecting the integrity of an artist's oeuvre: the authentication board and the catalogue raisonné. I believe that any foundation, part of whose purpose is to educate the public about a particular artist, has an obligation to take an active role in establishing the integrity of that artist's work. It is important to distinguish the real from the fake, because fakes undermine the integrity of an artist's work. And if one remains passive about fakes, they tend to proliferate. So doing nothing often unintentionally becomes a way of aiding and abetting fraud. The reason many foundations and estates avoid giving opinions is fear of being sued for defamation of property. In the United States, if you bring a painting to me and I say it doesn't look like an authentic work by that artist, you can say that I am defaming your property and sue me. In fact, I don't think anyone has ever won such a lawsuit, but defending yourself against such a lawsuit can be very expensive, so it scares people away from giving opinions about authenticity.

In the process of doing the catalogue raisonné, we had some vivid authentication issues. A highly public dispute arose in 2009 between the art dealers Marc Blondeau and Julian Weissman, who had formerly been associated with the Knoedler Gallery, and our Foundation. Blondeau had bought a work attributed to Motherwell entitled *Spanish Elegy*, dated 1953, from Weissman. Between 2007 and 2009 we firmly established that that painting and half a dozen related paintings were fakes, which resulted in a lawsuit. On the visual evidence, we believed that these paintings were fakes. And early in 2009, when we were allowed to see the forensic analysis of some of the paintings, it became incontrovertibly clear to us that a whole group of supposed Motherwell *Elegies* were fake.

By the time the lawsuit was settled two years later, in October 2011, additional evidence had come forth and we were able to have one of the works stamped as a forgery. (The bulk of the forgeries had been channeled through Weissman and the Knoedler Gallery, which closed its doors in the fall of 2010.)

LW: And how long did you have to hold back the information that you knew those paintings were not authentic?
JF: It's complicated, but basically from the time we strongly suspected that the paintings weren't real to the time that we were able to act publically was about a year and a half. It was a difficult time for us, but we wanted to make sure that we could forensically test at least some of the paintings in order to scientifically back up our strong suspicions. When the forensic tests were done, it turned out that certain parts of those paintings (binders and pigments) had not yet been invented at the time they were supposed to have been painted.

The way we are organized is that we have a Scientific Committee that meets twice a year, which examines all work submitted to us. We examine the works and decide if they're going to be included in the online supplement of the catalogue raisonné.

LW: How do you deal with the legal risk of continuing to give opinions?
JF: We have only been sued once on that score. When a work is submitted to us, we tell the person who submits it that there are three possible responses: that it is going be added to the catalogue raisonné, that it is not going to be added to the catalogue raisonné, or that we are not sure.

LW: Are you being successful with your efforts in helping other foundations gain awareness about the significance of authentication activities?
JF: We are being heard, which is a form of success. But whether we are actually being successful is more questionable. We are, however, having an effect. For example, I think that we were instrumental in provoking the new legislation that's being proposed now in the New York State Legislature.

In 2013, the New York City Bar Association's Art Law Committee presented a proposal for a change to the current legislation on the authentication of artworks. From this resulted a draft law that foresees that only individuals who have no financial interest are authorized to authenticate artworks.[2] This means that individuals who might, for instance, benefit from the sale of the artworks are excluded per se from providing expert opinions on authenticity. The draft legislation is currently before the New York State Assembly.

LW: The longer an artist has been deceased the more important it becomes to keep the academic and also the artistic dialogue about that artist going. How do you manage this?
JF: Because Motherwell was at the center of Abstract Expressionism—or as he preferred to call it, the New York School—he is usually placed in that context. But the artists associated with that movement worked in various ways, and Motherwell's oeuvre is especially rich in its range and variety. So one of our missions has been to make the breadth and depth of his oeuvre better known. We are actively working with museums to that end. In 2013–14 the Guggenheim Museum had a beautiful show of early Motherwell collages, both in Venice and New York. And in 2014 there was an exhibition at Guild Hall, in East Hampton, of paintings that Motherwell did between 1944 and 1951, when he was based in East Hampton. These marvelous early works were not widely known, and the exhibitions expanded people's notions about the range of Motherwell's art. Both shows, I should add, were inspired by the publication of the catalogue raisonné.

LW: How did you find the right balance between gift and purchase?
JF: Our aim was to place the works in the museums where we wanted them to be, so we gave those museums substantial discounts from fair market value. At the beginning, we had thought about giving works away, but we needed money for our programs, and we also realized that when you give things away they are valued less. If there is some skin in the game, it works better for everybody. So we had a gift/purchase program, which worked out very well for everyone. In fact, over the long run, the museums that participated in it have come out very well in terms of past cost to current value.

LW: And how do you finance the activities of the Foundation?
JF: Our annual budget is around $3.5 million, which we finance through sales and the investments of the endowment. Motherwell left a large body of work to

the Foundation when he died—all of his works that were still in his possession—and the Foundation not only got all of the works of art that he owned, but it also inherited his moral rights.

At the beginning, our emphasis was on placing works in museums with this gift/purchase arrangement. Now, we sell as little as possible and as much as necessary.

LW: Do you have a set of galleries you work with?
JF: We do not have an exclusive dealer. We work with several different galleries in the United States and Europe. So there is not an exclusive representation by one gallery. Motherwell liked the idea of having more freedom, not being tied down. The works that are for sale are chosen by members of the board who are very familiar with Motherwell's work.

LW: How many people are currently sitting on your board?
JF: At the moment we are seven.

Before Motherwell died he had named to the board of his foundation his financial advisor, Richard Rubin; his wife, Renate Ponsold; and me. Richard Rubin was President and CEO from 1991 until 2002, when I succeeded him as President. Motherwell also stipulated other people who would be named to the board upon his death. Most of those board members were people from the art world. Motherwell did not want any family members sitting on the board because he felt that he wanted professional people and he thought that having family members would also complicate things legally to some degree because they could become conflicted, or be considered what are known as "disqualified persons." His wife was the exception. As it turned out, she stayed on the board for only about six or seven years.

Among the people Motherwell named to the board upon his death were Dore Ashton, a professor of art history at the Cooper Union; John Elderfield, then Director of the Department of Drawings at the Museum of Modern Art; Lynn Kearney, an arts administrator in Chicago, who was a neighbor of the Motherwells in Provincetown; and David Rosand, a professor of art history at Columbia University.

---

2 See Nicholas O'Donnell, "Proposed Amendment to New York Arts and Cultural Affairs Law Would Protect Authenticators," in *Art Law Report* (April 30, 2014), http://www.artlawreport.com/2014/04/30/proposed-amendment-to-new-york-arts-and-cultural-affairs-law-would-protect-authenticators/ (accessed December 17, 2015).

The original board members were close to Motherwell during his lifetime, and are all within a certain age range. As some of those original board members have left or died, we have subsequently added new members: Pamela Auchincloss, a curator and art advisor; Steven Howard, an attorney; Katy Rogers, who is one of the co-authors of the catalogue raisonné of Motherwell's paintings and collages; and Morgan Spangle, who is our Executive Director.

LW: How would you describe the ideal board structure for an artist's estate?
JF: That is a difficult question to answer, as the circumstances vary depending on the artist. I think that you need a combination of people who are knowledgeable in different domains. It is good to have some members who are knowledgeable about the artist and the work, and who will endeavor to keep the idea of the artist's intentions foremost. One thing that you must deal with after the artist is dead is that you are not the artist. So while you will always try to act in terms of what you understand to be the artist's intentions and goals, you won't always be able to act in exactly the same way as the artist would have. The circumstances change, and the very fact that the artist is no longer alive to some degree alters the context in which decisions are made. This is something that can be hard at the beginning, especially if you were personally close to the artist, as I was with Motherwell.

You often start by saying: What would he have done? But after a while you realize that this is not the question. The question becomes more: What would be in the spirit of what he would be doing if he were alive now? Not what the historical Motherwell would have done twenty-five years ago, but what he might be doing now.

LW: What is your opinion about sunset versus perpetuity models for an artist estate?
JF: That's a very interesting question. The easy answer is that for some foundations it's wise to have a sunset clause, while others should go on indefinitely. The main factors are the nature of the financial resources, the nature of the oeuvre, and the kind of ambition that the foundation has, what it wants to accomplish. Sometimes, if a foundation has limited resources and its sole purpose is to promote the artist's work, they can fulfill their mission within twenty years after the artist's death. They can do a catalogue raisonné, promote exhibitions, place groups of works in collections that will enhance the artist's reputation, and then they can in good conscience say "mission accomplished" and walk away from it. For foundations that have fuller resources and larger ambitions I think the idea

of going on indefinitely is really good. For the Dedalus Foundation, I think that our programs are such that we can continue to do beneficial things in the world for a very long time. And we have planned ahead to ensure that we will have the financial resources to do so.

LW: What advice would you give living artists when they think about setting up an estate or a foundation themselves?

JF: For the artist, it's important to have someone to manage the studio that will keep good records and keep track of the work. And to set up an artist's foundation, the most important things are to get a good lawyer who is familiar with foundation law; get a good accountant; and get a good archivist, someone who can really organize things. Carefully consider the Board; they will be running things once you are gone. State your goals for the Foundation, acknowledging that, over time, circumstances will change.

I would also say: Don't throw things away. Don't even throw away cans or tubes of paint, they can become very handy down the road—as aids in documentation, in conservation, and even with regard to dealing with questions of authenticity.

Christy MacLear
Robert Rauschenberg Foundation

Robert Rauschenberg (1925–2008) was—as a painter, photographer, and object artist—one of the most important American artists of the twentieth century. He is considered as a forerunner of Pop Art, experimenting with materials and techniques and dissolving boundaries between styles. Objects from everyday life were integrated in the *Combine Paintings*, to which the icons of art history *Door* (1954) and *Bed* (1955) belong. Transcending genres, he collaborated with the musician John Cage and the ballet choreographer Merce Cunningham and established the association E.A.T. (Experiments in Art and Technology).

The Rauschenberg Foundation is one of the largest nonprofit artist's foundations in the United States and keeps Rauschenberg's work and philosophy of life, "art can change the world," alive. It initiates exhibitions at home and abroad and promotes interdisciplinary exchange between art and society as well as environmental protection by means of numerous grants for young artists, scholars, and institutions. Since 2012, the foundation has awarded 350 grants of up to $150,000 each.[1] In 2016, the Rauschenberg Foundation was the very first large nonprofit foundation to relax how it handles copyrights on the works of the artist and to facilitate license-free use of images for museums and educational institutions. The foundation's headquarters are situated in Rauschenberg's former studio on Lafayette Street in New York City. Since 2010, the former business manager of Philip Johnson's Glass House in New Canaan, Connecticut, Christy MacLear, has managed the Rauschenberg Foundation.

Loretta Würtenberger: How did the Rauschenberg Foundation evolve?
Christy MacLear: Robert Rauschenberg set up the Foundation that bears his name in 1990. This was only one instrument he used toward his philanthropic endeavors, others including the creation of an emergency fund for artists (Change Inc.), creating posters and prints for global issues, and even the fusion of art and international peace-keeping in his ROCI work.

After Rauschenberg's death, his will stipulated that all assets, after distributions, would go to the Foundation. Now, the Foundation manages all of Rauschenberg's artwork (which he had held), a philanthropic program within the values system of his life, and a residency we have in his former home and studio in Captiva, Florida.

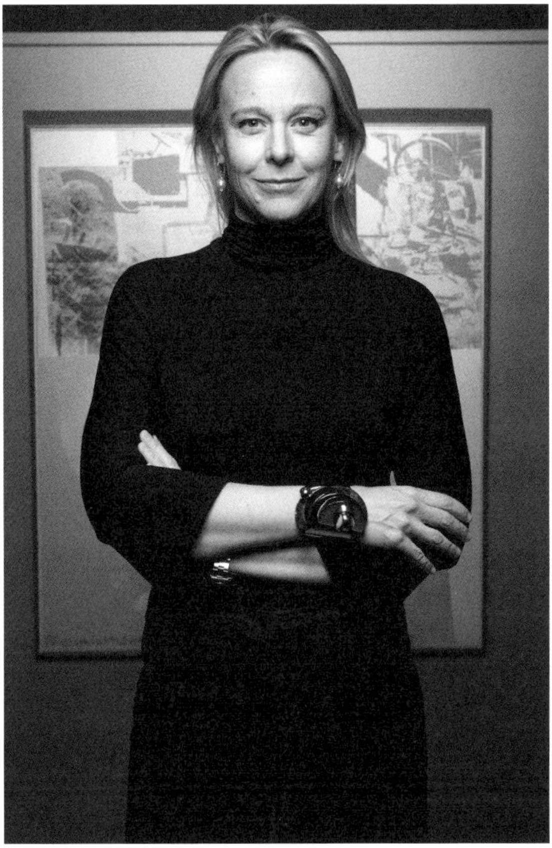

Christy MacLear

LW: How did you use the time before the assets were transferred to the Foundation? After Rauschenberg's death, it took four years to dissolve the estate trust and to transfer the assets to a foundation.

CM: To move from an estate trust with volunteer staff, with few assets, to one of the largest foundations, given the transfer of his estate, required a great deal of advance planning. I would characterize the work we did in advance in three areas: mission and vision focus, organizational preparation, and defining pilot projects.

One of the key elements for a foundation is to define the mission statement. This can be done in a very generic way (i.e., "to foster the legacy of the artist")

1 http://www.artnews.com/2014/03/26/how-rauschenberg-foundation-is-bridging-the-gap-between-art-life/ (accessed March 14, 2016).

or a very strategic way (i.e., "to provide support for projects which foster the legacy of the artist with a lens toward risk taking, collaboration and creative problem-solving"). It is important while the people who knew the artist best can help define the characteristics of the artist—allowing stewards in the future to make decisions 100 years from now.

The second area of business was to have the organization prepared to receive the assets. This included systems for the artist's staff to transfer to the foundation, such as payroll, insurance, budgets. We were transitioning the staff that had formerly worked with the artist to the Foundation. Not all staff would have a job in the new organization—as we no longer produced art—but we worked to ensure the long-standing knowledge of the work's production and curatorial expertise.

The final area was determining our strategic program—viewing our assets against our mission/vision to set a course. So for example—knowing we had the asset of his home and studio compound in Captiva, Florida, we considered all options for this asset—sale, a residency, or other programs. We defined a slate of pilots to test each idea—so, in the case of Captiva, launched a soft residency program to determine its use and impact. We did this across all of our assets. We had some grant programs, a pilot residency, used a warehouse in Chelsea as a project space, and had programs to circulate the Rauschenberg art. From that slate of pilots we were able to ascertain what worked, what mattered, where we could have impact or foster our mission best. That has been the focus of the early years.

LW: Another challenge was, and is, the building up of the foundation assets. To assist you with this, you opted for three galleries instead of one. What were the reasons for this decision?

CM: When the Trustees of the Estate managed the assets, they chose to work with Gagosian Gallery. This was a good choice—obviously an excellent gallery—and has a global reach with a centralized management. So this simplified the job of stewarding and transitioning assets to the Foundation.

After the art transferred to the Foundation we had several key needs: first to continue the exhibition schedule set by the gallery and second to sell the non-Rauschenberg work. The latter tactic was important to create an appropriate cash balance to our asset base. To sell the non-Rauschenberg work we worked with many galleries—Gagosian, David Zwirner, Matthew Marks, Dominique Levy, approximately twelve or so galleries. Selling this work created the base of our endowment, which helps us operate.

Once we had worked through the committed shows and diversified our assets we turned to look at our gallery model. RRF had the staff leadership and capability to manage multiple galleries, which we believed would serve a global audience in a very targeted way. So we chose a new course where gallerists with very deep geographic expertise could be tapped. They also had to be willing to take a long-term view of sales, which is more important to a Foundation (non-profit) than a gallery (for profit). We chose three galleries—Pace, Thaddeus Ropac, and Luisa Strina—to have deeper coverage in Asia, South America, and Europe as well as America.

LW: And are you the one managing the gallery relationships?
CM: We have someone who is with us now and works specifically on these gallery relationships.

LW: Coming from the art world?
CM: Yes. It really helps to line up the motivational structures. It comes down to building a legacy over time versus sales in the short term.

LW: Are you also involved in the secondary market?
CM: We are less involved in the secondary market but watch it closely. With all estates and foundations after the death of the artist there is a relaxing of prices. We see that it takes ten or so years for the prices to rise to levels that relate to the historic importance of the artist. So we, as a Foundation, watch the pricing at auctions relative to our documented private sale pricing. Private sale pricing is higher. That delta is important and narrowing but Rauschenberg is so important in art history, we are pleased to see curators and museums buying the work evidence of that role. We monitor, with the galleries, what is on the market, to ensure pricing, ownership (for the future catalogue raisonné), and even presentation.

LW: Are you planning an authentication committee?
CM: No. We don't actually have a problem with authentication, so we are fortunate that way. We are working on the planning for the catalogue raisonné, which will be an important part of the scholarship and assist any authentication inquiries.

LW: What are you going to do with Rauschenberg's archive?
CM: We wanted to keep the archive versus donating the archive.

LW: Why?

CM: The archive is the foundation for our curatorial activities, future scholarship, and the catalogue raisonné. We are fortunate enough to have legacy staff that was with Rauschenberg during his lifetime who can both organize and interpret the many items in the archive. This will be housed in our New York headquarters and be accessible to all scholars and researchers. We are also fortunate enough to be surrounded by a half dozen major universities (NYU, Cooper Union, SVA and others) so having the archive available to students and programs that draw them in will enliven scholarship and use.

LW: And my experience is that keeping the archive can be a good catalyst for the exchange between estates and academic researchers. You get insight into the processes of their work and not only into the results.

CM: Keeping the archives—processing them and making them available—is a considerable expense. Some artist foundations may find it more economical and have better reach/use if they sell or donate the archive. It's an important consideration about reach, use, and cost.

LW: Do you use social media to communicate the Foundation's activities?

CM: We have a strong effort in digital and social media. As a baseline we have made a significant investment in our website. Our intention is to have the framework for the digital version of a catalogue raisonné, so all artwork, images, and information would be accessible online. Beyond the website we do use most social media platforms but have found the most effective to be Instagram and Facebook. Additionally we have an e-news brief sent monthly to our subscribers and work with media to ensure our projects are covered, all to communicate our activities.

LW: You were talking about the catalogue raisonné. How long do you envision for it to be completed, and how many people have you staffed on this project?

CM: We have been working on the preparation for the catalogue raisonné for three years. We have built the website, been processing the archives, and are having the initial discussions about our approach. We will be doing both a print and a digital version and we believe this effort, once started, will take well over ten years.

LW: Had Robert Rauschenberg kept his estate in order? Did he make it easy for you to prepare?

CM: Yes, the Foundation received marvelous artwork records, but I won't actually attribute it to the artist but rather to the staff he hired. He had an assistant in Captiva who kept every letter; he had a registrar and a curator in New York who kept every exhibition note. He had a collections manager who had barcoded every single work of art to facilitate the move of the artwork into our storage facility. So the records we have are really remarkable.

LW: Coming to your board structure: I saw that there are family members, there are friends, and there are professionals. Did Rauschenberg himself envision the board's structure? Are you happy with the combination of family and third party people?

CM: When I started my position the board composition had a high degree of conflicts. There were staff members on the board, the estate trustees on the board, and then additional (less conflicted) board members. During his lifetime, Bob had chosen these people to serve on the board who helped facilitate the decisions he made. Once an artist dies, and it is no longer artist-lead decision-making, there are legal reasons why these conflicts of interest must be addressed.

We worked to move the staff off of the board first. Then we moved to have the Trustees of the Estate move off so they could focus on their job of transitioning the assets. Finally, we worked to build the board to have a well-rounded composition of skills and diverse experiences toward our mission. We have nine members of our board presently and believe we will be growing to approximately twelve over time, which remains a small but workable number to set strategic direction.

LW: Ideally, which skills and abilities should your board members bring to the table?

CM: We have a number of key roles which our board should fulfill: understanding of Rauschenberg, knowledge of the art through scholarship or the market, understanding of foundations and grant-making, financial planning experience, and experience and knowledge in the issues we provide grants in.

LW: How many committees do you have?

CM: We have core committees in Art, Philanthropy, Residency, Finance, which are flanked by some organizational committees: Nominating and Governance, and Audit. Beyond that we form task forces to deal with specific efforts that require focus but will expire based on a project—that included Estate Termination and Artist Rights.

LW: How often do they meet?
CM: The core committees meet at least four times per year—maybe more. The other committees (for example the Audit committee) may only meet once per year.

LW: Are they compensated for their activities?
CM: The board is not compensated. We do pay for their travel and hotel for board meetings and provide them with a discretionary grant to give to one or several organizations of their choice. This is our way of thanking them for their service but also putting philanthropy at the core of what we do.

LW: So they choose somebody who will benefit from the grant?
CM: Yes, but it has to be within the ethos of the Rauschenberg Foundation's value system. This helps ensure we are all involved in philanthropy and understanding the lens of our mission.

LW: Absolutely. That's great. Switching topics, what were your lessons learned after the lawsuit?
CM: We learned many lessons from the Estate Termination process. The most important lesson is for artists to put a cap on the Trustee fees. They can stipulate the maximum amount that a Trustee can make in stewarding the assets as per the will. The second lesson is that putting friends in charge may not always be the best course of action. I would recommend having a small team consisting of professionals and knowledgeable advisors. Friends, although well intentioned, may not have the skills and may, immediately after the death, be hard pressed to make decisions that involve change. That is not always the case, but a balance is important.

LW: Did Rauschenberg also leave instructions for the management structure of the estate? Was he explicit about his family being involved or not involved?
CM: No, he wasn't explicit about that at all. His son is our board chair and has all of the best intentions for the Foundation.

LW: It sounds like you have accomplished a great deal of all the relevant issues in a very short term. What are the next the challenges you are facing now?
CM: One of the less obvious challenges is financial planning. There is a need to address the tension between building long-term capital reserves (an endowment) versus art sales. Having a sense of your program helps define the ongoing annual

financial need and thus the endowment size required to operate in perpetuity. We have built a model that considers a slow and appropriate pace of art sales to allow for the building of an endowment over time. This helps move us from reactive to proactive, less hopeful and more planned. It also helps us focus on the work and how placement in key collections builds access as well as value over a long period of time.

LW: How do you do that?
CM: We are focused on access to the work (exhibitions and loans); gallery shows which create depth of understanding; and scholarship. Our programs are focused on these elements. Some example programs that accomplish this include our gift purchase program (to place works in museums in the first year we received the art) to our college art loan and grant program (to remove the barriers to great art being at our colleges and their companion scholarship introduction to students).

LW: What would be the one piece of advice, if an artist would come to you and ask you from your retrospective, post mortem work with an artist's legacy.
CM: I have led the start of a couple of estates now. One of the big questions people ask me is how much should the artist define the direction? It's very valuable to have latitude, but equally, if not more valuable, to have a sense of direction. It's exceptionally helpful if the artist can define the topics/issues/subjects that were critical to them and allow for the fluctuation of that over time. Rauschenberg was very open in terms of his interests, when faced with materials to define the direction of the foundation he checked every single box on the tax form: education, environment, AIDS medical research, etc. etc. It was almost too much, as if he wanted to be everything. So in this case we had to prioritize our focus based on our resources. Additionally, you have to assume that things will transform. So being too definitive is not good and won't allow for changes over long periods of time to adjust. With that in mind, one important criterion an artist can establish is whether the foundation is to operate in perpetuity or end at a certain point in time. This type of mandate impacts many strategic decisions and would be most helpful from the founders perspective, who has a sense of mortality versus those who come after and may have a desire for immortality.

LW: And what way are you going?
CM: The Rauschenberg Foundation is planning to operate in perpetuity. This decision requires in-depth financial discussions, scales our operating horizons, and adapts our sales or placement strategy on a very long timeline.

LW: And you still believe that there should be a cause for the foundation in 200 years?

CM: I believe so. Great artists legacies extend beyond 200 years ... and the issues that we can support may evolve but Rauschenberg can always be a part of those as a benefactor.

Rainer Judd
Judd Foundation

Rainer Judd heads the Judd Foundation in New York as its Co-President along with her brother, Flavin. She spent the majority of her childhood in Marfa, Texas, where Donald Judd (1928–1994) took up residence in the nineteen-seventies and set up his studio in the middle of the desert landscape, far away from the art establishment. He created many of his *Specific Objects*—three-dimensional, minimalist objects that cannot be assigned to the genre of either of painting or of sculpture—as well as other outdoor sculptures of aluminum and concrete on the around 25,000-hectare-large property. Judd had set up another studio in a former factory building at 101 Spring Street in SoHo, New York, which, following a longer renovation, has been open for visitors once again since 2013. Rainer and Flavin Judd were involved in their father's artistic work from an early age and assumed responsibility for his estate at the age of twenty-three and twenty-six, respectively. The siblings are among the founding members of the Judd Foundation and were on the Foundation's Board of Directors for seven years before becoming its Co-Presidents in 2013.

The Judd Foundation was established two years after Donald Judd's death as a nonprofit foundation according to American law with the aim of preserving Judd's living and working spaces as well as all of the artworks he installed in them. Judd exhibited his works in Marfa and New York along with works by contemporary artists, the majority of them friends of his, and designed many of the pieces of furniture himself. Today, the Foundation manages sixteen properties in New York and Marfa comprising a total of 12,000 square meters of exhibition space. To finance the preservation of the estate and the renovation of Judd's studio New York, in May 2006 the Judd Foundation auctioned off thirty-six selected works by Donald Judd through Christie's auction house in New York, realizing revenue of around twenty-eight million dollars.[1] Today, the building at 101 Spring Street is used as a visitor's center and exhibition venue. Another focus of the work of the Foundation is preparing a catalogue raisonné of Judd's works, which is being accompanied by a six-member expert committee. The members of the Board of the Foundation are currently Robert C. Beyer, Dudley Del Balso, Fairfax Dorn, Carl Ryan, Louisa Stude Sarofim, and Ellen Salpeter.

Loretta Würtenberger: How specific was your father about the way he wanted his legacy to be preserved?

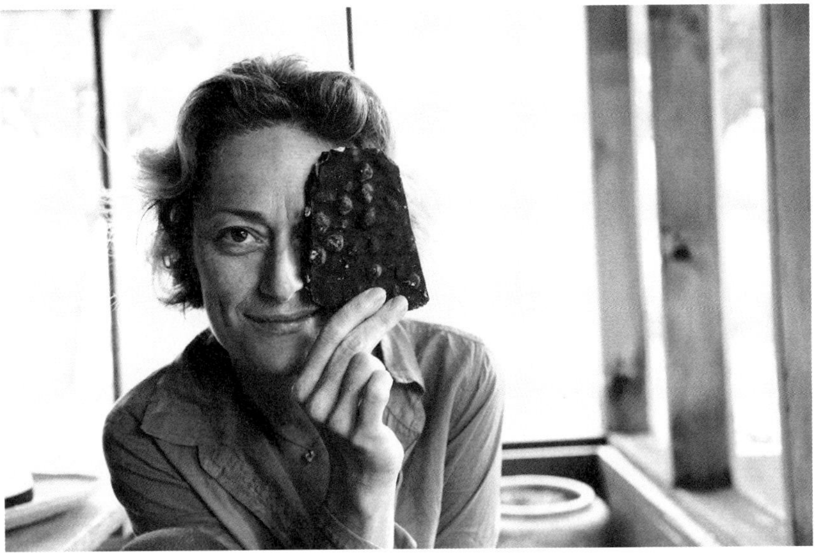

Rainer Judd

Rainer Judd: He was very specific in saying what he wanted. He wrote his first will in 1977. There he explicitly wrote about a "Donald Judd Foundation." But whether such a foundation was possible or how it might be achieved was not something he addressed in the will. The "how" of his dreams—that was something we had to deal with when he was no longer living.

> "Too often, I believe, the meaning of a work of art is lost as a result of a thoughtless or unsuitable placement of the work for display. The installation of my own work, for example, as well as that of others, is contemporary with its creation, and the space surrounding the work is crucial to it. Frequently as much thought has gone into the placement of a piece as into the piece itself. Accordingly, it is my hope that such of my works of art which I own at the time of my death are installed at 101 Spring Street in New York City, or in Marfa, Texas, will be preserved where they are installed."[2]
> —Excerpt from the Last Will and Testament of Donald Judd, 1991

1 Andrew Russeth, "Rainer and Flavin Judd Will Serve as Co-Presidents of Judd Foundation," in *The Observer* (October 26, 2012), http://observer.com/2012/10/rainer-and-flavin-judd-will-serve-as-co-presidents-of-judd-foundation/ (accessed December 18, 2015).

2 Last Will and Testament of Donald C. Judd, December 10, 1991.

LW: Did he give any guidelines?

RJ: The will speaks about the installed spaces. It was my father's wish to leave the spaces as he made them. That is the priority of the Foundation, to keep the spaces, and his art in the spaces where he placed them. Both his private living and working spaces in Marfa, Texas, as well as the New York residence and studio at 101 Spring Street.

LW: Was it clear right from the start for you that you and your brother would be so intensely involved and that you would be responsible for your father's estate?

RJ: We were both listed as executors since we were young, but there was no way for us to know what it would be like. I know it wasn't absolutely necessary that I, or both of us, stepped up the way we did, but sometimes life is like that. It was like things were aligned this way—in a way that we had been emotionally and educationally primed for. There is something about being Donald Judd's kids. There was nothing else we could do, except doing the right thing, for him and his world.

LW: When you became a trustee of the Foundation, was it clear what legal structure and organizational structure the Foundation was supposed to have?

RJ: Yes, there are very clear legal guidelines for administering an estate. For an estate you have to do an inventory, you have to pay estate tax, you have to go through all personal things.

The estate was created in 1994, and we created Judd Foundation in 1996 as an entity because according to the will a "Judd Foundation" was to be the beneficiary of the estate. According to the US guidelines for an estate you cannot give anything to the beneficiaries until all bills are paid, and we had bills for years. So it wasn't until 2000 that some assets could be transferred to the Foundation, a process that lasted until 2002. The whole estate now is part of the Foundation.

LW: Next to your brother and you, the Foundation's Board consists of six other members, how did you choose them?

RJ: We still talk about that to this day. We sometimes choose Board members in a non-traditional way and sometimes we choose them in a traditional way. We recently added Carl Ryan to the Board. Carl is a lawyer who worked with our Dad and was actually involved with the original estate and worked both with Marianne Stockebrand, my brother, and me. And he also knows a lot of land issues, as he owns a ranch in Texas. There is also Louisa Stude Sarofim, who is Chairman of the Menil Collection in Houston, and she took over the role of being a mentor. Dudley Del Balso is currently sitting on the Board, who worked with our Dad for years and was part of the original catalogue raisonné team. I think the unconventional way, is that we are interested in people who knew our Dad. It's not always about how much money they can give to the organization, but the expertise and insight they can give in a specific area.

My brother and I are what is called "lifetime trustees," I think that was written by our Dad. So we are the two Board members that have no re-election terms. Everybody else gets voted on. I was executrix at the age of twenty-three, so I've asked people for advice. I remember in the first year I went around to Paula Cooper and I saw a lot of people who had known my Dad and tried get advice on how to do things.

LW: What are the key success factors for leading a foundation together with other family members?

RJ: Although my brother and I couldn't be more different, we love each other and that makes a difference. We are also unified by both the love of our Dad and the love for his work. Our Board has become more sensitive over time to our involvement and our needs and what we want to do. They have done an incredible job of trying to understand who we are and what kind of involvement we are looking for. But if I can think of any good advice for siblings it would be: "Don't do things out of guilt. Do it out of inspiration."

In the Foundation, Flavin Judd, who works as an architect, designer, and writer, is mainly responsible for exhibitions with works by Judd and for preserving the buildings technically, while his sister launched an oral history project that has been being realized since 2007. The project documents statements by Judd's friends, colleagues, neighbors, and art dealers (for instance, Julie Finch, a choreographer and Judd's former wife, the gallerist Paula Cooper, and the artists Brice Marden and Lawrence Weiner), which tell of working together and encounters with Donald Judd—therefore giving rise to an impressive portrait of the artist. In addition to her work for the Judd Foundation, Rainer Judd works as a filmmaker, actor, and artist.

LW: Looking at the Foundation today, what are the most important tasks that you are currently engaged with?

RJ: The Foundation still has monetary goals and needs. If we didn't have monetary needs maybe I would be more involved with the Oral History Project. As a creative person I am very driven to understand ideas and words and Don's writings that were grounded in ideas of the sixties. There is still so much more I can learn.

LW: What memory comes to your mind when you think of your father today?
RJ: I have a very complex, multi-faceted person in my mind and heart. I often feel that other people have this snap shot of him that is ... very one-dimensional. It would be nice if a more nuanced take on him as an artist developed. That is what I want to work on.

LW: Which parts of his will were the most difficult to fulfill?
RJ: Cash flow was the most difficult for the first twelve years. I'd also say that the ranch land in Marfa had something to do with that because we had very large ranch payments and that was challenging for our cash flow. It took us many years to find a person to buy the land who would treat it well.

At the moment we are still doing a lot of work on the financial side. It's definitely interesting to think about what an artist foundation can do that hasn't been done before to create revenue. We have this beautiful building in Marfa that's an old hotel with a U-shape with twenty-eight rooms that we are interested in renovating and installing prints in, Don's prints, chronologically in a way he intended to install them.

LW: Is there one success in the past twenty years you are especially proud of?
RJ: There are a few things, definitely creating an endowment.

I was really proud because, after Don's death, we were pushed around since we were young and were told that we needed to sell 101 Spring Street. We were told that there was no way we could find the money to restore it. But we were stubborn and we didn't sell it and in 2013 we finished the restoration and opened 101 Spring Street to the public with an expanded public visit program. I'm very proud of that.

LW: How did you manage to finance all these projects, especially the preservation of Judd's living and working spaces in Marfa, Texas, and New York?
RJ: The breakthrough came, thanks to our Board, with a single art sale at Christie's in 2006 that was used to create an endowment. Since we have an endowment we can have a consistent operating budget. The costs for the restoration of 101 Spring Street were higher than expected so we are trying to reduce the operating

costs of the building and also to increase our income from other revenues, including visits in New York and Marfa, special events, and furniture. We are currently creating a system of special events for 101 Spring Street and reviewing the business plan for Judd Furniture. We also started a Patron program with multiple levels that allow people to engage with Don's spaces, and the Foundation, in different ways.

The abovementioned auction of Judd's works at Christie's made it possible to cover the costs of renovating the building at 101 Spring Street, which came to a total of twenty-three million dollars.[3] The Foundation is moreover responsible for maintaining the other properties, and in 2010 made the initial capital for the catalogue raisonné available—an extensive project that completely revises the first catalogue of works of 1975, covering his paintings and objects (edited by Dudley Del Balso, Brydon Smith, and Roberta Smith). For the project, the Foundation has had a new catalogue raisonné database developed, which documents all relevant information on Judd's artworks.

LW: Who decides on the sale of works? Is it you and your brother or is it the whole Board?

RJ: The whole Board. That's one of the decisions we must make unanimously. We have a few other things that are unanimous, such as making any changes in the installed spaces.

LW: You are currently represented by David Zwirner and Kukje Gallery; How do you collaborate with the galleries?

RJ: The galleries benefit a lot from my brother's understanding of how the work is intended to be shown. They are not involved in most issues related to the Foundation. We do not involve them with programming or any aspects of our visit programs in New York and Marfa. On the other hand they are extremely helpful with PR and marketing.

In comparison to when I was younger, there are very few galleries these days that are sensitive enough and truly fulfill the task of being educational entities.

---

3 "Donald Judd's Newly Restored Building at 101 Spring Street To Open in June 2013," Judd Foundation press release, http://hostedp0.vresp.com/1291741/598c58826a/ARCHIVE (accessed January 16, 2013, via www.juddfoundation.org).

Business/money making is only one aspect of a gallery. Nowadays the speed and size of some of the galleries is not conducive to quiet reflection. Whereas the environment in Don's permanently installed spaces allows room to think as well as imparting the sense of the studio, art, discussions, and philosophy of that time. It's like the difference between the city and the country. But it's also good, on the other hand, that so much money is being spent.

LW: How do you work with museums?
RJ: We are different than a lot of artist foundations because we are not here to loan works. Our mission is to take care of the works that are installed and to make them available to the public. And Don wasn't even that interested in the public ... but because we are a Foundation we need to be interested in the public.

LW: Are you actively collaborating with any museums?
RJ: We are lending works to DIA. We know which institutions have something coming up and we are very welcoming and helpful to scholars and curators coming from those institutions. But we haven't initiated museum exhibitions in the last few years.

LW: Had your Dad archived all of his work during his lifetime?
RJ: Dudley Del Balso, who sits on the Board today, the curator Brydon Smith, and Judd's former assistant, Roberta Smith, were organizing his writings. Dudley and other assistants kept very good fabrication records as well as correspondence with dealers and related records.

LW: Some parts of your archive are open for the public and others are kept closed. How do you differentiate those two parts?
RJ: The parts of the archive that remain closed are areas that have yet to be organized. Most of the archive is available including large portions of Don's published and unpublished writings, correspondence, photographs, gallery files, fabricator files, publications, exhibition ephemera, and family records. There will always be a small portion of the archive that will remain closed, such as Don's personal letters. Our staff is working to make the archive as accessible as possible.

In 2010, Judd's library was made accessible over the Foundation's homepage. Specially developed software makes it possible to know the titles and locations of the books—as the artist organized them himself. As an enthusiastic reader, Judd was fascinated not only by the content of books, their memory, but also by their object character. The library comprises around 13,000 books in over forty languages and offers a rich spectrum of knowledge about Judd and all aspects of his artistic work.

LW: You have digitalized your library. Are you thinking of digitizing the archive?
RJ: I am a little wary of digitization. Our main focus is on preserving and making accessible our analog archives as best we can. Undertaking large-scale digitization projects and maintaining that information for the long-term is really expensive.

LW: Are there any posthumous editions of Donald Judd's works?
RJ: The only things that are in edition are prints and a small amount of three-dimensional pieces. The only thing we reproduce is furniture.

LW: Are you involved in the authentication processes?
RJ: No. We consult people and provide information about their pieces, if available. The catalogue raisonné committee does a lot of outreach with collectors. But we don't authenticate, the legal risk is too high.

LW: What advice would you give other artist's children who have to administer estates?
RJ: Get a second opinion. For example, if an art dealer is saying, I give you this for that, just go and get a second opinion. Because even if you have known the person all your life and they fed you baby food, they're still a business person, and you as well should become a business person and get a second opinion. I would definitely recommend consulting with outside experts while not listening to others too carefully. I think lawyers should always be listened to with suspicion, logic, and reason. Lawyers as well as many institutional consultants are applying prescribed systems onto an artist foundation and they don't realize that artists have their own prescribed systems. There is often a gap of comprehension.

Barry Rosen
Eva Hesse Estate

Barry Rosen has been advising artists' estates for many years and is an outstanding specialist in this field. The estates that he looks after include those of Eva Hesse, Allan Kaprow, Lee Lozano, and Dieter Roth; he also works with the living artists Ida Applebroog and Dale Chihuly.

The Guggenheim Museum held *Eva Hesse: A Memorial Exhibition* in 1972, two years after the artist's death. In 1977 Rosen began working for her oeuvre. At the time, he was working at the Droll/Kolbert Gallery in New York, which Hesse's sister Helen Hesse Charash had asked to support her in working with the estate. A lot has happened since then—from the first show with Eva Hesse's work in the Droll/ Kolbert Gallery, to the organizing of her written estate, to the publishing of meanwhile two catalogues raisonnés (paintings and sculpture / the catalogue raisonné of drawings will be published in 2016) and providing the stimulus for diverse publications. Rosen initially considered one of the central tasks to be improving the inadequate documentation on Hesse, since, at the beginning of his work for her estate, there was only one monograph on the artist from 1976, in which works were misdated and dimensions and materials were labeled incorrectly. In 1979 followed the well-regarded exhibition *Eva Hesse: Sculpture* (Whitechapel Art Gallery, London; Rijksmuseum Kröller-Müller, Otterlo; and Kestnergesellschaft, Hannover), and since then, the artist's oeuvre has been presented in more than fifty-seven museum and gallery exhibitions around the world.

Rosen understood at an early point that estates have different priorities than museums and galleries. He sees his work as keeping the oeuvres of deceased artists alive, in particular through creating new perspectives on their work and the bringing together of curators and work with museums. This becomes exemplarily clear in his support for the performance work of Allan Kaprow: "It's very important to continue presenting these performances. Otherwise, his work will be completely forgotten."[1] Kaprow's happening *Fluids* was recently brought to life again in September 2015 in cooperation with the Nationalgalerie in Berlin.

Loretta Würtenberger: In your view, what is the single greatest challenge faced by artists' estates?

Barry Rosen: Clarifying the legacy. Encouraging focused exhibitions, building a context for advanced and continuing scholarly inquiry.

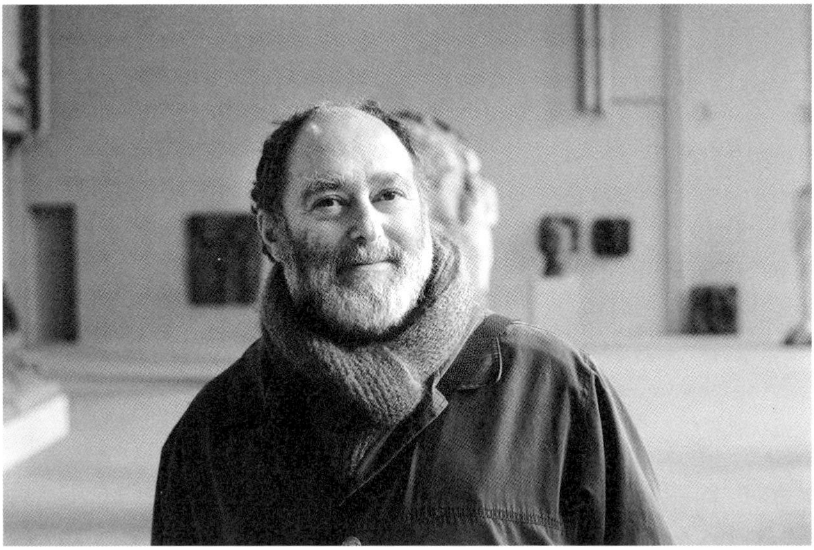

Barry Rosen

LW: Does the foundation form fulfill the practical needs of most artists' estates? Is a trust more flexible?

BR: In the United States, foundations are a very specific form, with very specific management responsibilities and fiscal duties. Foundations must have Trustees, are registered and must report annually to federal tax authorities (IRS) such things as current value of assets and annual spend down against value—or face a hefty fine. The works of art are owned by the foundation, not the heirs and are thereafter unavailable to family/heirs for personal use or personal financial gain.

A trust, as used here (US) is primarily understood as a vehicle for protecting assets and passing on assets, or the income generated, to heirs. As such, trusts behave much the same as individuals or corporations. They are free to generate income, and to spend it—within the by-laws established by the grantor. In this way beneficiaries have direct responsibility and benefits.

LW: Whole estates, or large bodies of works, given to existing public museums: good or bad?

1 Barry Rosen, cited in "Der Mann im Hintergrund," in *Monopol*, June 23, 2009, http://www.monopol-magazin.de/der-mann-im-hintergrund (accessed December 22, 2015).

BR: In most cases, large donations given to institutions without accompanying funds to support the very specialized work needed to support the legacy of that artist, become a burden on the museum; worse still, the artist and the works are basically unavailable, and so forgotten. (Scott Burton, Edward Hopper, Landshoff).

LW: How is it best to ensure continuity and longevity and focus?

BR: I very much feel that it is important to involve the family.

The story of Eva Hesse and her sister is a beautiful example of how a family member can play an important role in securing the legacy of an artist.

Famously, Hesse was just thirty-four at the end of her life in 1970. While close with her sister Helen, their worlds were distinct and separate: Hesse a brilliant artist active at the very hub of the then contemporary cultural whirl: Helen a professional woman with suburban family and two children.

Mrs. Charash inherited the full body of Hesse's work still in the studio. She also inherited, and very actively took on, a responsibility to Hesse's own ambitions for her work, and, significantly, a commitment to establishing an enduring legacy and scholarly discourse.

Her mentor in this, Donald Droll, the artist's dealer and dedicated friend, led the way by securing a major *Memorial Exhibition,* organized by the Guggenheim Museum in New York in 1972. This traveling show and accompanying catalogue with essays by Robert Pincus-Witten and Linda Shearer, curator of the exhibition, set the standard for Hesse museum exhibitions and scholarship. With all her major works on view for the first time, essays in the fully illustrated catalogue initiated a discourse around Hesse's art that went beyond that in the popular press of her lifetime.

In a program of support, including donations of works and gifts (of money), Helen enabled museums to acquire major Hesse works.

Supported by her share of a sale of several important Hesse sculptures to Victor Ganz in 1972, the Estate went on to commission and eventually publish, Lucy Lippard's ground breaking Feminist monograph, *Eva Hesse* (1976).

The *Memorial Exhibition* was followed several years later by a Whitechapel exhibition, *Eva Hesse: Sculpture,* (with a Continental tour) organized by Nicholas Serota in 1979. The catalogue's writer, Rosalind Krauss, continued and expanded on earlier writing about the artist's work.

A drawing exhibition, *Eva Hesse: A Retrospective of the Drawings,* curated by the legendary Ellen Johnson at Oberlin College led to the establishment of a study collection of Hesse's papers and the by-then famous diaries at Oberlin's

Allen Memorial Art Museum in 1982. Nearly 200 drawings are now included in the collection there.

During these first years Donald tutored Helen in how best to engage the art world, also in how best to support the growing world of scholars interested in Eva Hesse.

Around 1984 Donald retired from the New York art world and soon died, in 1985. Since, then Helen and I have worked together to navigate a rapidly growing, and very different, cultural landscape.

Unlike common practice today, the Estate of Eva Hesse has never asked for a photography or copyright fee for scholarly publications, nor fees of any sort from exhibition organizers.

Michael Ward Stout
Robert Mapplethorpe Foundation

In 1988, around ten months prior to his death, Robert Mapplethorpe (1946–1989) established a nonprofit foundation to protect his work and to support projects that were personally important to him. The artist was already suffering from AIDS at this point in time, but simultaneously found himself at the highpoint of his career: the Whitney Museum of American Art in New York dedicated a first extensive retrospective to him in May 1988, showing a broad overview of his portrait photographs and series of homoerotic images. Mapplethorpe died in 1989. In 1993, the Mapplethorpe Foundation made its first extensive museum donation, to the Solomon R. Guggenheim Museum, New York, therefore making it possible to set up the Robert Mapplethorpe Gallery and establish a new photo department. In 2011, the Foundation handed over Mapplethorpe's archive, including, in particular, early works such as Polaroids and over 200 drawings, collages, and assemblages to the Getty Research Institute in Los Angeles. The Mapplethorpe Foundation also administrates the copyrights for Mapplethorpe's works. It has supported numerous exhibitions and publications on contemporary photography, such as, most recently, exhibitions at the Tate Modern, London, at the Grand Palais, Paris, the J. Paul Getty Museum, Los Angeles, the Los Angeles County Museum of Art, as well as at the NRW-Forum in Düsseldorf or C/O Berlin. Since its establishment, the Mapplethorpe Foundation has supported medical research in the fight against HIV/AIDS and awarded grants totaling millions of dollars for research at universities and for the establishment of medical facilities including the Robert Mapplethorpe Laboratory for AIDS Research at Harvard Medical School in Boston, the Robert Mapplethorpe AIDS Treatment Center at Beth Israel Medical Center in New York, and the Robert Mapplethorpe Center for HIV Research at St. Vincent's Hospital and Medical Center in New York.

Michael Ward Stout was a close friend of Robert Mapplethorpe and today is president of the Robert Mapplethorpe Foundation. The artist portrayed him in his typical photographic style in 1986. Stout had already specialized in art and copyright at an early point in his career as attorney and represented numerous artists, such as the renowned Surrealist Salvador Dalí, as well as art organizations, authors, and photographers. Besides his work for the Mapplethorpe Foundation, he is also a member of the board of the Photography Committees of the Whitney Museum of American Art and the Solomon R. Guggenheim Museum, New York. He is also

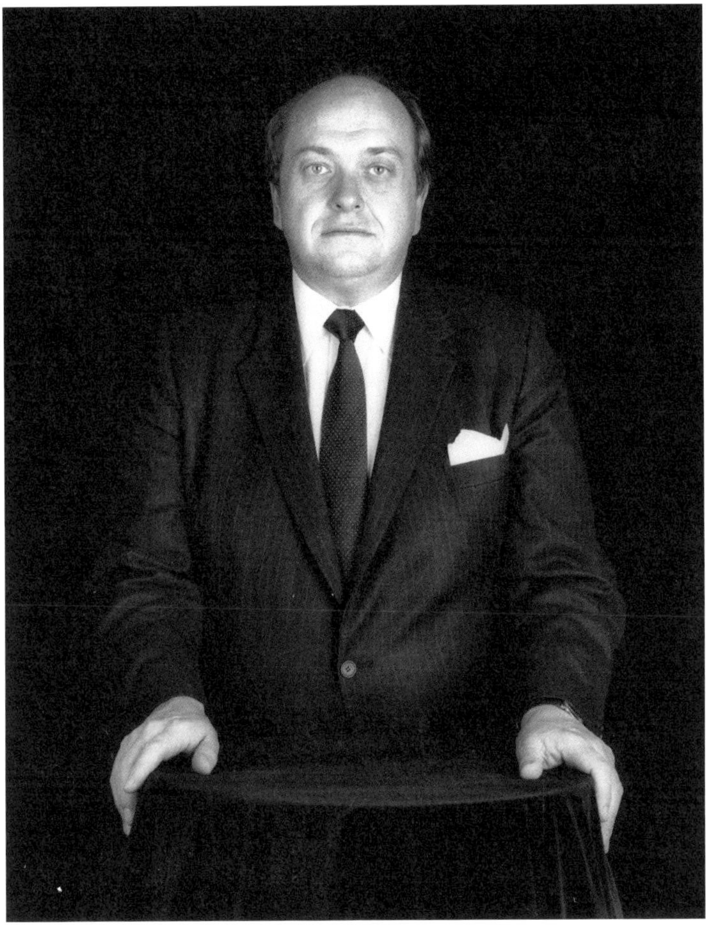

Michael Ward Stout

a member of the Library Council of the Museum of Modern Art, New York, and of the Board of Governors of the Center for Curatorial Studies at Bard College in Annandale-on-Hudson. He is, moreover, actively engaged in fundraising for the fight against AIDS and HIV infections and was a member of the Board of Directors of the American Foundation for AIDS Research for seven years.

The Board of the Mapplethorpe Foundation, which has its headquarters in New York, besides Michael Ward Stout, currently consists of the attorneys Burton G. Lipsky and Eric R. Johnson, Mapplethorpe's former assistant Dimitri Levas, and the photographer Stewart Shining.

Loretta Würtenberger: What was Mapplethorpe's motivation to set up a foundation?

Michael Ward Stout: I was Mapplethorpe's lifetime lawyer and we had the tragic luxury of discussing the details of his legacy, since he knew he was dying—even though he hoped he wouldn't die. Originally, the Foundation was tax motivated, but it was also motivated by his sharp business mind, and his determination to shape his own legacy. He was not motivated to leave any artworks or money to his family. Only during the very last two days of his life did he decide to leave one artwork to each family member, and $100,000 to one brother.

LW: How did Mapplethorpe choose the board of directors and which role did each member have?

MWS: He chose me because I was his lifetime lawyer and I knew a lot about his business, as well as about the commercial aspects of the art world. I had been an artists' lawyer for many years. He then chose a friend, Lynn Davis, who is a fine art photographer and was the closet person to him who knew the most about the photography world. It was clear to him that he was leaving the bulk of his estate to his Foundation in order to promote photography at the institutional level. She knew a lot about the museum collections in the United States and in Europe, and that interested him since he wanted his work to be in museums. Robert also chose Dimitri Levas who had worked side-by-side with him in the studio. He was the person who selected the flowers, provided the vases, and advised him on the frames. He shared Robert's aesthetic and he knew Robert's individual works better than any of us, each picture, each model, and the history of most. He was also a close friend.

Then Robert thought that if he were to die and I would be making financial decisions, I could be out-voted by the other two who were not as informed in the business world as much as I. Robert had a considerable inheritance from Sam Wagstaff, his long-term close friend and patron. For that reason he added Burton Lipsky, another lawyer, who was a tax specialist who helped make the structure of the Foundation. I find it very important that an artist make wise decisions about the board of directors. It's good if one has the opportunity to decide these important matters while alive. It is also important to compose a board of professionals—instead of a board of family members or other people emotionally close to the artist. They are often not qualified to run a foundation professionally.

LW: What advice would you give a living artist who wants to set up a board?

MWS: I think you need to have a lawyer on the board of a charitable foundation because you have to strictly observe the compliance rules established by the federal tax department and also those required by the New York State (or any other state) Attorney General's Office. There are very strict rules that affect, for example, self-dealing, meaning if you have a conflict of interest and you are a member of a board, that's very tricky if there are only family members on the board, who often own works themselves, while making financial and other decisions about the works owned by a foundation.

If you choose only your friends and family members as board members it's all very emotional. Mapplethorpe was very clever; each one of us had a professional role. His were not emotional choices. Family members can be involved but certainly should not have a majority vote. They are often resentful when all of what is left has gone to an organization and doubly resentful when people who are strangers to them are making decisions. One must remind family members that the estate has received a great tax deal. Hundreds of millions of dollars in many cases—as in the Mapplethorpe and some other artist-funded foundations—have passed to the organization without any death or estate tax. If everything had been left to the family, or other private individuals, the inheritance tax rates would apply, which, in the United States, are as high as sixty percent. Therefore, the artist's legacy would be bruised or maybe ruined because the art would have to be sold to pay the taxes, in the United States, within nine months of the date of death (subject to certain limited extensions).

Families typically do not have that kind of sophistication, they would not necessarily know all the rules a lawyer would know, about conflicts of interests, about what family members can do, about spending by a foundation, about expenses. These artist-funded foundations are actually running businesses. It's not like inheriting a portfolio of stocks and bonds and a bank account, an apartment and a country house, where an executor can sell everything and then start a foundation with a simple investment portfolio. When you are dealing with copyrights and intellectual property, which exists for seventy years beyond the date of death, and you are dealing with complex relationships with curators and museums, with collectors and the art market—these are the reasons why you need an experienced art business lawyer as a voting member of a board.

LW: From which other fields should the professionals on the board come?

MWS: They should come from inside the studio, preferably someone the artist has worked with, the painter's assistant, or a museum curator. Gallery owners are difficult because of the tax laws, which make the dealer a disqualified person because they are in a position to affect prices or the value of a foundation's assets

LW: The Mapplethorpe Foundation has existed for twenty-seven years. How has your role changed during those years? And what are the great challenges for the future?

MWS: There are challenges. Right after Mapplethorpe died, we, the board members, had thought that we would make the placement of the artworks a fifteen or twenty-year project. We were not interested in perpetuating or promoting our own positions. We wanted to handle the artworks and the legacy as carefully as possible and promote the artist by publishing books intelligently, mounting exhibitions at strategic venues, and making sales and gifts to museums in particular. We thought that would take fifteen or twenty years and then we would go out of business.

The challenge for us now is: How do we eventually wind down the business of the Foundation? We still have significant inventory, which could keep the Foundation going for another twenty or more years. We have made enormous gifts. For example, in 1993 we made a major gift to the Guggenheim Museum. It was a collection of approximately 200 pieces of the artist's best works, plus $2,000,000, a significant sum twenty-two years ago. We have made significant gifts to the Whitney Museum, and to museums in Europe (the Louisiana in Denmark, the Tate in London, the National Galleries of Scotland) and the Foundation gave artworks appraised at $38,000,000 to the J. Paul Getty Trust and Los Angeles County Museum of Art, a joint venture. Today, many unique early works are gone, but we still have many left.

LW: Could you tell me more about the structure of a gift / purchase combination to a museum?

MWS: It depends on the institution. For example, take our agreement with the J. Paul Getty Museum; in the nineties we worried about going out of business without having found a home for our tailored collection together with our archives, including negatives and contact sheets. We had tried to keep back one print of every image plus some unique works for this purpose. We spent fifteen years exploring the best home, including the Museum of Fine Arts in Houston, the Center for Creative Photography in Tucson, Arizona, the Boston Museum of Fine Arts, the Henry Ransom Center at the University of Texas, and finally chose the Getty Research Institute (GRI) and Getty Museum, together with the Los Angeles County Museum of Art (LACMA).

It's better equipped and it has more scholar access than any other museum. The Getty does not regularly exhibit contemporary art and is not specialized in twentieth-century photography, but, after the joint venture with LACMA, one creates a fantastic package.

After we made the gift arrangement with the Getty and LACMA, their directors and curators came back to us and asked for some very special things that were not included in the gift. We had held back many special things for our day-to-day business around the world. It's a very complicated inventory management system. However, we agreed that they could buy some unique or rare works on favorable terms, totaling three million dollars. The Guggenheim was a total gift; the National Galleries of Scotland now in its joint venture with the Tate Modern was part purchase, part gift. Again they wanted some works we weren't eager to give so we required a purchase.

LW: How do you deal with the remaining inventory?
MWS: We have decided against working with only one or two galleries because our needs are greater. We need several sale exhibitions per year. No single gallery could handle that. We need the income to support our grant making.

LW: Which decision did Mapplethorpe make about posthumous editions of his work?
MWS: Mapplethorpe discussed with us the fact that he wanted no posthumous editions but he did want us to finish the lifetime editions, which he authorized when he selected the first print of an image to be printed. In many cases he had printed six out of ten or five out of fifteen pictures (or whatever the edition total was) and we completed those editions beginning immediately after he died using his personal printer. We didn't sell any posthumous prints until 2006 because we didn't want to. It was the transaction with the Tate Modern and National Galleries of Scotland where they would not have proceeded with the project unless they could have eleven key images, which we could only supply by including posthumous prints, however, authorized by the artist.

I believe that as a charity our mission must be to expand and enhance the value of the Foundation's assets by earning money to support our charitable mandates. I think the world has changed with respect to the meaning of vintage and posthumous, and we should probably change with it. But I am not prepared to do that with Mapplethorpe's works. I think I would be the only one on the board making the argument, because the other board members are quite attached to what the artist said, what the artist wanted. Of course the artist I knew was very interested in monetizing his creations so when he saw that an image would also work in color he would print in color. If he thought it would work in platinum he would do that. We should never make those decisions. We only filled out the incomplete editions, exactly as envisioned by the artist and each print is clearly marked to indicate the date of printing. Who among us could decide which image looks better in color or in black-and-white? No one. Our sales indicate there is no difference in price between lifetime and posthumous prints. Collectors are buying beautiful images, and that is how it should be.

The Mapplethorpe Foundation conducts authentications of Mapplethorpe's works several times a year. Works whose authenticity is supposed to be confirmed can be submitted to the Foundation for examination. According to the Mapplethorpe Foundation's website, the fees for such an expert opinion come to $ 200.[1]

LW: If a living artist who wants to set up a foundation would come to you, what advice would you give to him or her?
MWS: Create the foundation while you are alive and form the board and have regular meetings. Observe how people behave while you are alive. Do not populate the board with family members and loved ones. Depending on the size of the board make sure that you have a majority in the hands of professionals. Of course it is fine to have a family representative but too many boards have too many family members and friends. It has been written about as the "entourage effect."

LW: What is your view about galleries that are representing artist estates?
MWS: My general view would be that it is not a good thing if a gallery or dealer is the executor or sole representative. Whether a foundation exists or not, there is certainly self-dealing that happens. Some galleries are very professional, and some not. There is, for example, the famous nineteen-seventies case of Rothko and the Marlborough Gallery.

---

1 http://www.mapplethorpe.org (accessed December 17, 2015).

Gisela Capitain
Martin Kippenberger Estate

The gallerist Gisela Capitain has been managing the estate of Martin Kippenberger (1953–1997) since the artist's death. She first met Kippenberger in Berlin in 1977 and was present at the founding of Kippenberger's office, a project space for exhibitions, readings, and concerts, in 1978. When they met, Kippenberger was twenty-four and Capitain twenty-five. A close, trusting relationship developed from their shared beginnings in the art scene. For Capitain, this was her introduction to contemporary art and to the life of an artist, as she says in retrospect,[1] and in her, Kippenberger found important support in managing and marketing his work. In 1983, Capitain moved from Berlin to Cologne and worked as an assistant at Max Hetzler. In 1986, she established her own gallery, which has since then represented artists such as Karla Black, Wade Guyton, Charline von Heyl, Zoe Leonard, Stephen Prina, Monika Sosnowska, and Christopher Williams. Her gallery has been the exclusive representative of Kippenberger's work since 1992. Their twenty-year friendship forms the basis for her work with Kippenberger's estate.

Martin Kippenberger was known for his intense lifestyle and way of working. In his lifetime, he sometimes realized more than a dozen exhibitions per year. Until his early death at the age of forty-four, he created a multifaceted and extensive oeuvre, comprising paintings, sculptures, installations, drawings, photographs, prints, posters, artist's books, and other publications as well as performances. His participation in the Documenta X in Kassel and Skulptur Projekte Münster made a substantial contribution to Kippenberger's great success in 1997. His daughter, Helena Hirsch, was born in 1989. In 1996, one year before his death, he married the Austrian photographer Elfie Semotan.

Gisela Capitain manages Kippenberger's estate in the spirit of the artist himself as an active platform for exhibition projects, scholarly research, and the development of an extensive archive. In 2014, Capitain published the first of four volumes of *Martin Kippenberger. Werkverzeichnis der Gemälde* (Martin Kippenberger: Catalogue Raisonné of the Paintings) in cooperation with Lisa Franzen and Regina Fiorito. Her gallery also manages the artist's copyrights.

Loretta Würtenberger: How did you get to know Martin Kippenberger? What was your cooperation like at the beginning?

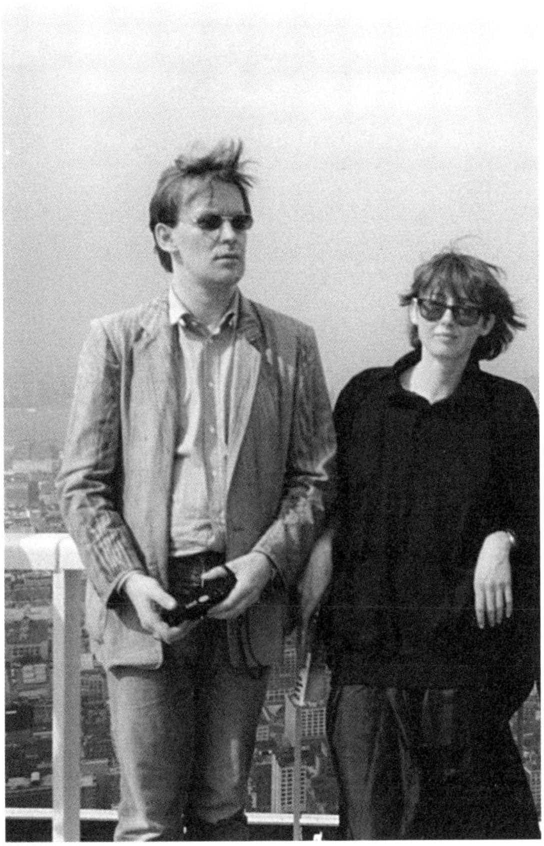

Martin Kippenberger and Gisela Capitain

Gisela Capitain: I met Martin Kippenberger in 1977. He established his office in Berlin in 1978, and at that point I began regulating his private affairs such as taxes, health insurance, accounting and banking matters for him. It wasn't that much work, but, as in the case of many artists, it was all managed quite chaotically. There was also still a small inheritance from his mother that had to be managed.

LW: How old were you when you got to know him?

GC: When we met, Martin was twenty-four and I was twenty-five. After the shared years at Kippenberger's office in Berlin, in 1980, he started his nomadic

1 "Interview mit Gisela Capitain," in *Vogue*, 8 (October 2013); http://www.vogue.de/people-kultur/kultur-tipps/kunst-interview-mit-gisela-capitain.

moving around from one place to another: from the Black Forest to Stuttgart to Cologne, in between Vienna, from Carmona in Andalusia to Madrid, later to Frankfurt; afterward Venice Beach in Los Angeles, back to Frankfurt again and then again the Black Forest. The last couple of years, he lived in Vienna or in the Burgenland in Austria. During this time, I was always his contact point for all his business affairs.

I was therefore also involved during the final months of his serious illness in Vienna. It was about a will, his sisters, final instructions. At that point, however, Kippenberger no longer still had enough energy to make fundamental decisions.

LW: Had you had an opportunity to speak with him about his estate beforehand?

GC: No. That wasn't an issue for him, although he was already hit quite severely by his cancer in the final two years before his death. He didn't want an exact diagnosis from a doctor, or medical treatment. He knew he had cancer, but wanted to approach the situation quite differently and used all his energy to spend half a year in Tokyo and to organize his last monographic exhibitions: a big retrospective at the Musée d'art moderne et contemporain in Geneva, another at the Museum Abteiberg Mönchengladbach as well as a smaller exhibition in Zurich.

After Kippenberger's death, his oldest sister and I were responsible for dealing with the formalities. Along with an attorney and an accounting office, we did our best to find a solution that was clear in terms of civil and tax law for his heirs, his wife, Elfriede Kippenberger-Kocherscheidt (Elfie Semotan), and his daughter, Helena Hirsch, who was represented by her mother at the time. His daughter wasn't even seven years old when he died in 1997.

LW: The two of them formed the testate succession.

GC: That's right. Everyone involved wanted a starting situation for the estate that was non-bureaucratic and constructive in the spirit of Kippenberger. We agreed to bring all the works together at one location. For various reasons, in the last few years, everything's come to be concentrated in Cologne: the storage space with the artworks, the archive including personal documents, my gallery, which, since 1992, has been exclusively managing all of this, including all the ongoing exhibition projects. Everything was managed and steered from here, and Cologne therefore became the central location for Martin Kippenberger's estate.

Kippenberger was denied long-term success during his lifetime. After his death, the prices for his works at auction increased, and the demand for exhibitions of his work grew. In 2003, one of Kippenberger's main works was exhibited posthumously in the German Pavilion at the Venice Biennale. In 2006, the artist received his first big retrospective at Tate Modern, London, and at the Kunstsammlung Nordrhein-Westfalen in Düsseldorf. Other important exhibitions were presented at the Museum moderner Kunst Stiftung Ludwig in Vienna and at the Van Abbemuseum in Eindhoven (2003/04), the Museum of Contemporary Art in Los Angeles, and the Museum of Modern Art in New York (2008/09) as well as at Hamburger Bahnhof–Museum für Gegenwart in Berlin (2013).

LW: At the time of Kippenberger's death the market value of his pictures was nowhere near as high as today. Has anything changed as a result?

GC: In 1994, in connection with a very important monographic exhibition in Rotterdam, there was a moment when we hoped that more recognition would come. Kippenberger had already been successful with a specific idea of painting in the mid-nineteen-eighties and acquired a particular reputation for himself due to his radical and provocative position at the time. In 1987, however, he turned away from painting and occupied himself with a completely new concept of sculpture. The consequence of that was a first slump in his career, which also ran parallel to the crisis in the art market at the end of the eighties and in the early nineties.

For this extensive exhibition at the Boijmans van Beuningen Museum in Rotterdam in 1994, Kippenberger created a very multilayered and extremely complex installation over more than two intensive years of work, *The Happy End of Franz Kafka's 'Amerika.'* That was *the* decisive exhibition for him, but without a happy end, and the continuing lack of success was a serious blow to him. He then began painting again, developed series of paintings, of which some works were purchased, but only for a fraction of what they would sell for today. It was then Catherine David's invitation to the Documenta X and Kasper König's for the Skulptur Projekte in Münster—both in 1997—that were decisive for him. It then became clear that he as an artist was and would remain an important and influential figure.

LW: At the beginning, an estate is naturally also a burden for the heirs, financially as well as emotionally. How did your role in managing the estate come about?

GC: My role resulted from the circumstances described and from the trusting relationship between the heirs and me. I was the only person who had an overview and was able to grasp all the things that had to be done. I was in the middle of things and was also able to take on the added new management work without a problem. That's why the two heirs asked me whether or not I wanted to take care of things. What was crucial was that everything was supposed to proceed in the spirit of Kippenberger. In one of his interviews, you can find him clearly stating that his work should continue being shown, whatever the case.

LW: How has your relationship to Kippenberger's estate changed until today?
GC: Until today, the relationship is based on very personal relationships to the heirs. In parallel, however, it's important to analyze and represent the interests of the estate on a purely objective and neutral level. There's always the danger of taking certain things too personally when the artist is directly involved, especially in the case of an individual as controversially discussed as Kippenberger.

There's a special responsibility with respect to the heirs and the work of the artist. It's possible to be very successful in developing an estate, and this success can be represented in figures. With growing success, however, expectations increase on both sides, for the heirs and collectors. The work is, however, accompanied by such a mass of bureaucratic and organizational details that you're are always brought down to earth again, to mediating the art.

Our aim is to support the assertions that Kippenberger made with his work and maintain their significance in the future. This task represents a much bigger challenge than the purely administrative work. The four volumes of the catalogue raisonné of the paintings, which we've been working on for six years, are one example of this. The first volume was published in the fall of last year.

LW: What's a central assertion for you?
GC: The fact that Martin Kippenberger is one of the most important and influential artists of his generation internationally.

LW: How would Martin Kippenberger have dealt with his estate himself? Would he be satisfied with how his estate is being managed today?
GC: What could I hope for more than that he would find what we are doing and how we are doing it good? The question of how he himself would have tried to organize his estate is nearly impossible to answer. I only know one thing: in contrast to popular opinion, he would have organized it conservatively, in a traditional art-historical way without jokes or gags. That became clear to me through

an experience with Kippenberger in connection with a group exhibition at the Kunsthalle Basel. The walls in the big exhibition space were clad with wooden panels of around 120 centimeters in height, and the curator proposed hanging Kippenberger's works around twenty centimeters above the edge of the panel with the lower edges all the same, as if all the pictures were standing invisibly on a rail. Kippenberger categorically rejected the suggestion and wanted the pictures to hang classically in the center. Therefore, as he had seen as a child at the Folkwang Museum in Essen, when he and his sisters were challenged by their father to find the best picture in the collection, and were then rewarded for doing so.

LW: How did you finance your work and the development of the archive at the beginning?

GC: We decided to only sell very little in the first years. An exhibition at my gallery in Cologne in 1997, which was already planned before he died, showed Kippenberger's *Medusa* complex of works of 1996, which consists of paintings, drawings, and lithographs. The only works offered for sale were the prints, to cover the first costs that were accruing. The estate tax was manageable.

Both heirs, based on their respective family situation, decided in advance not to establish a foundation. For a short period of time, there was the question of whether a public law foundation, perhaps connected with a German museum, might be of interest. The decision not to go down that path, however, was also related to the relationship of museums to Kippenberger's art and to him as an individual during his lifetime. Apart from a very few exceptions, he was neither recognized nor supported by institutions in Germany, and largely ignored by the general public.

LW: There is also a middle ground between establishing a foundation and managing an artist's estate privately. For example, you've taken on major tasks in publishing Kippenberger's catalogue raisonné and also supporting research on his work through his archive for nearly twenty years after his death. Not everybody had the desire to go a step further and, for instance, award grants as a foundation or support local art institutions.

GC: That's also how I understood my task and I've received a lot of support in realizing it from the heirs. Kippenberger was an extreme artistic personality, someone who presented himself publicly in such a provocative way as hardly anyone else had done. That shouldn't be disguised by the concept of a foundation. Establishing a foundation would also have blocked all kinds of projects and exhibitions that were brought to us shortly after his death.

After successful exhibitions internationally at Tate Modern in London and the Museum of Modern Art in New York, Kippenberger's works realized top prices in the art market. Among others, the renowned painting *Paris Bar* (1993) was sold at Christie's auction house in London for 2.7 million Euros in 2009.[2] A self-portrait of the artist *Ohne Titel* (Untitled), 1988 was sold at Christie's for over eighteen million Euros in 2014.[3]

LW: Do you still jointly decide on the sale of works today? Or has this changed in the past twenty years?
GC: Nothing has changed. We've reached a consensus on all sales from the very beginning, with the exception of the most marginal things such as the sale of posters or catalogues. Since our intention was to sell only a few works very selectively, weighing and agreeing on decisions together doesn't require that much work.

LW: There's surely also still a large body of work, isn't there?
GC: Many groups of works were already sold very successfully during Kippenberger's lifetime and are therefore no longer held by the estate. But of particular groups of works there are still enough works to be able to actively support exhibitions. Regrettably, the secondary market has developed a very limited view of Martin Kippenberger through ascribing an extremely high value to the self-portraits.

LW: For integrity reasons, you've deliberately maintained a distance to the secondary market, which nevertheless represents an important factor for artists being appreciated posthumously. Were you trying to provide a fresh impetus?
GC: Yes, naturally. You try to have an influence on the selection of international galleries the estate cooperates with, on the choice of institutions whose exhibitions the estate supports, on a precise system of substantiated knowledge about the artist's oeuvre that includes detailed information as well as the significance within the context of the oeuvre as a whole, on a scholarly archive that you make available to art historians and curators, and on an organizational machine that is able to provide substantial support for all projects. We guarantee professional expertise on Kippenberger's works. Kippenberger gave out a lot of unsigned works. The estate issues certificates for them in order to confirm the authenticity of a work and include it in the catalogue raisonné.

The past eighteen years have seen the development of a constructive collaboration with a few galleries and dealers who actively support the mediation of Kippenberger's works on the international art market. Ultimately, and this is extremely important, you do your best to develop trusting relationships with collectors in order to be able to obtain them as lenders for exhibitions and projects.

LW: What led you to withdraw from the secondary market?
GC: I kept my distance from it from the start in order to avoid conflicts of interest between the heirs and me. The essential concern is mediating works from the estate and not works that I might purchase on the market and then sell with a possibly higher profit margin. That would seriously violate the basis of trust between the two heirs and me. In my opinion, a good relationship of trust is the most important basis for working successfully with an estate.

LW: In the USA, there's the so-called sunset model, which specifies that the assets have to be depleted within a fixed period of time. From your point of view, what will happen with Kippenberger's estate in twenty to thirty years?
GC: My great wish is that all the catalogues raisonnés will be completed during that length of time. All four volumes on Kippenberger's paintings are supposed to be published within the next four years and, after them, the catalogue raisonné on the sculptures and the one on the installations. A catalogue raisonné on the drawings would be the final, and definitely most extensive undertaking, which we still don't dare think about.

LW: Are internal capacities one reason for that?
GC: Our capacities do not correspond to American circumstances. I would like to work on these catalogues raisonnés with a small team with a great deal of expertise and incredible dedication, which has gathered its experience over many years and is therefore also able to continue working independently later on.

LW: How big is your team today?

---

2 Brigitte Werneburg, "Freies Essen auf Lebenszeit," in *die tageszeitung* (February 22, 2013); http://www.taz.de/!5072779/ (accessed February 28, 2016).

3 "Kippenberger-Gemälde erzielt Höchstpreis," in *Monopol* (October 12, 2012); http://www.monopol-magazin.de/artikel/20105968/Kippenberger-Gemaelde-erzielt-Hoechstpreis-.html (accessed February 28, 2016).

GC: Lisa Franzen steers the project as a whole. Regina Fiorito, the director of the gallery for many years, and I support her in an advisory capacity, and a research assistant helps her. An external designer is responsible for the layout, in close consultation with us. We are publishing the four volumes as our own publication and having them distributed by the Verlag der Buchhandlung Walther König. The decision to work with Walther König was obvious because Kippenberger maintained a particularly good and productive relationship with him.

LW: Is the catalogue raisonné a joint project of yours in cooperation with Kippenberger's heirs?
GC: Yes, it's a cooperative project. We are involved to an equal extent in financing the catalogues raisonnés.

LW: After an artist's death, the perspective on his or her work often becomes limited. The market and later also curators and museums concentrate on one component of the artist's work, which then becomes the artist's trademark. How do you try to open up new perspectives on Kippenberger's work?
GC: All the extensive survey exhibitions that we have worked on up to now were conceived as introductions to or overviews of Kippenberger's complex production. The big obstacle for the reception of Kippenberger's work during his lifetime was indeed the fact that he created such an extensive and multilayered oeuvre, which looked so different again and again, that nobody was able or wanted to follow him, with just a few exceptions. Many simply lost an overview and judged his work as anarchic, excessive production. That was one of the major reasons why it was only possible to see two monographic exhibitions in German museums from the mid-nineteen-eighties until his death in 1997. "Before I hang in the museum, I'll probably see museum directors hanging." That's a Kippenberger quote.

Moreover, we also try to call attention to content-related levels in Kippenberger's work such as his use of language and to make this a focus for curators and art historians.

LW: You manage Kippenberger's copyrights. Have you already had to enforce the rights in order to prevent particular publications?
GC: In individual cases, we have to do so when the inquiries are unfounded or taken out of context. Such inquiries differ extremely in their content-related and formal quality.

LW: With the copyrights, it's also possible to support research on Kippenberger's work or to limit false claims.
GC: Up to now, we've primarily supported projects by museums and other institutions. Diedrich Diederichsen has been working for years on an extensive publication on Kippenberger's forms of production, working methods, and networks. In the fall of 2016, a monographic exhibition in Vienna will deal intensively with the theme of language and text in Kippenberger's oeuvre. We therefore support projects that broaden the reception of his work.

LW: Do you hold Kippenberger's entire written estate?
GC: We don't have all of his written estate, but nevertheless a large portion of it. In the exhibition *Martin Kippenberger—sehr gut / very good* at Hamburger Bahnhof—Museum für Gegenwart in Berlin in 2013, the letters that he sent from Florence to a female friend in Hamburg were presented, among other things. We naturally don't possess such private correspondence. His sisters and former girlfriends also have many letters. Some time ago, a private individual in Nuremberg sold very early letters by Kippenberger through a German auction house. Those letters have hardly any immanent significance for the work, but they do all show a personal stance of Kippenberger's that was very decisive for his understanding of art.

Kippenberger's installation *METRO-Net World Connection, Ventilation Shaft* (1993) was reconstructed posthumously at the Venice Biennale in 2003. Kippenberger planned to erect a fictive subway network spanning the world, for which he created stationary entrances and ventilation shafts. The curator of the Biennale, Julian Heynen showed the work inside the German Pavilion and was criticized for shifting it into an art context, since the work was originally conceived site-specifically, near a street.[4] The manager of Kippenberger's estate, however, gave her blessing for the reconstruction. She based her decision on very detailed information provided by the artist, who conceived the *METRO-Net* as a temporally and spatially open project.

LW: The reconstruction of a Kippenberger installation at the Venice Biennale in 2003 that was authorized by Kippenberger's estate was later severely criticized.

---

4 "Das soll Kippenberger sein?" in *Art. Das Kunstmagazin* (September 2003).

The work of an artist nevertheless needs to be kept alive and actively presented after his or her death. How do you see the question of posthumous reconstructions today?

GC: The reconstruction for the Venice Biennale was an extremely difficult decision. In principle, it was clear that we were permitted to reproduce the ventilation shafts in minimally different versions, because Kippenberger had already received invitations for various locations, and wanted to design each of them in a site-specific way. Unfortunately, he was no longer able to realize the projects himself. The inquiry from the curator, Julian Heynen, was therefore in the spirit of the artist.

We didn't stage anything in the German Pavilion that went beyond the work that Kippenberger had already created or that distorted the idea of the project—even if the critics in part saw things differently. Kippenberger had specified very precisely how the individual elements in the *METRO-Net World Connection* (1993) project were supposed to be designed. The entrance at the Documenta X in Kassel in 1997 was specified in great detail. The transportable ventilation shaft for Skulptur Projekte Münster was produced according to his ideas and its placement was decided on in cooperation with both Kasper König and Kippenberger's architect. The project in Venice was planned and realized in cooperation with exactly the same architect with whom Kippenberger developed Kassel and Münster. For them, there were wonderful drawings by the artist and the perfect construction plans by the architect.

The fact that we shifted the work to the inside of the pavilion was the point of contention. It was intended for the outdoors, parallel to a traffic route. The building regulations on the site of the pavilion are extremely strict, and we were not allowed to dig or add anything structurally, which left only the unusual and seemingly incorrect path inside, with the knowledge that the canals of Venice pass behind the site and the wide pedestrian promenade in front of the pavilion. Kippenberger himself had to give up his idea of positioning the transportable entrance at the Documenta in the Fulda River, and then decided for the meadow in front, therefore simply switched directions. That emboldened us to decide on the interior.

LW: Are there other works by Kippenberger that have been reproduced posthumously?

GC: No, with the exception of a carpet that Kippenberger developed for his complex of the Medusa works. It was executed anew in connection with an exhibition at the Akademie der Künste in Berlin based on detailed information provided by the artist. The same person who knotted the carpet the first time around made it again.

Kippenberger's works are represented in numerous international collections, including at the Kunstmuseum Basel, Hamburger Bahnhof—Museum für Gegenwart, Berlin, Museo Reina Sofía, Madrid, Museum of Modern Art, New York, Museum Ludwig, Cologne, Museum Brandhorst, Munich, San Francisco Museum of Modern Art, Stedelijk Museum, Amsterdam, Tate Modern, London, and Centre Pompidou, Paris.

LW: Have you considered giving groups of works by Kippenberger to a museum on permanent loan or selling them to museums in countries where Kippenberger's work is still relatively unknown?
GC: There have only been isolated inquiries about large groups of works. In addition, museums today are no longer really that interested in permanent loans, because, on the one hand, they find themselves burdened with an additional administrative task, and on the other also haven't only had good experiences with them. In 2006, we would've liked to extend the loan of *The Happy End of Franz Kafka's 'Amerika'* (1994) installation at K21 in Düsseldorf. An initiative started by Kasper König to purchase this work for a group of museums in North Rhine-Westphalia and then show it in alternation unfortunately failed due to the technical and conservation-related needs of the installation.

LW: Do you have contact with other estates?
GC: Other estates contact us relatively rarely, but we do have good contacts to Joel Wachs, the President of the Andy Warhol Foundation for Visual Arts, who I've known for many years.

Each estate has its own legal and fiscal peculiarities, about which little is said publicly.

LW: What will happen to the estate after your death?
GC: Then someone else will have to continue things. For some years, I've been familiarizing two of my employees with the work in-depth, and have high hopes for them, provided that the estate and they themselves agree. On a content-related, objective level, the estate can be managed without it being absolutely necessary to have known the artist. And after nearly twenty years, the impression of the person changes, the memories of those who knew him well change. We

encounter this phenomenon in the case of every question about particular facts about Kippenberger's work.

LW: When you look back at the last twenty years, is there any advice on the topic of estates that you would give to heirs or living artists?

GC: My advice to all heirs is to keep the management of the estate as small as possible and thus make the decisions as focused as possible. The more voices there are, the faster conflicts arise. In addition, a good relationship of trust between all parties is essential.

Hélène Vandenberghe
Estate of Philippe Vandenberg

The Estate of the Belgian artist Philippe Vandenberg (1952–2009) is managed by his three children Hélène, Guillaume, and Mo Vandenberghe. Set up as a private, non-incorporated Belgian partnership after his death in 2009, the estate maintains the artist's studio in Brussels as the central archive of his work. The work of the estate focuses on three areas: managing the artist's heritage and working space, facilitating research efforts around the artist's oeuvre, and making the oeuvre accessible through an ongoing dialogue with artists, curators, and the public. The children of Philippe Vandenberg form the nucleus of the estate. Depending on the project, be it an exhibition, a publication or a research program, they call upon a pool of specialists from different fields: museum directors, curators, art critics, art historians, researchers, visual artists, filmmakers, architects, collectors, and entrepreneurs to collaborate with.

Hélène Vandenberghe is a trained art historian and began her career as a curator in the museum of folklore (Huis van Alijn) in Ghent in 2000, followed by several years in the field of curating and project coordinating. From 2008 on she worked as artistic advisor to the CEO of the Centre for Fine Arts (Bozar) in Brussels. After the death of her father she has focused on the work with his estate. In 2015 she started working as a consultant for the Belgium government and other artists' estates.

Loretta Würtenberger: What was the perception of your father's work within the art world at the time of his death?

Hélène Vandenberghe: My father had a very turbulent career. As a brilliant painter, he started his career right after graduation from the Ghent Academy of Fine Arts in 1976. Soon he became very famous, both in Belgium and internationally. At the age of thirty-two he was represented by different galleries in Belgium as well as in the United States. His works were acquired by important collections, like the Guggenheim Museum and others. At the end of the nineteen-eighties, due to personal friction with the art world and some of its local protagonists, he decided to close off his studio. He retained one gallery in Belgium and had several important exhibitions there, but in general he remained very distant from the art world. At the end of his life he started to open up once again to the art world, resulting in a series of significant shows in Belgium, France, and New York. But he never found peace. He was always fighting the enemy within,

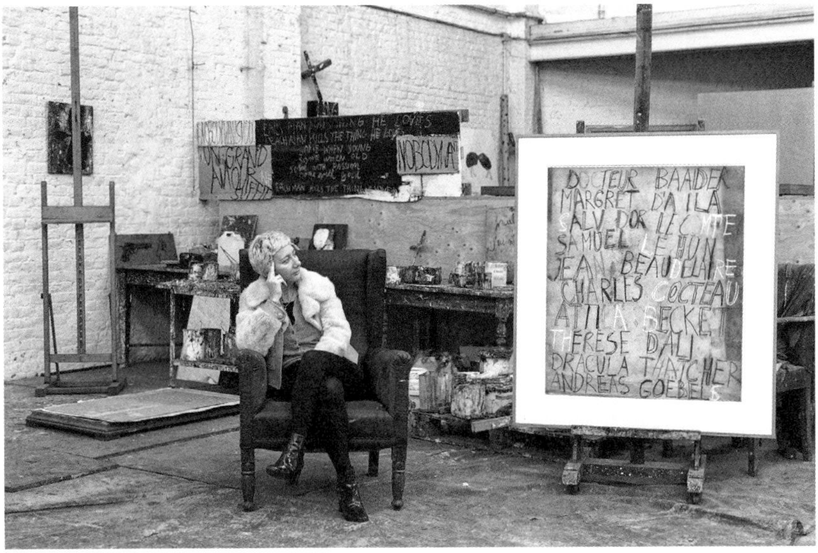

Hélène Vandenberghe

the adversary that he called "solitude." It requires a lot of courage to work the way he did, solitary in his studio, honest and not willing to make compromises. The life of a painter is often very lonely and hard. My father is a true example of an artist's artist. He was a major influence for many artists in Belgium, but he was also well respected in the Belgian art world at large.

LW: He was a very productive artist who left a lot of works. Did he mention any kind of wish during his lifetime as to how one should handle his artistic bequest? Or did he leave a clear will in this regard?

HV: My father didn't leave a will, but we did talk about what would happen with his oeuvre once he would have passed away. He was very concerned about that. For a lot of artists, art is a way to reach immortality. Hence the thought about what would happen to an artist's oeuvre after she or he dies is a very confronting one. It certainly is not an easy subject to talk about with others. My two brothers and I, however, were very close to my father. We promised him that he didn't have to worry, that we would take care of it. Yet at that moment we didn't realize how serious he was about it, as he took his own life about six months later in June 2009. It was very hard for us, but we kept our promise. There never was any conflict among the three of us. We started the estate as if it was the most normal thing to do. For six years now we have taken care of the work together, and we will keep on doing this. It's more than a duty to our father: it's an integral part of our lives.

LW: What was the first move you and your two brothers made concerning your father's estate?

HV: We closed the studio and we took the time we needed. That was crucial. We needed time to figure out in which direction we wanted to go and which steps we had to take. We halted every project that was running, blocked the sales, ended the contract with my father's gallery, and finally reacquired all the works they still had in storage. To close the studio to everybody was a difficult decision that made many people angry; today we realize that this was the best decision to make. It allowed us time and to keep every decision among ourselves.

The first year after my father's passing, both my brothers and I talked a lot; what would our father have wanted? What do we want? What are the possibilities? What structure do we need? Do we want a board? Who could be on the board? We also talked to some people in the art world we trusted: artists, curators, friend collectors, gallery directors, etc. We asked questions and we listened to what they had to say. We did not only question them about the best course of action, but also asked their opinion about the quality of our father's work. We wanted to know if it would uphold in an international context, and if so, where it could be positioned. These were often difficult but nevertheless crucial questions, as the majority of the international art world wasn't familiar with our father's work. As children of the artist we realized that we were too biased and that we were in need of an external perspective.

While crafting a general strategy and setting specific goals, we made sure that the works were physically safe. We converted the studio into a place where we could store and display the works safely while retaining the specific character of the working environment. My brother Mo, who is an architect, designed a plan that we implemented ourselves. It was a laborious endeavor, but the result is incredible. To this day artists and institutions ask us for advice concerning the storage of art works.

The same year we started with the inventory. We photographed and described every single artwork. My other brother Guillaume, who is a photographer and filmmaker, attended to this enormous task. It took us a long time to find an appropriate database that could meet with the international standards of registration, but once we found it we set up a digital catalogue that allows us to locate every single work in the studio and to make digital selections for books, exhibitions, sales, research etc.

After one year, in 2010, we outlined our short and long-term goals and planned the further steps we wanted take. To this day we still follow the very script we wrote down six years ago. It's amazing that we intuitively felt which steps were necessary.

Another key choice was that only the three of us were going to be in charge and make decisions. We decided not to have an external board. We take advice and we talk to specialists, but the final call is always ours. We made a contract between the three of us that stipulates how we want to manage the estate. It is fourteen pages long and it took us three years to finalize.

LW: And after that? Did you develop something like a management agenda?
HV: Our primary goal is to keep the international interest in our father's oeuvre alive. To achieve this, we focus on four interdependent aspects: conservation, research, presentation, and sales.

The first six years we focused on the long-term safety of the work: all the works are registered and properly stored, and whenever necessary restorative actions were needed they were taken. We started to collaborate with a new gallery, Hauser & Wirth. They help us to keep the work both safe and to give it international attention.

In the coming years we are focusing on disclosing the work to a wider public through research and exhibitions. We donated our archive to the library of the University of Ghent, where it will become accessible to the public after it has been fully processed and catalogued. Together with the art history department of Ghent University and other partners we are setting up an international research program around our father's body of work. The more the world learns about the work, the more it can be shared through books, shows, and projects.

Central in the disclosing of the work is the constant re-interpretation of the work. Every artwork lives in relation to his context. As the context changes, the interpretation of the work changes along with it. Creating this synergy is very important for keeping the work alive. We invite artists, curators, and researchers to the studio and then we talk about the work. It's interesting how many things come out of these meetings. A good work is able to be in dialogue with every new context. But the conversation will always be different. This in turn results in new shows, books, and research projects. It's a never-ending process that we wish to trigger.

LW: What do you think is key for the work with an artist's estate in general, and for an artist of the size / career level as your father's in particular?
HV: The attention that is needed to manage an artistic legacy can best be compared with the attention needed to manage a private collection. The core of the challenge for an oeuvre of a deceased artist is to perpetuate its place within the realm of contemporary art, as if the artist would still be alive. Since the oeuvre

is closed, however, a different approach is needed. In this regard, dealing with an artistic legacy is more similar to dealing with collections and the specific attention they require. Yet, the reach and resonance of the work remains situated entirely within the sphere of contemporary art.

Actually, neither the scope of the oeuvre nor the reputation of the artist has little effect on this. Every estate of a contemporary artist will have to deal with both sides. The workload depends on the nature and the scale of the goals you wish to reach. Since we still have a lot of work to do in the studio, a large part of our daily operations currently consists of handling the collection itself. But as the work of our father is steadily gaining international interest, we also put much effort into repositioning it within the contemporary art sphere. With this the gallery is a key partner.

LW: How do you finance the work with the estate? In the beginning, I suppose, your budget was not very large. Did you have financial supporters?
HV: It's true; in the beginning we didn't have a lot of money. But we did have an incredible collection of artworks, which in and of itself is priceless. It was important for us to remain true to ourselves and to focus first and foremost on our assets. We explored how these could be of interest to others and what bridges we could create. We collaborate with different art institutions, for which we get a lot of help to conserve and restore the works in return. We also work together with research institutions (art history departments, archives, departments of architecture and design) that are delighted to get access to such a variety of artworks in a single collection. Finally, we cooperate with several art schools. Many art students have come to visit and/or work in the studio and to create work inspired by its atmosphere and the works it contains.

From the beginning artists have been key interlocutors as well. Since they loved our father's work, many have helped us along the way. They are the best ambassadors for the work and through them we have come in contact with important curators, museum directors, researchers, and other key people of the international art world. The cooperation with other artists began just after the death of my father when people asked me to curate a show of my father's work. Because I am so close to the work I didn't think this was a good idea. So I asked Berlinde de Bruyckere, whom I knew really liked the work, if she wanted to curate the show. She came to the studio and ended up working for two years in the studio making a book and two big exhibitions in De Pont in Tilburg and La Maison Rouge in Paris. After Berlinde, other Belgian artists came, such as Dirk Braeckman, Walter Swennen, Jos De Gruyter and Harald Thys. It's very interesting to see what kind of work each of these artists choose. Depending on their own art practices they focus and bring out aspects in my fathers' work me and my brother's never saw. Sometimes new works came out of these visits and/or cooperation and are shown together. We worked together with the dance company Damaged Goods/Meg Stuart and it was beautiful to see the synergy between the performance and the work. For us this is a very important way to keep the work alive in the contemporary art scene.

LW: Do you get support from the government? Are there any programs in Belgium to support artists' estates?
HV: No. We really had to figure out everything for ourselves. I remember that I was visiting the cabinet of the minister of culture and nobody there knew how to help us. They barely knew what an estate was at that time and what position the government or their institutions should take on the matter. In Belgium, a lot of programs are directed at the work and practice of living artists, while the museums take care of the heritage of past artists. But an estate of an artist that still partakes in the contemporary art scene and at the same time needs the care of a heritage collection was largely foreign to them. Due to this lack of governmental support, together with another estate we started a platform with the name SOS Artistic Heritage. Our aim is to pull the artistic heritage in Belgium from its current isolation and social arbitrariness and to grant it a structural place within Belgian cultural policy at large. With this platform we hope to help other heirs, offer them guidance and answer their many questions that we have already faced and addressed in the past. At this stage we are working together with the cabinet of the minister of culture to determine what can and can't be done, as well as what needs to happen.

LW: You are a trained art historian. Has this fact influenced your work with the estate, and if so how? Do you feel more attached to it or even more knowledgeable?
HV: Yes, of course it influences my work within the estate. I know the importance of good conservation, restoration, registration, research, etc. I know how to write about an artist or work of art and how to communicate with the art world. I have experience working as a curator and in my last job I was the personal assistant of the director of the Centre for Fine Arts in Brussels (Bozar). I know a lot of people in the Belgian art world, which also helps.

But I would like to emphasize that I never would have been able to do the work we did, and still do, without the help of my two brothers. As I already mentioned, one of my brothers is an architect and in the estate he takes care of the studio and everything that has to do with architecture. My other brother, who is a photographer and filmmaker, knows every single detail of every work. I am the representative of the estate and I am working on the institutional strategies, the networking, and the ongoing projects. But the three of us decide everything together, and it works very well like this. Since we all have a different approach on the matter, we sometimes have long discussions, but in the end we always arrive at the best solution.

LW: You do a lot of social media marketing, such as Facebook and Twitter. Could you please share your experience with these media? How important do you think it is? What kind of feedback do you get?
HV: As children of our time we use the communication channels at our disposal and that inevitably includes social media. We have a Twitter account and a Facebook page where we put all the latest news regarding the work of the estate. This can be the restoration of a work, some installation shots for a new show, but also a quote we found in the archive or from some visitors in the studio. The homepage of our new website will have a wall of daily news on everything that happens in front of and behind the scenes. We think that these are important tools as they allow us to reach a wide range of people. As it is really important for us to keep the work of our father alive, we focus not only on the established institutions, but also on the people of our generation and the ones to come. They will continue the work in future years. As an estate we are not in a hurry and our objective isn't confined to a fixed timeline. We can wait a generation if necessary.

LW: What are your plans for the future?
HV: We are working further on our main goal of keeping the work of our father alive internationally. Together with bringing the work to the attention of a wide international public we want especially to spread his voice, his energy, and his plea for artistic audacity. In a world like ours, where fear reigns, we could certainly benefit from such a thing as artistic courage.

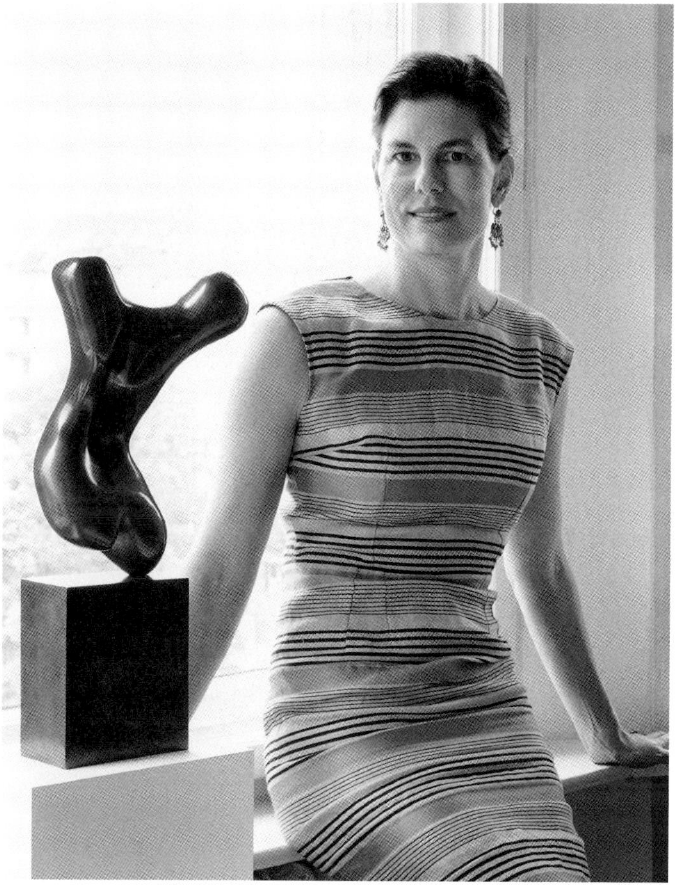

Dr. Loretta Würtenberger co-founded the Institute for Artists' Estates and has been working with artists' estates for many years, including those of Hans Arp, Sophie Taeuber-Arp, and Keith Arnatt. Having studied law, philosophy, and art history, she earned her doctorate in copyright law at the Max Planck Institute for Patent, Copyright and Competition Law in Munich. After serving as a judge in the district court of Berlin, she became an entrepreneur and was awarded the German Entrepreneur of the Year award in 1999. Dr. Würtenberger is a partner at Fine Art Partners and a founder of the Contemporary Arts Alliance Berlin.

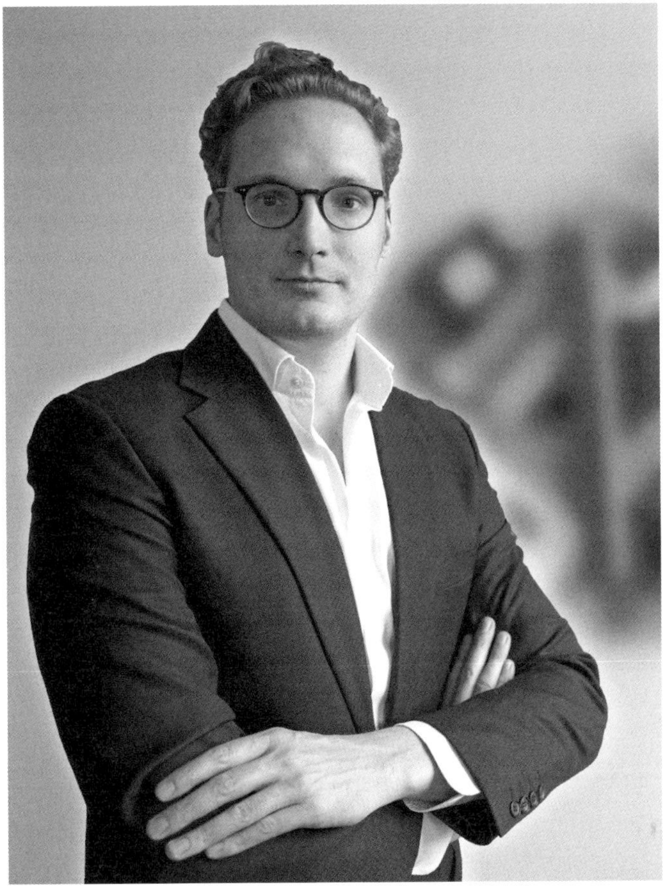

Karl von Trott is the director of Fine Art Partners in Berlin. He studied law in Freiburg, Munich, and Berlin and earned a Masters in Art Business at Sotheby's Institute of Art in New York. Before joining Fine Art Partners, he was a founder and managing director of an online marketplace for art and antique dealers.

Photo credits

Page 25: Installation by *Dieter Roth. Björn Roth* at Hauser & Wirth in New York, 2013. Chocolate castings for *Selbstturm*, 1994/2013. Courtesy Hauser & Wirth. Photo: Bjarni Grimsson

Page 39: Martin Kippenberger, *Bei Missfallen Gefühle zurück (Aussen Alster Hotel / Hôtel Touring-Balance)*, 1989.

Page 45: Robert Motherwell, *Elegy to the Spanish Republic No. 70*, 1961, The Metropolitan Museum of Art, New York. © bpk | The Metropolitan Museum of Art

Page 54: Robert Mapplethorpe, *Ken Moody and Robert Sherman*, 1984. © Robert Mapplethorpe Foundation, used by permission

Page 68: Donald Judd in Marfa, Texas. © Judd Foundation, courtesy Judd Foundation Archives

Page 71: Hélène, Guillaume and Mo Vandenberghe in Philippe Vandenberg's studio, their father's. Photo: Joke Floreal

Page 90: Paul Klee in his studio at the Bauhaus in Weimar, 1924. Zentrum Paul Klee, Bern, Donation Klee Family, Photo: probably Felix Klee

Page 92: The open warehouse of the Stiftung Arp in Berlin, 2014. © Stiftung Arp e.V., Berlin / Rolandswerth. Photo: Leo Pompinon

Page 98: Eva Hesse, *Accretion*, 1968 (detail), Kröller-Müller Museum, Otterlo, The Netherlands. Courtesy Hauser & Wirth. Photo: Abby Robinson, New York

Page 107: The studio of Donald Judd in Marfa, Texas. © Judd Foundation, courtesy Judd Foundation Archives, Photo: Elizabeth Felicella

Page 122: Archive and library of the Stiftung Arp e.V., 2014. © Stiftung Arp e.V., Berlin / Rolandswerth, Photo: Leo Pompinon

Page 128: Robert Mapplethorpe, *Calla Lily*, 1984. © Robert Mapplethorpe Foundation, used by permission

Page 136: Max Beckmann, *Selbst im Hotel*, 1922, from the portfolio *Berliner Reise*, Berlinische Galerie, on loan by the Land Berlin, Photo: Kai-Annett Becker

Page 143: Robert Rauschenberg, *Monogram*, 1955–1959. © Robert Rauschenberg Foundation

Page 159: Michael Baumgartner

Page 175: Mayen Beckmann. Photo: © Benjamin Weinkauf / BILD-Zeitung

Page 189: Richard Calvocoressi, in the background Henry Moore, *Two-Piece Reclining Figure: Points*, 1969/70 (LH606). The Henry Moore Foundation: gift of the artist

Page 197: Louise Bourgeois and her assistant Jerry Gorovoy in Italy, with marble pieces, Bourgeois had been working on in 1981.

Page 205: David Nash. Photo: Mitchell-Innes & Nash, New York

Page 213: Jack Flam

Page 225: Christy MacLear. Photo: © Carsten Fleck

Page 235: Rainer Judd, Marfa, Texas, 2014. Photo: © Vajra Olana Kingsley

Page 243: Barry Rosen. Photo: © Katalin Deér

Page 247: Michael Ward Stout. © Robert Mapplethorpe Foundation, used by permission

Page 255: Martin Kippenberger and Gisela Capitain, New York, 1984.
Photo: © Helene Winter, New York

Page 269: Hélène Vandenberghe. Photo: © Estate Philippe Vandenberg, Photo: Joke Floreal

Page 276: Portrait of Loretta Würtenberger with the sculpture *Torso* by Jean Arp.
Photo © Anne Schönharting

Page 277: Portrait of Karl von Trott. Photo: © Leo Pompinon

Editor
Loretta Würtenberger

Authors
Loretta Würtenberger and Karl von Trott

Editorial assistance
Sonja Claser

Editing
Aaron Bogart

Translations
Amy J. Klement, Sarah McGavran, Cordula Unewisse

Graphic design
Andreas Platzgummer, Hatje Cantz

Typesetting
Ulrike Poppe

Typeface
Sabon Next, The Sans

Production
Anja Haering, Hatje Cantz

Reproductions
Johann Hausstätter

Paper
Galerie Art Volume, 135 g/m²

Printing and Binding
DZS Grafik, Ljubljana

Published by
Hatje Cantz Verlag
Mommsenstr. 27
10629 Berlin
Germany
Tel. +49 30 3464678-00
Fax +49 30 3289042-48
www.hatjecantz.com
A Ganske Publishing Group company

ISBN 978-3-7757-5337-1
(English edition)

ISBN 978-3-7757-4132-3
(German edition)

ISBN 978-3-7757-5172-8
(E-book German)

ISBN 978-3-7757-5173-5
(E-book English)

Printed in Europe